FIFTH EDITION

Social Policy and Social Programs

A Method for the Practical Public Policy Analyst

Donald E. Chambers

University of Kansas

Kenneth R. Wedel

University of Oklahoma

PEARSON

Boston ■ New York ■ San Francisco
Mexico City ■ Montreal ■ Toronto ■ London ■ Madrid ■ Munich ■ Paris
Hong Kong ■ Singapore ■ Tokyo ■ Cape Town ■ Sydney

Senior Series Editor: *Patricia Quinlin*
Editorial Assistant: *Carly Czech*
Marketing Manager: *Wendy Albert*
Production Supervisor: *Patty Bergin*
Editorial Production Service: *GGS Book Services PMG*
Manufacturing Buyer: *Debbie Rossi*
Electronic Composition: *GGS Book Services PMG*
Cover Administrator: *Kristina Mose-Libon*

For related titles and support materials, visit our online catalog at www.ablongman.com.

Between the time website information is gathered and then published, it is not unusual for some sites to have closed. Also, the transcription of URLs can result in typographical errors. The publisher would appreciate notification where these errors occur so that they may be corrected in subsequent editions.

Library of Congress Cataloging-in-Publication Data

Chambers, Donald E.
    Social policy and social programs : a method for the practical
public policy analyst/Donald E. Chambers, Kenneth R. Wedel. — 5th ed.
    p. cm.
Includes bibliographical references and index.
ISBN-13: 978-0-205-57164-2
ISBN-10: 0-205-57164-6
    1. Public welfare administration—united states. 2. Social
problems—United States. 3. United States—Social policy.
I. Wedel, Kenneth R. II. Title.

HV91.C444 2009
361.6′10973—dc22

                                         2008011381

Printed in the United States of America

10 9 8 7 6 5 4 3 2 1   Hamilton   12 11 10 09 08

New to This Edition

Extensive updating of sources and references has been done in every chapter in order to bring current research to the attention of students. New data on poverty, poverty lines, TANF, Medicare/Medicaid, and child welfare legislation have been included.

Close attention has been given to updating the dramatic changes that have been made in the U.S. welfare system, especially those that have weakened the basic safety net: medical care, child welfare, immigration law, and practices.

- Includes a new section on the revolutionary move towards privatization of social welfare services in the past decade, discussing what we've come to know thus far about its advantages and disadvantages. (Chapters 6 and 7)

- Includes a new section on the recent devolution of social welfare responsibilities from the federal government onto the states with its accompanying difficulties and benefits for financing and service delivery. (Chapter 7)

- Includes a new section on "faith-based" service delivery, and the "charitable choice" idea. (Chapter 6)

- Includes a new section on the use of "proprietary contractors" in privatization of social programs. (Chapter 7)

CONTENTS

PREFACE

The General Approach of the Book

This book is about public social welfare policy, social welfare program designs, and the instruments through which they are expressed: governmental organizations, public departments, and welfare bureaus. The book is intended for use in courses that prepare students for practice in social work or in one of the many other human service fields. It is written with the young student-practitioner in mind, assuming little or no experience with social programs and nothing more than an ordinary citizen's exposure to social problems. No doubt there will be many readers who do not fit this description, readers with years of rich experience as paraprofessional human service workers. Instructors know that such students' personal accounts bring additional depth and flavor to the discussion of the material in this book; the text is written with a view toward facilitating that kind of enrichment.

Of course, writing a social policy text is a special challenge precisely because of the wide variability in the age, experience, and preparation of its audience. Although social policy texts have multiplied in the last decade, no single text has been totally successful. It is quite clear why success has been so long in coming: the task is simply too demanding. The text must be written with the simplicity and clarity appropriate for beginning-level practitioners, yet still deal with the extraordinary complexity of the world of public social policy and social programs. In a text for frontline practitioners, it is not appropriate to linger over the fine details of social policy abstractions or the more technical points at the heart of current academic debate. In addition, there is the distressing fact that the basic concepts in this field (by whatever name it is called—public policy, policy analysis, or public administration) are fundamentally vague and incomplete. Given all this, it would not be unreasonable to conclude that a textbook on this topic might be premature. That will be left to the tender mercies of those who can judge it best: the readers and instructors who use this book. The solution we have chosen is to present a general orientation to the topic and its major elements, to focus on its most basic structure, and to bring into sharp focus only the most central issues: social problems, programs, and policies. Our criterion for identifying these issues was to focus on social problems, social policies, and programs that are the main concern of organizations in whose employ the students who use this textbook are likely to find themselves. The following social problems and program areas are representative in that way: child welfare, health, poverty, and mental illness. There are other good candidates for inclusion—corrections, substance abuse, aging, and physical disablement, for example—so they are referred to in the textual examples and exercises. Instructors will find source material listed and annotated at the end of chapters.

The general approach of this text is designed for social work and human service practitioners (including their immediate supervisors) functioning as frontline practictioners—staff members of an organization whose task it is to enact social policy in direct encounters with citizens.[1] Such a practitioner selects and packages services and benefits, counsels and gives advice, makes referrals, and is supportive, among other things. It pays to keep in mind that direct-service practitioners also take away benefits and services and deliver other punitive measures that society deems appropriate under given circumstances. Of course, social practitioners do not deal in abstractions but with living, breathing people. For the conscientious and service-oriented practitioner, the consequence of a mistaken social policy or program design is not just an overstressed budget to be set right with an adroit accounting maneuver or a condition that can be dismissed with some statement like, "Well, we'll have to get that right in next year's legislature." The consequence is a hungry mother or child; a wronged, irate, and morally indignant citizen; a neighborhood terrorized by a violent psychotic; or a hospitalized child bruised, battered, and broken by an out-of-control parent. What street-level social practitioners most need to know about social policy and program design are those things that will increase their ability to extract resources and capacities from social programs that are necessary to alleviate or prevent any or all of the catalog of modern social horrors listed before. There are two general aspects here, and the major share of this book will be devoted to them.

First, orchestrating the resources and assets of a community so that they effectively serve needs requires a practitioner's clear-eyed grasp of the way a particular social problem is viewed by the staff who control the money, goods, or services that clients/consumers need. The sophisticated frontline practitioner knows that it is not necessary to agree with this viewpoint, but whether a client/consumer gets benefits he or she needs may well depend on the practitioner's ability to present those needs in ways that are compatible with the perspectives of program staff or administrators. For example, the practitioner must understand what the staff member or administrator takes to be the concrete indicators of a problem—its causes and its consequences—that are *really* important to relieve. The practitioner who understands and can use the method of analyzing social problems presented in Chapter 1 will be prepared to do that.

Second, working practitioners need to know some of the more important structural elements of particular social program designs: social program goals and objectives, service-delivery administrative system characteristics, entitlement rules, and so on. For example, an understanding of eligibility rules permits an advance estimate of the extent to which staff members are allowed to use their own discretion in awarding benefits or services of various kinds. Alternatively, understanding eligibility rules can yield important predictions as to what administrative level must be contacted before discretion is possible. The chapter on entitlement rules and other chapters on various other structural features of social programs are intended to prepare practitioners with sensitivity to social program features so they can anticipate such things.

This book does not take a detailed look at the legislative, judicial, and political processes, which are very important but worthy of a book all their own. The topic is a reluctant omission because it is so important, but long experience persuades us that few social practitioners are effective social or legislative advocates. We applaud the effort and involvement of practitioners in the political and legislative process but neither this text nor the courses for which it is intended can adequately address this specialty practice. It is a specialty that requires an expert grasp of social policy and program analysis, one that involves so much more than can be done justice here. Instructors who want to focus more on the legislative, judicial, and political processes will want to add supplementary material to their courses.

Finally, our particular objective in writing this book was to put together a method of analysis that ensures that students are taught how to judge whether a social policy or program could be good or bad for their clients/consumers—and to provide them with particular and explicit criteria by which to generate those judgments. Thus, program designs and features can be judged *in advance* to have such serious design faults and side effects that they cannot possibly achieve their goals. These evaluative criteria are included in each chapter for each program or policy operating feature. Many, if not most, books on social policy lack them entirely or rely on the traditional concepts of social justice and costs and benefits, where lack of definitions of these terms can lead to much mischief; for example, costs-to-whom, benefits-to-whom, adequacy for what specific purpose. This book takes some pains to illustrate how the social problem analysis provides a concrete context for defining those ideas and applying them to the pressing realities that practitioners deal with in everyday life.

The Organization of the Book

This book is organized around two major aspects: social problem analysis and social policy and program analysis. It opens with a presentation of the central importance of social policy in the professional practice of social work and other human services. Because social policies both create and constrain the possibilities in any social practice, students must grasp the fact that understanding social policies is not a matter of choice. The major task of Part One is to show students how social problems can be analyzed using four interrelated but different aspects: problem definition, causal explanation, ideology and values, and identification of gainers and losers.

Part Two introduces the reader to a straightforward method of analyzing a social policy or social program. The intention is to help the student quickly grasp the minimum fundamental elements involved in a program or policy. More complex or sophisticated policy and program issues can follow in later courses.[2] The following elements are used in this analytic scheme:

1. Policy and program *goals and objectives*
2. *Forms of public benefits*
3. *Eligibility rules* for receiving benefits or services
4. *Administrative service-delivery system* (including program design[s]) through which benefits or services are delivered to consumers)
5. The method of *financing* the program benefits or services
6. Identifying of important *interactions* within and between the preceding elements

Chapters 2 through 8 are devoted to the study of these basic program elements. Sometimes classification schemes are developed to help the reader cope with confusing variations, such as those for types of eligibility rules and for types of benefits and services. In each chapter, a unique set of evaluative criteria is presented; for example, clarity and measurability are two of the several criteria for goals and objectives, just as accountability, response time, and consumer participation are criteria for the service-delivery system.

The use of this method of analysis is demonstrated in Part Three in which the example is a particular social problem—child abuse—and a particular social program intended to deal with it. Chapter 9 opens with an analysis of social problem viewpoints; a brief review of various judicial decisions that have shaped present policy and program efforts in this area; and a concise description of historical issues, former program and policy efforts, and competing political agendas. By using the analytic method, a particular program dealing with child abuse is described and shows how the evaluative criteria for assessing the merit of the program are to be applied.

Acknowledgments

Because I was never taught by nor even conversed with the three people who have had the greatest influence on forming my ideas of what should be in this book, this is probably the only occasion there will ever be for acknowledging their influence and delivering my thanks for their contribution. The intellectual ground from which this book is taken uses concepts that Richard Titmuss first set to paper during his years at the London School of Economics and uses an analytic approach that Evelyn Burns, an LSE product herself, used in her 1948 classic *The American Social Security System.* If this book succeeds in its aim, it is simply because it applies some of their ideas to the contemporary U.S. social policy context, a very different world from that of Titmuss and from that of Burns. Finally, this book is indebted to Martin Rein whose marvelously clear essays on value-critical policy analysis enabled me to think in a quite different way in the 1990s about how to teach students to make clear, practical, and unashamed value-based judgments on whether social policies and social programs are good for the clients/consumers they are intended to serve.

Other ideas that framed this book are likely to have come from that extraordinary group of teachers with whom I have been blessed and who have been (under)paid to teach me at various times over the course of almost forty years and two careers. For the most part, they have been gifts to me out of the abundance of the universe.

There is Professor Claude Henry, who taught me the wonder of ideas in the great literary classics; Professor Maude Merrill; Professor Garnet Larsen, who introduced, with great patience and forbearance, the subject of social policy to a very young, impertinent graduate student; Elizabeth Ossorio, who taught me about perseverance and wisdom in the research process; William E. Gordon, a scientist teaching social workers; and Richard Rudner, a philosopher teaching about science.

More immediately, I would like to acknowledge the help of those who read the manuscript in one form or another of the first four drafts. Their fair and generous criticism is sincerely appreciated: Bradford Sheafor, Colorado State University; Anne Weick, University of Kansas; Winifred Bell, Cleveland State University; Mary Ellen Elwell, Western Maryland College; John M. Herrick, Michigan State University;

Milton S. Rosner, Ohio State University; Mitchell A. Greene, University of Northern Iowa; Arthur J. Cox, East Tennessee State University; Joseph Kuttler, Tabor College; Gary L. Shaffer, University of Illinois at Urbana–Champaign; Jane F. R. C. Bonk, Lutheran Family and Children's Services of Illinois; Charles Rapp, University of Kansas; Rebecca Lopez, California State University–Long Beach; Murray Gruber, Loyola University–Chicago; Sharon Eisen, Mott Community College; David Iacono-Harris, University of Texas–El Paso.

For their comments and suggestions on the fifth edition, I would like to thank the following reviewers: Roger E. Boyd, Southern Illinois University, Edwardsville; Alice K. Butterfield, University of Illinois at Chicago; Iris Phillips, University of Southern Indiana; and Ruth White, Seattle University.

I want to extend very special thanks to my (former) doctoral student, now colleague, Mary Katherine Rodwell, Virginia Commonwealth University, for her careful reading and intellectual contributions to many of the chapters. In the same way, I am indebted to John Pierpont, teaching colleague at the University of Kansas, whose ideas about policy matters and experience in using this method of policy analysis shaped the second edition in quite important ways. And I am indebted to Richard Wintersteen of the University of Minnesota–Mankato in just the same way in regard to the third edition.

I would like to thank my former editors at Macmillan Publishing Company for their efforts in the making of previous editions of this book, particularly Linda James Scharp, editor; Steve Robb, production editor; and Loretta Faber, copy editor. I would also like to thank Carly Czech, Allyn and Bacon, and Connie Strassburg, GGS Book Services, for their assistance on this edition.

Special thanks go to my late wife, Mary Anne, who taught me so much about life and law. Also, special thanks to James Bonk, without whose helpful assistance while I was in Central America I could not have managed. And, finally, I would like to thank Marylee Brochmann, University of Kansas, for her patient reading, support, and judicious suggestions (and helpful argument) during the third edition revision.

D.E.C.

NOTES

1. Michael Lipsky, *Street Level Bureaucracy: The Dilemma of the Individual in Public Services* (New York: Russell Sage Foundation, 1980), pp. 4–10.

2. Notice that no great attention is paid here to the distinction between *policy* and *program*. Although that distinction can deserve much attention in some contexts, it is not taken to be crucial here in this book for frontline practitioners—other than to note that policies are taken to be general rules or guides for action, whereas programs are taken to be the general human and organizational apparatus, or the instruments, through which policies are implemented.

PART ONE

Creating the Context for Social Policy Analysis
The Social Problem Context

A man said to the universe:
"Sir, I exist!"
"However," replied the universe,
"That fact has not created in me
a sense of obligation."

—Stephen Crane, *War Is Kind*

Introduction: The Problem of Policy for Practitioners

The objective of this book is to help readers develop skill in the critical analysis of modern social welfare policies and programs. The motive is to preserve the sanity and dedication of social practitioners who, on behalf of clients or consumers, must daily interpret, enforce, advocate, circumvent, or challenge those policies and programs. Much of the working life of professional practitioners is spent in the context of those policies and programs. If practitioners are not employed on the staff of an agency administering such programs, they serve clients/consumers whose lives are affected vitally and daily by those programs: the client/consumer whose child is detained in a local juvenile detention center or the client/consumer whose Social Security disability benefit is suspended because a judgment of work capacity has been changed. Without being concerned about such policies or being prepared to analyze the nature of their strengths and shortcomings, no social worker can aspire to a professional calling.

1

Social work is unique for its simultaneous focus on the client/consumer *and* the social environment. Like family, community, psychological, and work factors, social policies and programs are a critical feature of the client/consumer surroundings and demand every bit as much care and attention from the working professional. For better or worse, the lives of all private citizens are subject to serious and widespread invasions by governmental social policy. For those whom social workers serve, it poses a special stress because it affects lives already burdened with fearsome and demoralizing social problems: hunger, illness, physical or mental disablement, violence, discrimination, or disease.

Stephen Crane's lines at the beginning of this chapter are a moving rendition of the idea that immense forces are at work in the world, forces that have no concern for their effect on the fates of particular individuals. Crane means to call our attention to the idea that an earthquake or a volcano does not consider the suffering it causes to individuals in the cataclysmic changes it wreaks—changes begun long before those individuals were born, changes whose effects will outlive human memory.

Crane's point can be extended to modern social welfare policies and programs. Public policies generally are not designed with the needs of *individuals* in mind; rather they are designed for *groups of people* who share a common social problem. It is of utmost importance for social work practitioners to understand that because of this feature, *social policies and programs will fail some, perhaps many, individuals on some occasions.* This fact of life is a pervasive problem and a prominent part of the work of most program administrators. It also identifies an important area of social work practice for those who work with individual clients/consumers: finding ways to meet clients'/consumers' urgent and unique needs that cannot, at first glance, be met through existing programs. Examples are not difficult to find:

> John Samuelson is a construction worker. Every year for the past five years he has received notice from the county attorney's office that Mildred Singer has filed suit against him for nonsupport of a child she claims is theirs. Each time a suit is filed, John loses about five working days' pay because of the time it takes to talk to his Legal Aid attorney, give depositions, and appear in court. Each year thus far, the local judge has dismissed the case for lack of evidence because John has denied paternity on the basis that the baby was born ten and one-half months after he left Mildred. Mildred has admitted that she lived with other men during the time her child could have been conceived but nevertheless has identified John as the father. John once received a letter from Mildred admitting that, contrary to her allegation, she believed another man to be the baby's father, but John's wife destroyed the letter in a fit of jealousy. John agreed to take a blood test that, with 99.9 percent accuracy, tells whether a specific man can be *excluded* as a child's father.[1] The test declared that John could very well be the father. The judicial policy is to consider the test accurate, within a less than 0.1 percent margin of error. John now must pay $200 per month in child support until the child is eighteen. In fact, Mildred (now the mother of three) does not wish to press nonsupport charges against John (now the father of four), but federal policy requires applicants for TANF (like Mildred) to press nonsupport charges as a condition for continuing to receive financial assistance.

Note that in this case, it would be a peculiar moral position to argue that it is somehow wrong to enforce a public policy that makes fathers financially responsible for their children, pursues fathers across state lines to do so, and makes an accurate paternity test available. The reason, in this instance, that these public policies come to grief is that they did not anticipate the incredible complexity that characterizes the lives of individual ordinary citizens. Legal procedures assume—reasonably in most instances—that people will present *all* evidence in which clearly it is in their self-interest to do so. A test that is 99.9 percent accurate makes very few mistakes indeed; the fact that it *might* have made a mistake in this instance must be viewed in the context of the 99.9 percent of the other cases. Most people would be willing to accept the small risk of injustice done to John. Here is another example:

> Nancy Willard's arms were burned off below the elbow when she caught them in the corner of a plastic injection mold. (Hot plastic disintegrates flesh and bone instantly.) Nancy was a dependable and efficient worker who earned $18 per hour. The law in her state requires all employers of more than six people to carry workers' compensation insurance to provide for just such accidents. Nancy is twenty-eight years old and the mother of two children. The plant she works in spends a lot of money to keep it accident-free and has an excellent record—only two other serious accidents in its ten-year history. State law specifies that Nancy must agree to a lump-sum settlement of $50,000 in compensation for the loss of both arms below the elbow. Nancy's average annual earnings were $35,000—$32,000 net after taxes. She also had $3,000 worth of fringe benefits per year (medical and life insurance, uniforms, and bonuses).

There is nothing intrinsically wrong with the idea of worker-injury compensation or with public policy that requires lump-sum settlements. The problems here are with equity and adequacy that flow from the individual attributes of Nancy Willard. Were she sixty-four with one year to go before retirement, a $50,000 settlement would be adequate compensation for loss of one year's work. At the age of twenty-eight, however, she will lose most of thirty-seven years of wages earned at full working capacity, because with prostheses to replace her arms, she probably will work at only minimum wage. Furthermore, she will lose all her earnings for a one-to-two-year period—the time it will take for surgery, prosthetic fitting, and training. This period alone will cost her perhaps $30,000, or one year of net income. (Her employer's insurance company is required to pay her medical bills.) The $50,000 lump-sum settlement will replace only a small fraction of her long-term economic loss, *and that settlement assumes that rehabilitation will be successful and that she can return to work.*

It is clear from these examples that, despite a practitioner's best efforts and good policy and program design and administration, some clients' needs will go unmet. That knowledge will be the cause of much hard feeling, bad public relations, and personal distress on the part of the social worker. If a client goes hungry for a week, loses a child, or loses a job that required months of effort to obtain, simply because public policy could not deal with the unique circumstances of his or her life, it cannot be easily forgotten or suffered willingly—nor should it be.

Neither are clients'/consumers' lives measurably improved by drawing sweeping conclusions that such instances are the result of the corruptness of the welfare system or its personnel. Although some features of some welfare systems can be shown (on certain moral assumptions) to be corrupt—and surely there is evidence that some personnel are corrupt—it is neither useful nor accurate to generalize along those lines. What is intended to be shown by the preceding illustrations is that there are natural limits to the effectiveness of social policies and programs. The more unique a citizen's situation is, the less likely it is that policies and programs will meet his or her need.

Therefore, the question might arise, "If so much deprivation continues because social welfare programs and policies cannot take individual circumstances into account, then might it be better if all programs intended for groups of people were replaced with programs intended for, and consciously designed to meet, *individual* needs?" This solution might entail a social welfare system in which persons in need applied for any kind of assistance to one—and only one—social worker who had access to the resources of *all* available programs. If the client/consumer needed financial assistance, the social worker would decide not only whether but also how much to give. If the client/consumer needed medical care, the social worker would tell the client/consumer where to get it and would pay the bill. In fact, this vision might be sufficiently detailed to suggest that all monies from all current programs be put into one big pot and allocated to each social worker in proportion to the number of clients/consumers he or she served. The key constraint on largesse would be that the social worker must ensure that the pot lasts long enough. The vision might even anticipate that because each package of services and benefits would be individually tailored, no general standards of need would be necessary. Furthermore, no paperwork would be necessary because the social worker would be accountable only to the client/consumer (and to the fiscal officer, to ensure that all monies went to clients/consumers). The issue here is that this is a legitimate, even plausible, style for the delivery of social benefits.

Although it is intrinsically appealing, this custom-tailored approach to social policy is not without problems. For example, every social worker will likely have different standards for determining how much money, medical care, housing, and so on is needed. That would result in noticeable differences in benefits among people similarly situated. That would be a natural enough effect, for treating people individually was the basic idea behind this way of doing things. Consequently, we have a dilemma here: If we construct our social welfare system to be adequate in the sense that it meets unique needs and circumstances, it will be inevitable that some will need and, thus, will get more than others, an inequity. But if we construct it so that it is exactly equitable (everybody gets the same benefit no matter what), it will always be inadequate for those who need more. Equity and adequacy are two criteria by which modern social welfare programs should be evaluated. A third criterion is efficiency.

No doubt there are ways in which these inherent conflicts among equity, adequacy, and efficiency could be overcome and still keep social programs sufficiently flexible to take unique client need into account. We would encourage the reader to think along those lines because that is the way better policy solutions are developed.

However, the search for better solutions also reveals the limits of social welfare program design and demonstrates an important principle about social policies and programs: *Every policy or program that solves the social needs of one client/consumer or client/consumer group will create additional problems for another client/consumer or client/consumer group in need.* Social policy and program solutions are inherently imperfect to some degree and constantly require revision. Far from being the occasion for disillusionment, it is this very fact that creates the opportunity for service by dedicated professional practitioners to people in need. Social policies and programs left to their own devices are unguided missiles, guaranteed to harm the unwitting and unwary. That danger can be tempered only by frontline practitioners devoted to seeking humane and rational interpretations of social policies directed toward human needs. It is the practitioner's responsibility to know the policy system well enough to do that, and it is to that end that the following chapters are directed.

NOTE

1. K. G. Anderson, "How Does Paternity Confidence Match Actual Paternity?" *Current Anthropology*, 47(2006): 513–520.

CHAPTER

1

Analyzing the Social Problem Background of Social Policies and Social Programs

The Nature of Social Problems

Earlier, the point was made that social welfare programs are solutions to social problems. Notice that not all "problems" are social problems and that they are not all equally important. Some argue that the "importance" of a social problem depends on two things: (1) the power and social status of those who are defining the problem and urging the expenditure of resources toward a solution and (2) the sheer number of people affected. Thus, the more people affected and the greater the social power and status of those urging a solution, the more important the social problem.

Examples of "big" and "little" social problems abound. Social problems often arise as a consequence of rare diseases with strong social effects—retinitis pigmentosa, for example. A relatively rare congenital defect that prevents those afflicted from seeing in the dark, retinitis pigmentosa is a medical problem surely, but it is also a social problem because it creates serious social consequences: For all practical purposes, the sufferer is blind during more than half the hours in a day. The disease is a small problem to most people because the number affected is comparatively small. To those so afflicted, however, it is a very big problem indeed, and they can cite persons of great social stature who have the defect. But, to date, no one with widespread credibility (power and status) has presented the problem to the public as a matter of concern, so that to the world at large, it will remain a minor problem until it either affects more people or is redefined as socially important by a public opinion maker.

Less exotic examples of big social problems include unemployment, because it affects so many people; health, because potentially it affects everyone; what used to be called mental retardation, because after Rose Kennedy (mother of a U.S. president) became a public advocate of the issue, federal appropriations for the problem increased magically.

Whereas not all problems are social problems, of course, many do have important social consequences: When someone loses a job, it is a *personal* problem only for that individual and his or her immediate family; when a machine operator loses a job because of modern standards of worker safety or product quality, it is a *technological* problem; when there is a declining market for the things the machine produced, it is a *business* problem; when consumers no longer have money to buy what the machine produces, it is an *economic* problem. When, as a result of any or all of the foregoing problems, many people lose jobs and are unemployed, or when people of power, wealth, and social status become concerned about the effects of these problems, such concern becomes a *social* problem. Usually, an existing policy or program solution to the problem will remain in place at least until the personal, technological, business, or economic problem that created the social problem is solved. The social program may continue past that time; for example, social programs such as unemployment compensation were created to meet human social problems created by first-order economic, business, or technological problems.

In summary, social problems are those concerns about the quality of life for large groups of people where the concern is held as a consensus populationwide, and/or the concern is voiced by the socially powerful or the economically privileged. In general, it is these types of problems that spawn social policies and programs as corrective measures. Although this account of social problems is certainly not the only one, it is arguably the one most relevant to those who must understand social problems as a prerequisite of understanding social programs operated by the social welfare institution.

The purpose of this book is to help readers understand social policies and programs, and that understanding cannot be complete without the ability to analyze the social problem that the policy or program is intended to correct. This next section demonstrates how attention to four specific aspects of social problem viewpoints or statements will yield that basic understanding.

Social Problem Analysis

Understanding a social problem is not quite the same thing as understanding the truth of "how things really are." It is not quite the same thing as understanding how bridges keep standing or trees grow. *To understand a social problem is to understand how and what another person (or group) thinks and believes about the social events being defined as a problem.* When you do that, you are doing an *analysis* of a social problem. A central aspect of social problems is that, although the events that identify or define them may be the same no matter who views them, the way in which those events are interpreted is likely to vary considerably. That a family of four has, say, $16,242 annual (gross) income is, on the face of it, an unambiguous fact but one bound to be interpreted differently by different observers. Whether the fact is interpreted as a social problem depends on the value bias and ideology used to render that judgment. For example, a person might believe that beef, beer, alcohol, or tobacco is vital or that no child should share a bedroom. In that case, then, $16,242 per year is unlikely to provide for those minimum standards for four people, and the straightforward conclusion is that a $16,242 annual income is an indicator of the presence of a social problem called poverty. However, notice that these standards clearly are value-biased; they are founded on cultural preferences; most people outside North America or Europe survive on far less.[1]

Note also how the reason for the existence of the social problem can vary with the viewer. Based on one kind of idea about how the economy and labor markets work, one person might say that this low income was the result of the skill this worker offered to an employer, the employer's need for it (how good business was), how good a worker the person was (productivity), and how many other people offered the same skill and effort (competition). Another person might say that the low income that creates this social problem is caused by the tradition among employers to pay workers according to the social status and prestige of the work they do and the families from which they come. The point in the initial stage of social problem analysis is not to decide whether the viewpoint presented is right, but to sort out what is being offered by way of explanation.

It should be clear from the preceding examples that the way social problems are understood is highly variable and depends on the viewer. On that account, there is no such thing as the "right" or the "only true" social problem viewpoint. Social problem viewpoints may be factual or not, clear or muddled, complete or incomplete, logical or illogical, or even useful or useless, but they are not right or wrong in some absolute sense. An unemployed person who has seen savings wither to nothing, while debts mount and children go hungry, will view the general problem of unemployment as excruciating, whereas those who believe they are paying high taxes so that the unemployed can loaf will not view it that way. Those who are outraged at a society that permits unemployment will view the problem differently from those for whom unemployment is merely a newspaper item. Unemployed persons stress food for children, whereas taxpayers stress the cost of that food and current events followers stress the difference between this year's and last year's unemployment figures. No one is wrong in any absolute sense here, and the basic issue for the person who wishes to understand social policies and programs is the viewpoint on which every social policy and program is based.

The social problem analysis does *not* begin by judging whether something is right or wrong; rather it must await a clear understanding of the social problem viewpoint itself. The final thing to do in a social problem analysis is to make moral judgments about the argument; the first thing to do is to specify what the viewpoint is and how it differs from others. The reason for bearing down so hard on this idea is twofold: (1) Social problem analysis is a demanding task, and (2) at the end of the chapter, you will do analyses of the social problem viewpoints of other persons. In doing the exercises, another caution for the beginner is *to be sure to hold your own views very much apart while doing each social problem analysis.* Your own views are very important, but you will find that initially it takes some discipline to avoid letting them get in the way of the viewpoints of the writers whose materials you will analyze.

The remainder of this chapter is taken up with a discussion of the four dimensions to consider in doing a social problem analysis:

1. Identify the way the problem is defined.
2. Identify the cause(s) to which the problem is attributed (its antecedents) and its most serious consequences.

3. Identify the ideology—the values, that is—that makes the events of concern come to be defined as a problem.
4. Identify who benefits (gains) and who suffers (loses) from the existence of the problem.[2]

There are other aspects of social problems, of course (history and legal status, for example), and they will be discussed in later chapters.

Problem Definition

It is essential to begin a social problem analysis by determining its distinguishing marks or identifiers, that is, to state the *concrete observable signs by which its existence is to be known.* A social problem can be identified in a wide variety of ways. For example, one way to identify the problem of drug abuse is by noting the use, intentional exposure to, or ingestion of *any illegal chemical substances* in a nonmedical way (not prescribed by a physician). Thus, the nonmedically prescribed use of an illegal substance identifies this social problem. Another way is by defining drug abuse as an addiction; for example, defining drug abuse as occurring when most daily life affairs and social encounters are organized around the problems and pleasures of obtaining and using a chemical substance. Here the indicator of the existence of a social problem is determined not by the use or the legality of the chemical, but by its preeminence and the amount of time devoted to it in the user's life. The indicator here is an observer's judgment of the prominence of drug use in daily life.

Obviously, it makes an enormous difference whether the former or latter definition of the problem is chosen. For example, the first definition includes the occasional marijuana smoker and the long-haul trucker's use of amphetamines. The latter definition does not include such instances but *does* include all alcoholics and many tobacco-users. Not only would conclusions about the qualitative nature and the number of people affected differ in each case, but also conclusions about what kinds of people comprise the social problem group would differ radically. Clearly, it can be seen how different social programs would be depending on which view of the social problem is adopted. Using the first definition, we are likely to see a law enforcement approach, for example, the "War on Drugs." Adopting the second definition we might expect to see addiction prevention and treatment programs.

Even though social policies and programs are usually designed to solve social problems, sometimes (as noted earlier) *the social policy or program creates social problems of its own.* For example, and justifiably, long stays in mental hospitals are said by some to not only worsen the condition of a number of individuals with mental disabilities but also create "insanity" in some patients who were never "insane" in the first place. Another example (less clear) is the case of no-fault divorce. The no-fault divorce policy was created to allow for an amicable divorce process and greater flexibility in the law for determination of alimony, child custody, child support, and allocation of property and by most accounts it has done that. It also makes divorce easier to get. It is the latter point that critics of the policy believe has led to increased rates of divorce,[3,4] and economic hardships for divorced women and their children.[5] A third example, which we will consider in greater detail, is the federal minimum wage.

Hourly wages are subject to economic changes over time. Other factors being equal, wage erosion has very negative effects on the working poor, and we see poverty rates rise. Minimum wage policy is intended to reduce the burden of poverty for the working poor by requiring employers in covered employment to pay a minimum hourly wage. A federal minimum wage covers employees who work for certain businesses or organizations ("enterprises") that have at least two employees and do at least $500,000 a year in business; or are hospitals, businesses providing medical or nursing care for residents, schools and preschools, and government agencies. Individual coverage when there is no enterprise coverage includes workers involved in "interstate commerce." Domestic service workers (such as housekeepers, full-time baby-sitters, and cooks) are also normally covered. Some states and some U.S. territories have their own minimum wage laws as well and in some cases can result in expanded coverage and higher minimum wage rates for workers.

The federal hourly minimum wage was first established by Congress in 1938, and it has been increased nineteen times since then. In 2007 the federal minimum wage was set by Congress at $5.85 an hour. Critics argue that the federal minimum wage creates unemployment. Walter E. Williams believes the federal minimum wage is a foolish and expensive undertaking. He presents his argument on this subject follows.

Minimum Wage—Maximum Folly[6]

Federal minimum wage laws represent a tragic irony. In the name of "preventing worker exploitation," "providing a living wage," and "reducing poverty," these measures in fact impede the upward mobility and increase the dependence of the most disadvantaged among us. National leaders, including black leaders, fail to recognize that many economic problems faced by a large segment of the black population are the result of *government-imposed restrictions on voluntary exchange.*

The Strange History of Unemployment for Black Youth

Today's youth joblessness is unprecedented: nearly 35 percent among blacks and 16 percent among whites, nationally. Black youth unemployment in some major cities is estimated to be 50 percent. In dramatic contrast, black youth unemployment in 1948 was 9.4 percent and white youth unemployment was 10.2 percent. In further contrast to today, until 1954 blacks in every age group were *at least* as active in the labor market as whites were.

These facts demand that we challenge the official and popular explanations of current black youth joblessness. Employers have not become more discriminatory. Black youth of earlier times were not better skilled or educated than their white counterparts. Neither can we attribute the problem to slow economic growth. Even during the relative prosperity of the sixties and seventies, black youth unemployment rose— both absolutely and in relation to white youth unemployment. The real explanation lies in the limitations of law itself. By increasing the minimum wage, Congress has caused a significant loss of job opportunities for young blacks. When employers are required to pay a minimum labor *price* of [$5.85] an hour, they have no economic incentive to hire workers whose labor *value*, in the production of goods or delivery of services, may be only $4.00 an hour. Congress can legislate a higher wage, but it cannot legislate that workers be more productive. Because Congress has not yet seized complete control of personnel operations in private firms, the minimum wage law thus discriminates against the low-skilled.

Basic Economics and Practical Politics

A law that reduces opportunity for some almost always increases it for others. To see how the minimum wage law accomplishes this, recognize, as economists do, that low-skilled labor and high-skilled labor can often be substituted for each other.

Imagine an employer can build a particular fence by using three low-skilled workers each earning $42 a day ($126 total labor cost per day), or by using one high-skilled worker who earns $110 a day. To minimize labor costs, the employer hires the high-skilled worker.

But suppose the high-skilled worker suddenly demands $155 a day. The fence firm then hires the three low-skilled workers, and the high-skilled worker loses his job.

On the other hand, the high-skilled worker may understand politics and economics. He may now join with others like himself and lobby for a minimum wage law of $50 a day (claiming noble motivations like "prevention of worker exploitation" and "provision of a living wage").

Once the $50 minimum wage is law, the high-skilled worker can demand and get his $110 a day—because it now costs $150 to build the fence using low-skilled labor. By law, the high-skilled worker's competition is priced out of the market.

Williams argues that aside from causing unemployment for some, minimum wage policy has additional negative consequences. He believes the policy is an *"incentive to discriminate."* "If an employer must pay a minimum of [$5.85] an hour no matter whom he hires, he may as well hire someone whose color he likes."[7] Williams further indicates that the policy discriminates against young people because it discourages employment of low-skilled workers—and it is usually young workers who have the least skills.

If joblessness merely deprived young people of pocket money, we might shrug it off as another consequence of foolish government intervention. But early work experience produces more than money. It produces pride and self-respect. It lets a worker make mistakes when they are not terribly costly—when there are probably no dependents counting on the worker for continuous income. These labor market lessons are critical, particularly for minority youths who attend grossly inferior schools, where these lessons are not learned.[8]

Williams adds that much of the crime and other antisocial behavior among many of today's youth may be attributed to lack of job opportunities. And he attributes high unemployment among youth to minimum wage policy.

Note in this example how the focus is on *unemployment*. What is central for Williams in the material quoted here is that the minimum wage law by creating unemployment "impedes upward mobility and increases the dependency of the most disadvantaged." Employment is important for Williams because it is the key element in upward mobility and economic independence. Thus, the central social problem defined here is unemployment, the immediate cause of which are certain features of the minimum wage law; the central values that are thought to be threatened here are upward mobility and economic independence. Note that Williams does not tell us exactly what he means by unemployment. It is clear that he is not as concerned about the level of pay as the *number of available low-paying jobs*. He believes that this is the major problem among black youth. Others might disagree. The federal minimum wage law was amended in 1996 in a way that may have changed his analysis. The amendment established a subminimum wage per hour for employees under twenty years of age during their first ninety consecutive days of employment with an employer. The effect of this policy change on the argument would be a concern to the present-day policy analyst.

Social problem analysis should state the concrete measures and indicators of the social problem of concern more clearly than Williams does. Definitions that are specific, concrete, and measurable are useful in these respects:

1. Everyone then knows precisely to what he or she refers.
2. It is possible to construct comparable estimates of incidence and prevalence so that quantification, importance, and change over time can be judged.
3. It makes it possible to discuss causation. Unless the problem is clearly defined, it is fruitless to discuss causes: What is it that is being caused? It is also fruitless to speculate about "solutions" under these conditions.

Note that here a definition is not "good" or "bad" because you either agree or disagree with it. It is common to have serious disagreement about how a given social problem should be defined. For example, many people have disagreed violently with a definition of institutional racism (a serious social problem, surely) that refers to differential access to institutional resources on the basis of color. That definition implies that if people of color have lower-quality education (for whatever stated reason), it is first-order evidence of white racism. Such a definition is one of the central issues around which the whole school-busing-to-achieve-integration argument has revolved. Are blacks and Latinos the victims of white racism because, for example, their school districts have less taxable property yielding less tax revenue, which results in fewer resources for education in that district? Based on the preceding definition of racism, the example unequivocally constitutes racism. Following some other definitions of racism, particularly those that define racism as overt and intentional discrimination based on color, this would not be an example of racism because no "intentional" discrimination can be distinguished.

The point is that both definitions are "good" insofar as definitions go, regardless of which you think is the better. The criteria for definitions revolve around clarity, not "truth"; therefore, both definitions are satisfactorily clear. On ideological or value grounds, we would argue that the first definition is preferable to the second, but that is a different issue than whether it is a clear definition.

Earlier, the statement was made that the importance of social problems—in fact their rise to public consciousness—depends not only on the social status of those who speak publicly about them but on the sheer number of those who are affected as well. Because of the latter factor, you should expect the problem-definition section of careful social problem analysis to give attention to a presentation of the quantitative dimensions—the sheer size—of the problem: estimates of the number of persons (or families), estimates of the percentage or proportion of the total population affected; estimates of the demographics of the problem (e.g., the numbers and percentages of the different ages, sexes, and geographic localities affected). In looking again at the Williams presentation of the social problem of minimum wage, you will see how carefully he has quantified the problem for us. He notes that in 2005, youth joblessness was nearly 35 percent for blacks and 16 percent among whites nationally.[9] He adds demographic data showing that unemployment for black youths in particular cities is as high as 50 percent. He could have carried this kind of analysis even further as you might imagine. Quantifications such as these are often very important in judging the adequacy of social programs and policies to solve the social problem. Without such data, it is impossible to determine whether, for example, the eligibility rules or other features of the program are directing program benefits and services to the people who have the problem or are directing the most benefit or service to those who are affected the most. Furthermore, adequacy of funding for the program cannot be assessed without some idea of how many people are affected. Do not be misled by thinking that quantification is important only in regard to this example concerning minimum wage and youth unemployment; quantification is crucial in the analysis of any social problem. Child abuse, for example, cannot be properly understood without some idea of how widespread it is or the types of people and families in which it appears the most frequently.

Another way in which to deepen the understanding of social problems is to present common variations within the problem category itself. The author of a social problem presentation is very likely to refer to several subtypes of these and expend some effort at distinguishing among them. For example, in discussions about the social problem of crime, distinction is made among the legal subtypes of crime: premeditated homicide, felony murder, manslaughter, and assault. These are legal categories, but the practical public policy analyst can use them to speak of different causes for different subcategories, to speak of different ideological issues, to speak of different prevalence data for each, and so on. In fact, it is not uncommon for the discussion to direct itself mainly to a single subtype, particularly where the broader problem is not well understood or is particularly complex. For example, you are most likely to read about sexual abuse apart from a discussion of child abuse in general. The task of social problem analysis is to track the subclassifications being used, that is, how much and in what regard a narrowing of focus has occurred. One reason for this careful tracking is to avoid being misled by later data that are presented about the problem. Sometimes, for example, social problem presentations will focus only on a subtopic but will present data on the *whole* social problem. Sometimes this is intentional mischief; other times presenters themselves are unaware of the error.

Causes and Consequences

Another factor to consider in doing a social problem analysis is what causal explanations are offered as to why a social problem has come to exist. But sometimes the focus is not on explanation at all, rather on predicting *consequences* that will follow from the social problem. Sorting out this pattern of attributed causes and consequences is at the core of analyzing a social problem viewpoint for causation. A primary goal of the analysis is to discover whether it is the causes (antecedents), the consequences (effects), or both that are of utmost importance to the particular social problem presentation being analyzed. One way to separate antecedents from consequences is to try to diagram, to capture what is being said by setting down on paper what appears to be the causal pattern the author is asserting.

Causal patterns can be described in many ways; one simple method is to describe what will be called causal chains. A *causal chain* consists of a set of events (or variables or factors) arranged in a time sequence that shows the social problem event that is to be explained—what comes before the event and, therefore, is said to "cause" it and what comes after the event and is said to be a consequence. Causal chains are to be read from left to right so that the "event-to-be-explained" is always some variable to the right of the center of the chain. If only antecedents are of concern, the social problem event-to-be-explained will always appear on the *far* right of the causal chain. Let us now focus only on such causal chains as these, for simplicity. Figure 1.1 presents a simple causal chain "explaining" high unemployment rates (follow the arrows).

It should be clear that this is neither the only, nor even a complete, explanation for unemployment, only one plausible explanation. Remember, the object here is to find the expressed *belief* about the causes of the social problem. This causal chain could also be used to explain poverty and economic deprivation because poverty can be a result of the fact that people are just not working and earning wages. However, another author concerned with poverty and economic deprivation might explain it on the basis of high prices rather than low wages. That causal chain might look something like the one in Figure 1.2.

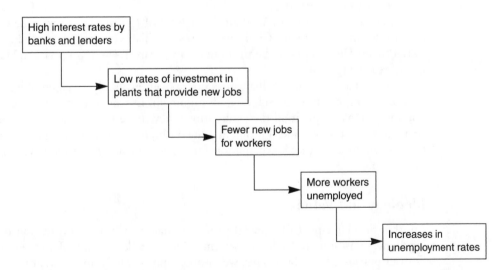

FIGURE 1.1 A simple causal chain explaining high unemployment.

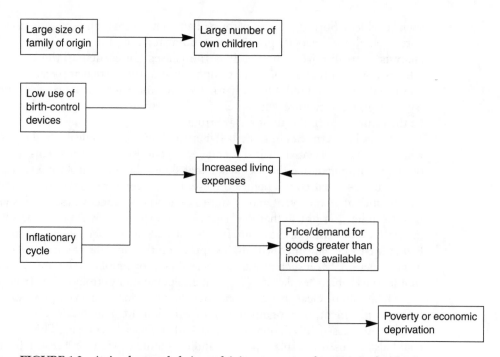

FIGURE 1.2   A simple causal chain explaining poverty and economic deprivation.

Some causal chains or "explanations" can be very complicated. We can put both these diagrammed causal chains together and add some other features to generate a broader and more complex explanation of poverty. Thus, Figure 1.3 shows how *both* high prices and low earnings produce poverty; it also shows some of the reasons for high prices and low earnings.

Let us now return to Williams's analysis of the minimum wage law and its relation to unemployment. Could we express Williams's argument in the form of a causal chain? We would suggest the example in Figure 1.4 as appropriate to Williams's line of reasoning.

Note that although Williams has not spoken explicitly of an employer's profit motive, it is crucial to understanding his argument. Discussions of social problems do not always make explicit all the assumptions they make in presenting their explanations for the cause of a social problem. One of the reasons for making a special effort to understand an author's explanation for a social problem is to uncover "hidden" assumptions.

Ideology and Values

Another crucial aspect of a social problem analysis is the identification of major ideological positions and value biases embedded in a description of a social problem. For our purposes here, by a *value*, we mean simply a conception of what is preferred. Values express a vision of how things "ought" to be. Note that value statements can be

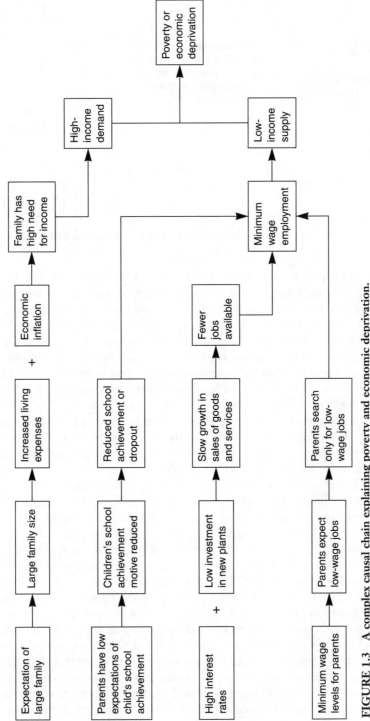

FIGURE 1.3 A complex causal chain explaining poverty and economic deprivation.

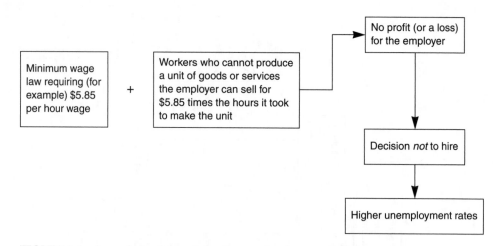

FIGURE 1.4   An analysis of the minimum wage law in a causal chain.

simple or complex, but in the end, they need no justification because they are personal or cultural preferences. For example, if poverty as a social problem is identified by a lack of minimum nutritional standards, a value stance is implied that prefers that no one be hungry. However, if poverty as a social problem is identified by some large difference between annual incomes of certain types of citizens, a value stance is implied that prefers that income be more *equally distributed*, without respect to the differing needs of individuals or any concept of how social merit should be rewarded.

Value statements are usually expressed in phrases using the words *should, ought,* or *must.* For example, the statements "No one should be hungry" or "Employers should not refuse a job because of an applicant's racial background" are value statements using *should* terms. Value statements are usually more numerous and more complex than can be stated in single sentences. On that account, and for our particular purposes, let us use the term *ideology* to refer to sets of value statements.

Sometimes it is difficult to disentangle value and knowledge statements. Ideology is built from value statements, and explanations and causal chains are built from sentences that describe what *is* the case about one thing or another. These latter sentences are "factual" statements, statements asserting what exists. Recall that value statements are sentences about what is to be preferred. So, it is one thing to say "No human being *should* be hungry" (a value statement, a statement of preference), but it is another thing to say "From 12 to 15 percent of the U.S. population lives in conditions of poverty in which they *are* hungry some part of each week" (a statement of fact). The operating terms are italicized. Again, value and ideological statements feature verbs such as *should, ought,* or *must;* knowledge and factual statements feature verbs such as *are* and *is.* The reason it is sometimes difficult to disentangle value and knowledge statements is that they concern the same event; it is important to distinguish between the two statements because they are intended to deliver two very different messages. The correct reading of the message of the value statement gives the reader of a social problem description advance information about *outcomes* that the author will advocate.

The correct reading of the message in the factual statements of the causation analysis will give the reader advance information about the kind of program interventions or policy or legislative changes the author will seek.

Let us now return to the Williams material on minimum wage just to search for examples of the difference between value and knowledge statements. Our conclusion was that Williams's causal argument necessarily entailed a statement about employers' profits. That is a factual statement as it stands—that is, we are saying that Williams implies that employers *do* consider the effect on their profit in making hiring decisions. Note that it would be a value statement if it involved some term such as *should* or *ought:* "Employers *should* consider profit . . . , and so on, in their hiring decisions." The point is that his argument does not say that; all it says is that employers *do* consider that issue.

Unfortunately for us, the value statements in the Williams excerpt are not distinguished by the presence of the revealing verbs *should* and *ought.* Therefore, to identify his ideology, we must construct statements whose meaning is not substantially altered by transforming them into statements containing *should* and *ought* terms. For example, we *cannot* take such a statement as "Black youth unemployment in some major cities is estimated to be 70 percent" and transform it into the statement "Black youth unemployment in some major cities should be 70 percent" and contend that we have not changed the meaning radically. However, we can take a sentence from the first paragraph of the excerpt and transform it into a value statement without altering its meaning. Thus: "Federal minimum wage laws represent a tragic irony. . . . [T]hese measures in fact impede the upward mobility and increase the dependence of the most disadvantaged among us." We can restate this sentence as a value statement as follows: "Impeding upward mobility and increasing the dependence of the most disadvantaged among us are effects of the minimum wage law that we should not allow." What we have done is to take a cue from the phrase "tragic irony" and interpret it to be equivalent to saying that there are effects of the minimum wage law that *should* not occur.

Gainers and Losers

The focus of this aspect of social problem analysis is on three things: (1) *who* loses and gains, (2) *what kind* of gains and losses are involved, and (3) *how much* value is entailed. The reason to examine this angle is that it is not always obvious what losses and costs are of concern; different groups value different kinds of losses and costs. We do not trouble to take a stand about a social problem unless we are concerned about a loss of some kind, so in almost any social problem description, some attention is paid to the issue of losses and costs.

The first principle here is that social problem costs (losses) are seldom, if ever, shared equally among citizens. The first question is, "Who loses most?" In some ultimate sense, there is probably no citizen who is not affected in an indirect way by all social problems. The issue is to identify those who pay the biggest costs. For example, it is quite clear that the group that pays the biggest cost of the very high rates of crime in inner cities is made up of the local inner-city residents themselves. It is they who are robbed, raped, mugged, and murdered. There are also *indirect* costs shared by all taxpayers, for example, emergency room costs of violent crime. On the other hand, by any measure, the most prominent victims of the "white-collar crime" of tax evasion are the middle-income classes, who pay the biggest share of the taxes collected by the U.S. Treasury. They bear most of the cost of the social problem because they must pay most of the extra tax needed to make up for the evaded taxes.

One of the important costs of the social problem of maintaining the health of the population is the dollar costs of medical care for the aged. Those costs are paid largely through Medicare, a Social Security subprogram financed by the Social Security health insurance withholding tax paid by those now in the workforce. The amount withheld from the preretirement wages of those now receiving medical care was always far less than present average costs, so current recipients cannot be said to have paid for the Medicare benefits they now receive. That is not necessarily because of their unwillingness to do so but simply because (1) many people retired before Medicare was enacted, (2) the costs of medical care have risen enormously in recent years, (3) wages were less inflated in earlier years and, therefore, (4) contributions for Medicare were less. In addition, no one foresaw the incredible advances in medical care now available—for example, the expensive medical technology developed mainly for the older population: bone and joint transplants and heart bypass procedures. The unpredicted costs here are paid from the contributions to Social Security by those who now work and pay withholding taxes. Note carefully that what has been said is not yet a judgment of the justice of the way these charges are distributed; such judgment will evolve from the *shoulds* and *oughts* of the value and ideology analysis.

Sometimes, very small details designed into public programs make an important difference in who ends up paying the biggest share of the costs. Consider again the example of wage losses for workers permanently and totally work-injured who receive workers' compensation benefits. Lost wages are the amount a person could be expected to earn (at present wage levels) from the date of injury to the date of retirement. It is a cost to the *worker* when not all of the loss is repaid by the workers' compensation program. It is a cost to *taxpayers* when the workers' compensation benefit is not paid at all or is so insufficient that some other public welfare benefits must be paid to keep the worker with disabilities and his or her family afloat. However, it is a different case when a company buys workers' compensation insurance coverage that is sufficient to pay the worker's full lost wages but *increases the price of its product or service to pay for the insurance.* Thus, it turns out that the *consumer* is actually paying for the worker's injury. These examples show why it is important to take careful notice of who pays social problem costs; existing social program details can and often do make substantial alterations in what would appear to be the obvious pattern of cost bearing for social problems.

After considering who loses from a social problem, the next issue to consider is the type of loss involved. In the preceding examples, money (or income) was the prominent kind of loss of immediate concern. Other concerns—pain, discomfort, inconvenience, time, and geographic dislocation—are examples of other types of losses that sometimes are discussed in presenting social problems. One obvious example is found in discussions of the social problem of abortion. For some, the concern is the loss and costs of the extinction of human life; for others, the concern is each woman's loss of autonomy over her body and its products. Much of the argument here turns on precisely what type of loss is viewed as important. Similarly, the social cost of a brutal beating might be said to be pain, disablement, discomfort, injustice, shame, and terror—which could be said of most violent crimes, including rape. Although some of these social costs can be said to be subjective in some sense, none would argue that they are unimportant, incalculable, or uncompensable.[10]

Sometimes, social problems incur costs that revolve around the loss of *potential gains* rather than immediate losses, monetary or otherwise. For example, one of the costs for the parents of a child with severe developmental disabilities may be in what those parents are prevented from doing for their other children, their own future employment, or further education. Other social problems also can incur status costs; for example, a cost of crime or mental illness to the families of those involved can be negative social labeling that results in losses in both social status and personal esteem.

Finally, consideration must be made of the magnitude of costs—*how much* (whether money or some other measurement). It is convenient to express social costs in dollar terms because that measurement is easily interpreted by a wide audience. There are widely accepted ways of translating almost any kind of loss into dollar terms. The value of life is translated daily into dollar terms when civil courts hand down judicial decisions—for example, on whether a physician was guilty of malpractice in a patient's disablement or death or whether a certain dollar value relieved "pain and suffering." One way economists translate subjective losses into money losses is by imagining (or gathering data on) how much most people would be willing to pay either to get rid of the effects of particular pain or suffering or status loss or how much they would demand to take on the problem intentionally. One simple test is to ask yourself, for instance, how many dollars it would take to get *you* to take on the care of a person in a persistent vegetative state in your own home or to have it generally known that a close family member is imprisoned for a serious crime. Estimating the *magnitude of social costs of a social problem* is an important process in understanding a social problem because doing so provides at least one standard by which a problem's "importance" can be measured both absolutely and relatively to other social problems.

If the first principle is that social problem costs are seldom shared equally among citizens, then the second principle is that *some people and some social groups actually benefit from others' social problems*. It is quite possible that some social problems are not solvable in any important and immediate sense simply because they create benefits that others are reluctant to give up. The general—albeit unsavory—idea here is that indeed some people do profit from others' misery. The extent to which this idea is true is debatable, but it does not seem wise to assume that such is never (or only seldom) the case. The most obvious evidence of this truth is the documented fact that a small number of people profit handsomely from others' addictions (liquor, tobacco, pharmaceuticals, illegal narcotics, and such). Less obvious is how this principle operates in relation to other more controversial social problems like unemployment, physical disablement, and aging. For example, it is not merely cynical to observe that forcing more welfare recipients into the workforce will increase the pool from which employers can draw low-wage employees and will most likely reduce wages.

Employers of unskilled labor would certainly seem to profit from reduced welfare benefit levels and high unemployment.

It would be unfortunate to conclude that only employers benefit from the existence of social problems. One rather well-known line of social analysis views racial and ethnic prejudice and discrimination as one means of establishing an "underclass," a scapegoated "bottom-of-the-social-ladder" group, against whom all other classes and types can be measured and positively valued. Theoretically then, wherever racial discrimination reduces competition from persons of color, whites must gain in terms of money and status. Some believe that the big gainers from the social unrest and racial tensions of the sixties and seventies were not working-class blacks but the black middle class, who achieved gains in income and increased their entrance at educational institutions and their starts up career ladders. That is not a bad thing, only a comment on the disparate distribution of social gain from social problems. Another commonly discussed example is the ability of the health corporations to profit from disease. And, in fact, all professional practitioners profit from social problems; if there were no social problems, there would be no need for social workers or human service personnel at all. But, be careful with that claim. Showing that a professional makes a profit isn't enough to establish that professionals themselves contribute to continuing the existence of a social problem. Professional profit is not a serious issue unless it can also be shown that personal profit rather than benefits to clients/patients or consumers have first priority.

Understanding who profits from the existence of a social problem can reveal the forces that act against its elimination. It is very likely that where a shortage of good housing exists and profits are being made from existing stock, associations of rental property owners, in serving their own interests, will oppose the building of public housing. Similarly, it is unlikely that the American Medical Association will support the creation of a large number of medical schools—despite evidence that all citizens get medical care at reduced cost if the patient–physician ratio were decreased. It is equally unlikely that traditional craft unions (plumbing, carpentry, toolmakers) will admit minorities for fear they will become job and career competitors—especially in a stagnant economy in which the threat of competition willing to work for less wages is keenly felt. The point is that the social problems of unemployment, housing, health, and racism all have some built-in resistance to solution simply because they generate strong economic and status rewards for other citizen groups.

Using the Conclusions of Social Problem Analysis to Design Social Policies and Programs and to Judge Their "Fit" to the Social Problem

When political scientists, students of government, or sociologists study a social policy or program, their interest is centered on explaining it as a fact of social life—that is, how the policy or program came to be, what broad social function it serves, or why it appeared in one form and not another. The social practitioners for whom this book is intended have different questions in mind because their interest lies in how social policies and programs can be instrumental in solving, or helping solve, social problems for their clients. How much difference does this program or policy make to those who suffer from the effects of the social problem?[11] *Qualitative judgments about the merit of a social program or policy cannot be made without reference to the original understanding of the social problem.* The idea here is that social policies and programs should be judged against the needs and causal analysis implied in the conclusions of the study of the social problem. Social policies should not be designed in the abstract or in relation to more or less random ideas about the nature of the social problem toward which they are directed as a solution.

Table 1.1 contrasts the components of social problem analysis with the basic elements of social policies and programs. What is the relationship between the two?

Consider eligibility rules, in their most elementary sense, as policies that tell who should and should not get benefits or services. Then ask the question, "Does a problem definition influence how such a rule could be constructed?" The most

TABLE 1.1   Each Social Problem Analysis Component Specifies an Aspect of a Social Policy and Program Element

Problem Analysis Component	Policy and Program Basic Element
1. Problem definition (terms)	Specifies the terms that must be used in the *eligibility rules* determining who is/is not entitled to benefits or services and specifies the general *goals* to be achieved.
Subtypes	Specifies the specific *target populations*.
Quantifications	Can specify the priorities on the basis of which one *goal* rather than another is chosen when size of the problem is believed to be the determining issue.
	Helps estimate financing needed.
2. Causal analysis	Specifies the particular *types of benefits and/or services* that must be delivered to address the problem.
	Specifies the *type of personnel* required to deliver the services or benefits when causation implicates cultural factors or implies a particular expertise and/or training or experience of the helper.
3. Ideology and values	Can determine choice of type of *eligibility rule* (e.g., means test rather than insurance principle).
	Can determine *goals* by establishing priorities to serve preferred subcategories of the problem.
	Determines *amount of financing* made available.
4. Gainer and loser analysis	Can specify method of *financing* in which dollar loss is clear, ability to pay is obvious, and responsibility for loss can be assigned (e.g., workers' compensation).

straightforward answer is that ideally an eligibility rule should make services and benefits of the program available *only* to those who have the problem, a determination based on who meets the terms of the problem definition. Conversely, the rule should make it *impossible* for those who do not meet the terms of that definition to receive benefits and services. For example, if the social problem of concern is long-term hospitalization of chronically psychotic individuals, then an appropriate eligibility rule might be found in the current American Psychiatric Association's *Diagnostic and Statistical Manual of Mental Disorders (DSM-IV-TR)*. Thus, the eligibility rule might restrict benefits and services to individuals with "Delusions, hallucinations, or . . . disturbances in the form of thought."[12]

The "fit" with which we are so concerned here is not just a matter of its being logically "neat," because the lack of fit has serious consequences. For example, a program can either overlook needful citizens (underinclusion) or is more expensive than it should be (produces overwhelming cost) because program benefits or services are wasted on those who do not have the problem and do not need the benefits. Furthermore, without a clear eligibility rule in place, it is impossible to determine whether a program or policy had an impact on the problem and, thus, whether the causal explanations in the analysis were right. Data on the results of the program are useless if contaminated by (1) inclusion of those whose problems the program was never intended to solve or (2) data from an ill-formed eligibility rule that excludes either too many or the wrong people. In the example of long-term hospitalization of individuals with psychosis, no one would be able to tell whether people with a chronic psychosis and a history of long hospitalization could be helped by a programmed intervention that involved their living outside an institution independently if, for example, nonpsychotic chronically delinquent youngsters and senile elderly people were accepted into the program by an ill-fitting or misapplied eligibility rule. Not only might important resources be misdirected and, therefore, unavailable to those for whom they were originally intended, but also the chance to learn something about the validity of the ideas in the social problem analysis would be lost.

A few eligibility rules are not constructed out of their relationship to the social problem. The fact that any honorably discharged veteran is entitled to free hospitalization in any Veterans Administration hospital is clearly a welfare benefit according to the generally accepted definition (a material gain resulting from the direct or indirect redistribution of someone else's income).[13] This is not to say that the benefit is undeserved, but only to make the point that the eligibility rule is *not* based on the conclusions from a social problem analysis. Rather, the basis for this eligibility rule is society's desire to *reward* those who in serving their country risked their own lives.

The problem-definition aspect of social problem analysis also prescribes the terms in which the program goals and objectives must be stated. For example, a city's summer recreation program that was originally intended simply to provide adult supervision for out-of-school children transforms its goal into a grand statement about "providing for the child's total well-being during the summer period." There is nothing wrong with concern about children's total well-being (although strange that it is only during the summer period), but in this instance, the goal is misguided because it is unfaithful to the original conception of the problem.

Before leaving our consideration of how qualitative standards for policy and program design can be derived from problem definitions, recall that there is a subsection of the problem-identification aspect called *subtypes*, which allows for variability within the social problem to be noted and reviewed; for example, there are key differences between sexual abuse, neglect, and physical abuse within the larger social problem category of child abuse. Once a subclass is declared, there should also be some awareness of its numerical—that is, its *quantitative*—importance. These issues from social problem analysis should guide judgments about whether the goals of the policy or program are directed toward the *whole* social problem or only one of its parts; if the concern is with a subtype, analysis should help determine whether its size warrants priority relative to other subtypes. Size is not the only determiner of priorities, but it is important to understand that magnitude provides the basis for a claim on public resources.

Now let us pay some attention to the relationship between causal explanation and the types of services or benefits delivered. Earlier, we showed how the most powerful kind of causal analysis proceeds by identifying the factors (variables) believed to be the crucial determiners of the problem. Where that is the case, it should be obvious that the types of benefits or services should be those that are powerful in reducing the influence of those determiners. For example, if the social problem of concern is the physical abuse of children and the causal analysis identifies severe economic stress as the major determinant of abuse, then among the benefits provided by the policy and program must be money, goods, or their equivalent to relieve economic stress. If the causal analysis identifies as the key cause of maternal child abuse, the presence of a nonnurturing, abusive mother who never shows her daughters how to rear children without physical abuse, then the program or policy design simply must provide the substitute parent model that abusing mothers did not get in their own homes.

Even though it would seem that no rational policy or program designer would violate this simple, straightforward, and obvious idea, that is just not the case. Some programs, despite their objective to alleviate child abuse based on an understanding of the problem as described in the preceding theory, in fact only teach about child-development stages. As uplifting (even useful) as that might be, such a program must be judged to be a bad fit and an irrational policy. Even the casual observer of social policy and programs does not have to look hard to find bad examples along this line: One program design is based on a causal analysis that identifies (reasonably enough) the major factor in poor social adjustment of some developmentally disabled children as their isolation from ordinary children in ordinary classrooms. However, this same program develops a policy to scatter special education classrooms for these children throughout ordinary neighborhood schools—but it staggers and limits the daily schedule of the special education classrooms so that pupils with disabilities have no chance to associate with mainstream schoolchildren either in the classroom or elsewhere. The fit between the causal analysis and the policy solution is lost because the type of benefit intended as a solution consistent with the causal analysis turns out not to be the one implemented.

Another possibility is that the causal analysis may direct the program or policy to employ only certain types of personnel to deliver benefits or services; that is, the causal analysis creates certain standards for the administrative service-delivery system. As will be discussed in Chapter 6, personnel specifications are an important feature in benefits and services. A common example is a causal analysis that explains that some subgroups of certain ethnic or racial minorities do not apply for important health or school-based services because of the cultural and language barriers created by nonethnic or nonminority personnel. When that causal view is taken, a heavy obligation is laid on the personnel policies of the delivery system: Sufficient ethnic or minority personnel must be online if the services are to be delivered effectively.

The analysis of major gainers and losers as a result of social problems is also a source of rational expectations for social policies and programs. These conclusions are particularly relevant for specifying methods of financing. When the loss involved is a tangible material or financial loss, one obvious method of financing is implied: The gainers should repay the losers. In fact, that is exactly what is behind the "victim restitution" programs operated in relation to the social problem of crimes against property (e.g., theft, larceny, and misdemeanors). The causal explanation usually invoked by these programs is that offenders repeat such crimes because (1) doing so costs the offenders nothing out of their own pockets and (2) offenders never have to encounter their victims face to face in terms of being held accountable for their criminal acts. Victim restitution programs, both the direct program cost and the cost arising from the adverse effect(s) of the crime, ideally should be paid for by the offenders themselves. This financing feature is entirely consistent with the causal analysis. Another example is the workers' compensation program, the goal of which is to compensate workers injured on their jobs so that their income will not suffer irremediable damage. Workers' compensation legislation characteristically assumes that the cause of the income loss is the workplace incident (even though the personal blame for that accident is not assigned and its determination is not made a part of the program or policy—a no-fault system). Because the workplace "caused" an income loss, the policy pursued in legislation is to place responsibility on the employer to provide insurance payments to pay the cost of replacing the injured employee's lost income.

Summary

Chapter 1 discussed the central importance of social policy in the professional practice of social work and other human services. Social policies both create and constrain the possibilities of any social practice. Central to that understanding is an ability to ferret out the view of the social problem taken by legislative bodies, policy and program designers, political critics, and program and policy administrators. An analytic framework—that is, a set of concepts by which the fundamental dimensions of *any* view of a social problem can be understood—was presented. This framework takes into consideration four activities:

1. Identify the way the problem is defined.
2. Identify the cause(s) to which the problem is attributed and its most serious consequences.
3. Identify the ideology and the values that make the events of concern come to be defined as a problem.
4. Identify major gainers and losers with respect to the problem.

These activities were discussed and examples were given so that readers can learn to analyze social problems. The chapter closed with a discussion of how to use the results of the problem analysis to make judgments of the merit of the program and to design programs anew.

EXERCISES

1. Reread Williams on the minimum wage, pages 11 and 12, and the causal chain drawn for it in Figure 1.3, page 17. Add "maximizing employer's profit" as an explanatory factor (antecedent) to the diagram. Then think how it would affect the total diagram and Williams's causal argument overall.

2. There are both direct and indirect costs paid by those who lose and gain from the existence of a social problem. Pick a social problem and show both its direct and indirect costs.

3. Social problem costs, when they seem to involve things that cannot be priced in a handy marketplace (physical pain, for example, or fear of street violence or a neighboring district full of prostitutes and drug dealers, perhaps), can be estimated by imagining that there is such a market where you can pay (expressed in dollar terms) as much as you would be willing to pay to have it disappear (and assuming you had the money). Identify a social problem that annoys you and your friends and estimate what you personally would be willing to pay to be rid of it. Then present the scenario to friends, and collect their "price."

4. Do an analysis of the social problem viewpoint expressed in the following historical document. Use the four social problem analysis categories discussed in this chapter.

Dangers in Half-Dime Novels and Story Papers, 1883[14]
Satan stirred up certain of his willing tools on earth by the promise of a few paltry dollars to improve greatly on the death-dealing quality of the weekly death traps, and forthwith came a series of new snares of fascinating construction, small and tempting in price, and baited with high-sounding names. These sure-ruin traps comprise a large variety of half-dime novels, five- and ten-cent story papers, and low-priced pamphlets for boys and girls.

Again, these stories breed vulgarity, profanity, loose ideas of life, impurity of thought and deed. They render the imagination unclean, destroy domestic peace, desolate homes, cheapen woman's virtue, and make foul-mouthed bullies, cheats, vagabonds, thieves, desperadoes, and libertines. They disparage honest toil and make real life a drudge and burden. What young man will serve an apprenticeship, working early and late, if his mind is filled with the idea that sudden wealth may be acquired by following the hero of the story? In real life, to begin at the foot of the ladder and work up, step by step, is the rule; but in these stories, inexperienced youth, with no moral character, take the foremost positions, and by trick and device, knife and revolver, bribery and corruption, carry everything before them, lifting themselves in a few short weeks to positions of ease and affluence. Moral courage with such is a thing to be sneered at and despised in many of these stories. If one is asked to drink and refuses, he is set up and twitted till he yields or is compelled to by force. The idea of doing anything from principle is ridiculous in the extreme. As well fill a kerosene-oil lamp with water and expect a brilliant light. And so, in addition to all else, there is early inculcated a distaste for the good, and the piercing blast of ridicule is turned upon the reader to destroy effectually all moral character.

Satan is more interested in the child than many parents are. Parents do not stop to think or look for their children in these matters, while the archenemy is thinking, watching, and plotting continually to effect their ruin.

Thoughtless parents, heedless guardians, negligent teachers, you are each of you just the kind that old Satan delights to see placed over each child. He sets his base traps right in your very presence, captures and ruins your children, and you are each of you criminally responsible.

Take further instances of the effect of this class of publications, and then say if my language is too strong. Does it startle and offend? To startle, to awaken, to put you on your guard, to arouse you to your duty over your own children, is my purpose. *Your child is in danger of having its pure mind cursed for life.*

From infancy to maturity the pathway of the child is beset with peculiar temptations to do evil. Youth has to contend against great odds. Inherited tendencies to wrongdoing render the young oftentimes open to ever-present seductions. Inherited appetites and passions are secretly fed by artificial means, until they exert a well-nigh irresistible mastery over their victim. The weeds of sin, thus planted in weak human nature, are forced to a rapid growth, choking virtue and truth, and stunting all the higher and holier instincts. Thus, many a child of dissolute parents is born with natural desires for strong drink, and early becomes intemperate. In his thoughtful moments he loathes drink, and yet there comes upon him a force he is powerless to resist. So, too, the incontinence of parents brings into the world children inheriting morbidly susceptible natures—natures set like the hair trigger to a rifle—ready to fall into shame at the slightest temptation.

We speak of youth as the plastic state—the period of all others when the human soul is most easily molded and character formed. Youth is the seed-time. Maturity gathers in the crop. Youth is the fountain from which the waters of life flow. *If parents do not train and instruct their children, the devil will.* Whether parents deem it important to watch the child or no, there is one who deems it so important that he keeps a constant watch. *The devil stations a sentry to observe and take advantage of every point open to an evil influence.* He attacks the sensitive parts of our nature. He would destroy the finest and most magnificent portion of our being. The thoughts, imagination, and affections he is most anxious to corrupt, pervert, and destroy.

I unhesitatingly declare, there is at present no more active agent employed by Satan in civilized communities to ruin the human family and subject the nations to himself than evil reading.

If gambling saloons, concert dives, lottery and policy shops, poolrooms, low theaters, and rumholes are allowed to be kept open; if obscene books and pictures, foul papers, and criminal stories for the young are allowed to go broadcast, then must state prisons, penitentiaries, workhouses, jails, reformatories, etc., be erected and supported. Expensive courts and high-salaried officials must be employed at the taxpayer's expense, to care for those youths who are ruined, or to protect society against them.

Parents do not permit their children to make a playhouse of a sewer, nor to breathe its poisoned gasses. It is not popular to set diseased meat before the public in any of our numerous hotels or restaurants. Infected clothing may not be offered for sale, much less hawked about the streets. Yet worse evils than these are tolerated and encouraged, even while they are scattering moral death and physical suffering among those whom it is the especial duty of every civilized government to shield and protect—the young.

NOTES

1. P. Pinstrup-Anderson, *World Food Trends and Future Food Security*, Food Policy Statement Number 18 (Washington, DC: International Food Policy Research Institute, 1994).

2. These broad analytic categories were put together by David Hardcastle, a professor at the School of Social Work, University of Maryland–Baltimore, from the work of a variety of sociologists and other students of social problems. We have expanded them and added the details in the material that follows, creating substantial alterations to 1 and 4.

3. The overall 2005 divorce rates in the United States were around 40 percent, but not a very good predictor of who is likely to be divorced because divorce rates vary widely by income, geography, education, race, age, and other demographics. D. Hurley, "Divorce Rates: Not as High as You Think," *New York Times*, sec. F, April 19, 2005, p. 7, P. A. Nakonezny, R. D. Schull, and J. E. Rogers, "The Effect of No-Fault Divorce Law on the Divorce Rate Across the 50 States and Its Relation to Income, Education and Religiosity," *Journal of Marriage and Family*, 57 (1995): 477–488.

4. P. R. Amato and D. D. DeBoer, "The Transmission of Marital Instability Across Generations: Relationship Skills or Commitment to Marriage?" *Journal of Marriage and Family*, 63(4) (2001): 1038–1052.

5. A. M. Parkman, *Good Intentions Gone Awry: No-Fault Divorce and the American Family* (Lanham, MD: Rowman & Littlefield, 2000) pp. 99–150.

6. From Walter E. Williams, "The Minimum Wage Vision," *Washington Times*, October 26, 2006, p. 3; Walter E. Williams, *SmithKline Forum for a Healthier America*, 1(6) (September 1979): 1–6. Dollar amounts have been adjusted to reflect inflation. Reprinted by permission of the author and VanSant Dugdale Advertising, Baltimore, Maryland. Notice that in the past decade the consensus among economists that supported Williams' argument has weakened. J. Stiglitz, "Employment, Social Justice and Societal Well-Being," *International Labor Review*, 149 (2002): 1–2; P. Lewis, "The Economics of the Minimum Wage," *The Australian Economic Review*, 30(2) (1997): 204–207.

7. Williams, *The SmithKline Forum*.

8. Ibid.

9. The data on unemployment in 2005 in this section were taken from Community Services Society of New York, *No Recovery for Youth: Black Men Have Yet to Fully Regain Employment Lost in Recession* [press release], February 26, 2007, www.cssny.org/news/releases/2007_0226.html.

10. The reader may notice that these examples all concern individuals and, thus, may be concerned that this contradicts earlier statements that social problems concern *groups* and not individuals. That problem can be resolved by remembering that all the individuals here are assumed to be members of a larger group in which all suffer from the same problem.

11. Notice that this criterion for judging a policy or program is not entirely practical from the viewpoint of the government or society because the standard concerns what the policy or program does for *those in need*. Unfortunately, in any view, the interests of the state do not always coincide with the interests of those in need, with those who suffer from a social problem. For instance, it may be easiest, and certainly the least costly, for society at large and a government to ignore sick, disabled, and poverty-stricken individuals. The focus on the interests of those in need is a bias here and is consistent with the value positions of the social work profession. The profession takes as one of its goals the elimination of "barriers to human realization." Social problems of concern to the profession are those believed to be major barriers to many people. See "The Working Definition of Social Work Practice," *Social Work*, 3(2) (April 1958): 5–9.

12. *Diagnostic and Statistical Manual of Mental Disorders (DSM-IV-TR)*, 4th ed., text revision (Washington, DC: American Psychiatric Association, 2000).

13. Richard A. Musgrave, *The Theory of Public Finance* (New York: McGraw-Hill, 1961), pp. 111–112.

14. From Anthony Comstock, "Dangers in Half-Dime Novels and Story Papers," in Robert H. Bremner (ed.), *Traps for the Young* (Cambridge, MA: Belknap Press of Harvard University Press, 1967), pp. 21–28, 238–242, first published in 1883.

PART TWO

A Style of Policy Analysis for the Practical Public Policy Analyst

[P]rovidence never intended to make the management of public affairs a mystery, to be comprehended only by a few persons of sublime genius, of which there seldom are three born in an age.

—Jonathan Swift, *Gulliver's Travels*

Introduction

The first part of this book closed by showing how conclusions from the social problem analysis might indicate for the practitioner-analyst how particular features of a policy or program were (or should have been) shaped. The next step is to look closely at an actual operating policy or program design to identify its major features. Thus, the first section of Chapter 2 will present a way of looking closely at (of describing analytically) social policies and programs. It proceeds by first searching for the six fundamental elements in social policy and program designs. These are fundamental in the sense that they can be found explicitly or implicitly, in one form or another, in every social policy or program. Each element will be discussed, examples will be given, and concepts and classifications will be presented to sensitize the observer to their various forms. Once these elements are identified, a judgment is made to answer the most basic question: Are these program or policy features "good"?

2

An Overview of a Style of Policy Analysis

A Value-Critical Approach

This chapter is intended to lay the groundwork for understanding the basic tasks the practitioner as policy analyst will confront. To that end we will discuss the distinctions among the value-analytic, the value-committed, and the value-critical methods of policy analysis. Arguments will be presented in favor of the value-critical style for the use of social work and human service practitioners. Criteria for making professional judgments about the "goodness" of social policies and programs in using the value-critical style will be presented. We will also discuss how personal value preferences are taken into account. These evaluative criteria will be used throughout the succeeding chapters.

Martin Rein calls the "analytic-descriptive" method of policy analysis the *sheer description* of a social policy or program, which is a necessary step taken prior to a value-critical analysis. It proceeds by taking the policy or program apart, piece by piece, "where the intellectual challenge is to identify common features that are (or aren't) congruent or logically consistent with each other."[1] But, for the practical policy analyst, description is never more than a means to an end because the most important step in analyzing program and policy features is to arrive at a judgment about them, that is, whether they are, in a particular sense, "good," "right," or appropriate beyond logical consistency. Policy analysis that remains at a descriptive level, leaving this question unanswered, cannot be a complete, much less a good, analysis. Coming to judgment is always a value-laden business and a practitioner as analyst should not apologize for that fact; a judgment that would try to be otherwise—somehow value neutral—is hollow because human judgment must always use values as a foundation. This "coming to judgment" creates a *value-critical policy analysis* as distinguished from the analytic-descriptive approach.

The method of analysis presented in this book advocates using *both* approaches serially. It is analytic-descriptive in proceeding first to instruct the reader how to do close description by *disaggregating* the social policy or program into parts (policy elements and the three contexts) and examining them one by one. It follows Rein in advocating the crucial second step, which consists in critically evaluating all of the parts and how they fit together as a whole using strong, value-based criteria by which to make judgments of their goodness, fitness, and appropriateness. In some ways, the analytic-descriptive approach is a way to see clearly how things *should* work. Because in the real world things almost never work out as planned, this second-step, value-critical approach then throws the conventional view (how a program should work) into question and adopts a critical and skeptical view of how programs *actually* work—or don't work.[2] It seeks to uncover shortcomings, inconsistencies in logic, and ambiguities in the everyday program operations.

Michael Howlett's policy review is a good example of an analytic-descriptive analysis that comes short of a value-critical analysis.[3] At issue are policies addressing the need of poor people for low-cost housing. In Howlett's review there is no room for consideration of what policies can or cannot do for poor folks; for example, the analysis never considers how cash, as opposed to in-kind housing benefits (housing project apartments), gives different advantages and disadvantages to the people for whom they are intended.[4] When his analysis considers things such as complexity of operations and goes no further, it favors the interests of public administrators over poor people.

Value-critical analysis looks to ferret out policy problems through the use of value-based (biased) criteria, the function of which is to highlight problematic policy and program features. The analyst should expect to encounter conflict and divergence between the perspectives of two groups whose career interests are often quite different: (1) legislators who passed the enabling laws and (2) the middle managers and practitioners who implement the program derived and funded out of the law.[5] This kind of policy analysis is similar to what Habermas calls "cross-frame discourse."[6] Out of this dialectic, implications for action arise and it is precisely the intention and purpose of this method of policy analysis to generate action from its results. The hope is to present a method that will result in reader discontent with the old and a strong motive to create something new and better, to develop a better (more useful-for-clients) way of doing things.

Rein points out yet another approach to analyzing social policies and programs (one this book will not emphasize) called the *value-committed* approach. This approach

> starts with a strongly held position about how things *ought* to be . . . [and why they aren't] and then works out the implications of this commitment for action. . . . Some Marxists and many social activists, but definitely not all, fall into this category.[7]

On several counts, value commitment is an important dimension for social work and human service practitioners. There are moments when they can be called by any one of the three approaches. A calling to activism is recognizable in the roots of the social work profession—a calling to actively pursue particular strongly held positions based on fundamental professional values about how things ought to be against a very different real world. Note that in following that course, the policy discourse will then *not* be about operating details of policies and programs, but about more fundamental social and structural problems.

Under certain circumstances, a value-committed approach is irresistible. An example from Central America serves to clarify: From some particular value-committed points of view, there is an inherent injustice in a society in which 95 percent of a nation's assets and income are received by 1 percent of its people, particularly in the face of unemployment rates of over 40 percent, a poverty rate that by local standards approaches 50 percent, and a level of armed violence that makes death and civilian casualties a daily occurrence. For the social work practitioner as value-committed analyst, then, the argument should *not* be whether a policy of in-kind benefits like governmental commodity distributions (e.g., beans, cheese, flour, or meal) is the best way to keep people from starving (not that hunger isn't an important policy issue). Rather, for the value-committed practitioner, the argument *should* be whether this kind of income maldistribution is *just;* the policy argument should be over what is the best means of radically altering it. An appropriate comparison that expresses the futility of small-scale adjustments against a catastrophic environment is that the prevailing state of affairs is "like rearranging chairs on the deck of the sinking *Titanic.*" Examples closer to home might be migrant workers in fields sprayed with pesticides or workers involved in the production of nuclear power. For purposes of the value-committed approach, the argument *should not be* whether workers' compensation benefits should be administered by a public or a private profit-making insurance system (as it is in most states) but about whether some operations of high-injury industries should be permitted at all if they produce injuries at such a high rate or level of seriousness that any workers' compensation system design will be deficient.

The value-committed approach will not take the world at face value but will seek to impose its vision onto the world and change conditions so that they are more in keeping with the ideal world envisioned. Social workers and other human service practitioners need Rein's distinction among the three types of policy analysis in order to think clearly about which type they will opt for in any given situation. The decision is difficult because a number of questions must be weighed: "What is the 'real' state of the world with respect to the presenting social problem?" "What fundamental values are at stake?" "Is there plausible reason to believe that any audience exists to respond to the policy implications of a given activist approach to the social problem (i.e., will the approach have any chance of success)?"

The merits and difficulties of the value-committed approach will not be discussed in detail here because it seems a better fit with pure political activism, which is beyond the scope of this book—although the professional practice of social work does include that aspect. The point here is that professional practice goes beyond exercise of strongly held ideological conviction of the value-oriented approach. Certainly, social work practice includes political activism, but the social worker who wears the policy analyst's hat cannot *simultaneously* wear the political activist's hat. In this style of policy analysis, the two hats are mutually exclusive. Professional practitioners are called to commitment to a rationality that prizes alternative viewpoints and advocates taking them into account. They also are called to commitment to an objectivity that features multiple perspectives. However, *multiple perspectives are not a major feature of the value-committed approach because it assumes that the "truth" is already known and value choices are already made.*

Social work and other human services are currently much enamored of practice using multiple perspectives about the human condition, so the value-critical approach has a nice fit with the current professional preoccupation in its emphasis on multiple perspectives on the human condition.[8] The value-critical approach also fits the current professional preoccupation in its assumption that no facts are independent of theories and value biases. Whereas certain kinds of facts are very unlikely to change, the value-critical approach takes the view that the *selection* of facts taken under consideration does vary with the theory used; the approach further posits that it is the very purpose of theory to highlight some facts and ignore (or suppress) others. Note that for the purpose of analysis, the value-critical approach is, like all professions as a matter of fact, both conservative (in its view that the status quo might be worth saving) and radical (in calling the status quo into question).

The value-critical approach also has appeal because it can (and should be) grounded in practice experience. The questions practitioners raise are not just theoretical or just value-driven. In conducting the analysis of a social policy or program, social work and human service practitioners must bring to bear their own practice experience and, not least, the experience and perspective of their clients.

One element of the value-critical approach is that it requires teasing out the value biases and frames of reference that lie behind social problem analyses and their associated policy and program designs (ideology, causation, etc.). It develops a useful skill in unearthing competing values and frames of reference, a skill practitioners might use when confronted with conflict at any level—personal, familial, organizational, communal, or political. Practitioners need to develop this skill to be able to sort out their own organizational world. After all, each practitioner conducts her or his practice surrounded by competing values and frames of reference. For example, as indicated earlier in this chapter, organizational administrators have a frame of reference about implementing legislation or court mandates that may differ completely from that of the practitioner (the *frontline* practitioner) whose frame of reference about the social program design and the social problem comes from an entirely different world: street corners, interacting families, or the corridors of public schools and hospitals. Part of the business of practice is to find some rationalization for practice behaviors or program designs to bridge these competing interests and frames of reference. Social work and human service practitioners at either administrative or direct service levels don't anymore directly implement legislation than do physicians directly implement medical care out of textbook solutions or Medicare, hospital, legal, even ecclesiastical regulations. Thus, one of the important and persuasive attributes of value-critical policy analysis is that it forces practitioners to analyze for multiple and competing values and frames of reference, to make hard choices among them, and to take even their own frames and values into question as they confront the reality of the social world in general, the world their clients/consumers live in, and the daily operating world of organizations, laws, and public expectations.

Still, there is a utility to all this ambiguity in public policy. Social workers and human service professionals need to realize that it is precisely the *lack of specificity* of legislation, court decisions, historical tradition, and organizational regulation that is, in some important sense, the source of their freedom to practice while remaining faithful to their own personal values and professional frames of reference. Where legislation and regulation are precise and specific, practitioners have little discretion and their tasks are like automated decision making. Although practitioners' freedom will be seriously restricted whenever it conflicts with or bursts the bounds of plausible relation to legislation or regulation, nonetheless, it is commonly the judgment of experienced practitioners that *there is almost always more freedom to practice at the limits of organizational rules and regulations than is ever used by most social work and human service practitioners.* The point is, practitioners can protect themselves as well as maximize their freedom to practice simply by having a keen awareness of the relationship between their own values and frame of reference about a social problem and the programmatic features designed to cope with it. A key part of the practitioner's task is to bridge the two, and it is both an offensive and defensive practice strategy to be prepared to do so. The general principle is that a practitioner who can give a rational account of the relationships between what she or he is doing and the various frameworks that administrative or political superiors are using is less likely to experience a serious attack on his or her competence and autonomy. Martin Rein is very clear on this point:

> We more typically start with practice (action) and then design policies to justify what we do. The sequence is then from practice (action) to design to purpose. *Thus, policy rationalizes and legitimizes actions that arise from quite different processes.*[9] (emphasis added)

The advice here is not to suggest that a seat-of-the-pants behavioral style is really the way social work or human service is best practiced but only to underscore that practitioners and organizations (and street-level bureaucrats) muddle through, work things out, and try to do everything they can to be successful—then repeat what experience shows to be successful. Most likely they *did* begin with a guiding idea for practice, but that idea was shaped by the lived realities of both clients/consumers and helpers. The notion is that policy formed out of practice experience serves a useful function in helping shape the resulting program and practice design. It creates a freer stance from which to conduct a professional practice; here practitioners create programs and are not simply the routinizing, bureaucratic implementers, the tools of higher organizational powers.

The major problem for this approach lies in locating and working with a set of criteria by which to make the value-critical judgment. Particular sets of criteria for each policy element will now be advocated, criteria that seem to be absolutely necessary (though probably not sufficient, of course). Other criteria could be proposed certainly, but those proposed here will force the analyst to give attention to certain features of social policies and programs that are absolutely essential if the analyst is to understand the whole. It is left to the reader to ferret out the peculiar set of underlying, fundamental value biases in the criteria presented here. One such bias is the assumption of the authors of this text about rationality, that is, the best social program being one that is internally rational and logically consistent among its parts: for example, logically consistent with the judicial decisions, which by law it is obligated to follow, logically consistent with the social problem analysis used by the legislature when the enabling legislation was enacted, and logically consistent with the social problem analysis of the agency administrating the program or policy.

So, our list of evaluation criteria will begin with *whether the basic elements of the program and policy are consistent with its social problem analysis.* It can be said that the solution to inconsistency with the social problem analysis is not always to change program features, but one can change the social problem analysis! This is in line with two ideas: (1) Policy as well as social problem analysis can emerge from practice, not always the other way around, and (2) theories are not ultimate truth and should be shaped by practice and empirical experience as well as abstractions.

   Other evaluation criteria used here will include traditional ones: equity, adequacy, and efficiency (originally developed for use in economics). Also included are criteria that may be less familiar: trade-offs and access/coverage effects (as we have labeled them). Note that whereas these criteria are intended to be used for critical evaluation of more than one policy element, there are other criteria that are unique to a *single* policy element.

   The next section will give a brief overview of how to do an analytic description of policy and program using the six policy elements. We will then discuss how to do the value-critical aspect of the analysis, using suggested evaluation criteria to judge the ultimate merit of the operating characteristics.

The Policy and Program Analysis Process: An Overview of the Six Fundamental Policy Elements

Six policy elements form the cornerstone of every policy and program presented daily to citizens and clients/consumers. It is these policy elements on which the practical social policy analyst ultimately will base judgments about a policy or program. Ordinary sources for information about them cannot always be relied on; and, given the size and complexity of modern social welfare programs, agency staff members, administrators, and policy manuals, are not always accurate or completely informed. The six policy elements to be discussed are as follows:

1. Goals and objectives
2. Forms of benefits or services delivered
3. Entitlement (eligibility) rules
4. Administrative or organizational structure for service delivery
5. Financing method
6. Interactions among the foregoing elements[10]

   Why study these six rather than others? Because these are the six without which a social policy or program cannot be operated; that is, they are necessary to implement a program or policy system. It is simple enough to do a mental experiment to test out this idea: Suppose you have something very valuable to give away and you neither wish to bury it nor give it to kin or friends. How will you dispose of it? If you want to do it rationally, you will have to ask six questions to reach a decision.

1. What purpose or *goal* do you wish to achieve in giving this gift?
2. Given those goals, *who* is entitled to the gift?
3. In what *form* would the gift be given, assuming you could easily transform it into cash or some other form?
4. Whom will you select to *deliver* it?

5. Do you want to give the whole gift at once or just the interest earned from principal, or do you wish the recipient(s) to help with *financing* by putting up some of the money?
6. If the gift is given in cash, will the recipient(s) spend it for the *purpose* intended (i.e., interactions in this case between goals and form of benefit)?

These same choices have to be made whenever policies or programs for the general good are to be put into effect. In an ideal world, of course, no such choices are necessary because there is an unlimited supply of what everybody needs. Unfortunately, however, in our faulty paradise, a world in which it is *not* the case that everybody has enough, social welfare policy and programs are necessary.

Social policy is concerned with the six elements enumerated because, in the final analysis, they are the basis on which social policies and programs ration and distribute benefits, select beneficiaries, and attempt to ensure that money, goods, and services are used efficiently, effectively, and without waste. Some public commentators remark sarcastically that social welfare policy and programs are futile because they attempt to bring paradise to an inherently imperfect world; the reality is quite the opposite—the benefits of paradise are self-selected, self-rationed, and occasioned by justice. *In the real world social welfare policy is about selection and rationing in an attempt to correct injustice.* Social welfare policy is about a concrete empirical world and the attempt to moderate its sometimes cruel and inhumane effects. We will talk more later about how the challenge to social policies and programs is to be successful in moderating one cruel effect without creating another, more cruel effect.

Table 2.1 lists two additional types of information for each operating characteristic: *subtypes* and *evaluation criteria*. When the practical policy analyst studies the policy elements of particular social welfare program or benefit systems, it becomes clear that there are only a limited number of ways in which those criteria are expressed; for example, only about a half-dozen (more or less) subtypes of entitlement or eligibility rules are apparent. That is not to say that an inventive mind couldn't think of others or that certain programs (domestic or foreign) might not have others. Column 2 of Table 2.1 summarizes the main subtypes of policy elements—for example, the main subtypes of forms of benefits are cash, commodities, personal social services, and so on. This summary provides a quick and handy reference for describing the main features of any social welfare service or benefit program. The subtypes listed in Table 2.1 are intended for use by the practical policy analyst who daily encounters a world full of new and old social programs and policies that he or she must evaluate in order to know whether they are useful to clients/consumers.

These subtypes are not mutually exclusive; that is, a particular social welfare program or policy may use more than one kind of entitlement rule or financing method. For example, Supplemental Security Income (SSI) is a federal program that pays monthly benefits to people who are age sixty-five or older or blind or have a disability who pass a *means test* for income and resources. A means test covers only one part of eligibility. Note that age status is an eligibility criterion for some individuals to qualify. The exercise of *professional judgment* is factored in for persons to qualify as blind or disabled. *Diagnostic criteria* are applied to others who may be eligible for disability benefit

TABLE 2.1 **Policy Element Subtypes and Evaluation Criteria for a Value-Critical Appraisal of Social Policies and Programs**

Basic Policy Element	Subtypes	Evaluation Criteria
Goals and objectives	1. Principles or purpose 2. Long term/short term 3. Intermediate/ultimate 4. Manifest/latent	1. Criteria specific to goals and objectives (a) Concern with outcomes, not services provided (b) Clarity, measurability, manipulability (c) Inclusion of performance standards and target specifications 2. Implications of goals and objectives for adequacy, equity, and efficiency 3. Fit of goals and objectives with the social problem analysis: problem definition and variables (consequences) in causal analysis
Forms of benefits and services	1. Personal social services: expert services 2. Hard benefits: cash, goods, commodities 3. Positive discrimination 4. Credits/vouchers 5. Subsidies 6. Government loan guarantees 7. Protective regulations 8. Supervision of deviance 9. Power over decisions	1. Criteria specific to benefits and services (a) Stigmatization (b) Target efficiency (c) Cost-effectiveness (d) Substitutability (e) Consumer sovereignty (f) Trade-offs (g) Coerciveness/intrusiveness (h) Complexity and cost of administration (i) Adaptability across users (j) Political risk 2. Implications of benefit/service for adequacy, equity, and efficiency 3. Fit of benefit/service form with the social problem analysis
Eligibility rules	1. Means/asset tests 2. Administrative rule 3. Private contract provision 4. Prior contributions 5. Professional discretion 6. Judicial decision – *Court ordered* 7. Attachment to workforce	1. Criteria specific to eligibility rules (a) Over-/underutilization (b) Overwhelming costs (c) Stigma/alienation (d) Disincentive for work (e) Incentives for procreational and marital breakup and/or generational dependence

Basic Policy Element	Subtypes	Evaluation Criteria
		2. Fit with social problem analysis: problem definition/target group specifications 3. Implications of eligibility rules for adequacy, equity, and efficiency
Administration and service delivery	1. Centralization 2. Federation 3. Case management 4. Referral agency 5. Indigenous worker staffing v Professionals 6. Racially oriented agencies 7. Administrative fair hearing 8. Due process protections for clients' procedural rights 9. Citizen participation	1. Evaluation criteria specific to administration/service delivery (a) Has an articulate program/policy design (b) Integration/continuity (c) Accessibility (d) Accountability (e) Client/consumer empowerment (f) Consumer participation in decision making (g) Coping with racial, gender, and ethnic diversity 2. Fit with social problem analysis 3. Implications for adequacy, equity, and efficiency
Financing	1. Prepayments and the insurance principle 2. Publicly regulated private contracts 3. Voluntary contributions 4. Tax revenue appropriation 5. Fees for service 6. Private endowment	1. Evaluation criteria specific to financing (a) Continuity in funding (b) Stability in broad economic change: inflation/depression and demographic change 2. Fit with social problem analysis 3. Implications of this administrative type for adequacy, equity, and efficiency
Interactions		(No unique evaluative criteria)

entitlements. *Qualified professionals* determine whether a physical or mental problem keeps an individual from working, or when deciding if a child is disabled; SSI looks at how his or her disability affects everyday life. In addition to federally financed SSI benefits, many states also add money to the basic benefits. Furthermore, SSI-eligible individuals may also be able to get assistance from the Food Stamp program, Medicaid benefits, and additional social and rehabilitation services.

How each operating characteristic is evaluated is discussed in the following section.

Criteria for a Value-Critical Appraisal of Social Policy and Programs

Column 3 of Table 2.1 lists evaluation criteria by which the policy analyst can judge why and how a particular program has implemented each policy element and, ultimately, the worth of the program and policy system. For example, a mission statement (if available) gives the policy analyst descriptive information on the purpose of a policy or program. A mission statement tends to be very general and ambitious—a call for action, so to speak. Goals are also general (abstract) statements that may elaborate on the direction of policy or program initiatives to fulfill a mission and, at a minimum, can be evaluated on the basis of clarity. Objectives are concrete, stated more specifically as intended outcomes to achieve goals. The policy analyst will want to evaluate whether objectives are measurable and manipulable, identify a target population, give reference to time parameters, and use other such criteria. Forms of benefits and services may be examined from a number of perspectives, particularly regarding the extent to which they are appropriate for addressing the presenting social problem. A means test (eligibility rule) should be evaluated on the basis of whether it creates stigmatization, alienation, or off-target benefits. Administration and service-delivery evaluation criteria guide the analyst in determining whether benefits and services effectively reach the client/consumer. Finally, financing evaluation criteria address the adequacy of resources committed to resolve the social problem and who commits resources and in what manner.

The method of policy analysis contained in this book actually suggests three general but very different types of criteria for evaluating the features of social program and policy systems. The first type *uses the social problem analysis as a referent,* the evaluation issue being whether the policy or program has any potential for making an impact on the social problem it was intended to solve. In this mode, the practitioner asks certain questions:

- Do the entitlement rules direct benefits at the entire population defined to have the social problem, or do they only reach a subgroup?
- Do the goals and objectives of the program or policy system fit a social problem as defined?
- Can this form of benefit produce a significant impact on the causal factors believed to produce the social problem?
- Does the policy or program recognize or build on the strengths or assets of those affected by the social problem?

The second type is made up of *those traditional value perspectives—adequacy, equity, and efficiency.* For example, one might ask: "Is delivery of commodities rather than cash as a form of benefit a more *efficient* (cost-effective) way to solve the problem of nutrition?" An example of the *adequacy* criterion lies in the question: "Is the counseling adequate to the task of creating change of sufficient magnitude?" Similarly, a practical policy analyst might be evaluating a particular service delivery type against both an equity criterion and an adequacy criterion when she or he asks: "To what extent does the case-management style of service delivery increase the ability of the policy and program system to relate to the ethnic and racial diversity of its target population?" It is more than a little useful for the practitioner to be aware of what root questions are being asked (whether adequacy, equity, or efficiency questions) when a program and policy system are being judged for merit.

The reader should be alert to the possibility that many of the questions about adequacy are answered in the context of evaluating the fit of a policy element with the social problem analysis. *In fact, one of the most important functions of a social problem analysis is to provide an internally consistent basis for judging whether the policy/program design/policy system is a "good" one.* For example, a good social problem analysis will describe who is affected and (obviously) the policy or program solution must address those very people in order to be judged adequate. And recall that a good social problem analysis will describe the consequences at the heart of why the problem is considered to be a social problem—obviously, in order for the policy or program design to be judged adequate, it has to (plausibly) make an impact on just that problematic condition. The basic question is whether it is believable (or whether there is any evidence) that the program design can do that.

The adequacy/equity/efficiency criteria were developed by economists. When they use them, it is out of a concern for large-scale economic matters: changes in the characteristics of the national workforce, profitability of big industrial employers, gross domestic product, the national wage scales, and the like. Those are surely important matters but not very useful to social program implementers and designers because they are not factors within their reach. No one likely to read this book would design or implement a program intended to raise the national worker wage scale—though that might, indeed, go a long way toward the solution of some social problems. Economists, bless their souls, do have a good deal to say about how that might be accomplished, though they aren't often right on target. The economists' perspective is to judge the adequacy of public policy by how it contributes to an economy that rewards and encourages capital investment and the creation of national wealth. It is nearly inescapable that economists believe that what benefits wealth holders almost always and necessarily benefits workers and the general population. Although that might be true over some long time spans, it is often not the case for the near term of a few years, the time scale social practitioners and their needful clients/consumers work with. They are concerned with immediately presenting problems. Sadly, and as anyone knows from having read reliable accounts of large-scale unemployment resulting from large corporations profiting from shifting production overseas, corporate downsizing, and mergers, much of the profits in the U.S. economy goes into the pockets of those already wealthy, whereas the national income share of the middle and working class remains stable or decreases.[11] *Thus, judgments of policy/program adequacy for the practical policy analyst/practitioner uses the social problem analysis perspective, and its ideological/causal perspective focuses on the consequences for persons and citizens, not on the effects on the economy.*

The reader can find the economists' focus on equity useful, that is, on whether a policy or program design does treat similarly situated program participants in the same way. Inequities are sometimes (legitimately) designed into policies and programs, of course, but the point here is that inequities need to be searched out, identified, and examined for their consequences, intended or not. And the same can be said of efficiencies. Even though there are prominent exceptions, for the most part, the program or policy that is most efficient or cost-effective is the best choice—if for no other reason, the least cost alternative allows the always scarce social welfare dollar to go to more people in need.

The third type of criteria with which to evaluate policy elements for their worthiness are those used *only* for a particular policy element. Good examples are "includes target specifications" or "performance standards," which can be used *only* for evaluating goals and objectives. Notice that it would make no sense to ask whether some benefit form like a "voucher" has "target specifications." Target specifications are peculiar to goals and objectives.

In summary, then, the evaluation criteria the practical policy analyst should use for deciding the merit of the policy elements in a program, service, or policy system will always include the following:

1. The fit of the policy element to the social problem of concern
2. The consequences of the policy element with regard to adequacy, equity, and efficiency for clients/consumers and program participants
3. Criteria that are uniquely useful for a single policy element but not others

We will save a more detailed look at evaluation criteria for the specific chapters on each policy element that follow this overview.

Summary

Chapter 2 contrasted three styles of policy analysis: the analytic-descriptive, the value-committed, and the value-critical methods. While recognizing that political occasions will arise during which it is essential, the value-committed approach is rejected because it is not open to new data or conclusions. This fact argues for the value-critical style, which forces into the open whatever ideology is inherent in the analytic method used and the fundamental value commitments of the analyst in whose hands the method rests. Taken into the open, the effects of ideology can be observed and accounted for. Although useful, the sole use of the analytic-descriptive method fails in policy analysis because it commits the analyst to untenable assumptions: for example, that judgments about the goodness or merit of a social policy or program can be made in a value-free way. Such assumptions are unrealistic because any judgment of social program merit requires judgment of social worthiness—which simply cannot be made absent a strong value commitment. The virtue of the value-critical method is that it forces value commitments into the open and, therefore, gives both the analyst and his or her audience great freedom in using (or not using) the data produced from the analysis. This approach also enables practitioners to decide whether they are in agreement with the conclusions, to sort them selectively, or to freely substitute their own value biases and draw different conclusions. That sort of freedom can be used at different levels—either with regard to particular social program or policy operating characteristics or with regard to summary judgments.

Value commitments inherent in this preferred method of policy analysis are rationality, logical consistency, and reaching conclusions by a contrast between various value perspectives and between program means used to realize them. Other basic value commitments inherent in the analytic method are adequacy, equity, and efficiency.

EXERCISE

1. *Complete the following mental experiment:* Your physician has just told you that you have a fatal and incurable illness. You have just eight weeks to live. On returning home from the physician's office, you decide not to go berserk today (perhaps tomorrow), at least not until you open your mail. There is an envelope with a strange return address on it, foreign stamps in fact. Opening it first, you learn that you have inherited several million dollars, being the last living heir to a European fortune. A quick calculation shows that you cannot possibly spend it all in eight weeks. Then you decide you do not want to give it either to friends or relatives—your closest friend recently offended you and your closest relative died three years ago. Use the six basic policy elements to decide how you want to dispose of the money.

NOTES

1. M. Rein, *From Policy to Practice* (Armonk, NY: M. E. Sharpe, 1983), p. ix.

2. Ibid., p. x.

3. M. Howlett, "Policy Instruments, Policy Styles, and Policy Implementation: National Approaches to Theories of Instrument Choice," *Policy Studies Journal*, 19 (1991): 1–21.

4. Ibid., pp. 6–9.

5. M. Rein, "Value-Critical Policy Analysis," in Daniel Callahan and Bruce Jennings (eds.), *Ethics, the Social Sciences and Policy Analysis* (New York: Farrar and Rinehart, 1983), pp. 83–111. See also A. Weick and L. Pope, *Knowing What's Best: A New Look at Self-Determination* (Lawrence: University of Kansas, 1975), mimeographed.

6. J. Habermas, *Theory and Practice* (Boston: Beacon Press, 1976).

7. Rein, *From Policy to Practice*, p. x.

8. A. Weick, "Reconceptualizing the Philosophical Base of Social Work," *Social Service Review*, 42 (1975): 218–230.

9. Rein, "Value-Critical Policy Analysis," p. 87.

10. Elements 2, 3, 4, and 6 were used by Evelyn Burns in a book titled *The American Social Security System* (New York: Houghton Mifflin, 1949) and we assume that (collectively) they are original with her. Her ultimate sources may lie somewhere in the British tradition of social policy studies, of course. Many contemporary authors use N. Gilbert and H. Specht, *Dimensions of Social Welfare Policy* (Englewood Cliffs, NJ: Prentice Hall, 1974). We have added new operating characteristics in the belief that they are important to a thorough analysis: Goals and Objectives and Interactions among Elements.

11. "2004 Income in U.S. Was Below 2000 Level," *New York Times*, Business sec., (November 28, 2006), p. 5. This article uses IRS data to show that "only those in the top 5 percent of incomes had significant income gains. The average income of those on the 95th to 99th rungs of the income ladder rose by 53 percent, almost twice the average rate."

CHAPTER

3

The Analysis of Policy Goals and Objectives in Social Programs and Policies

"[B]ehind every political agreement there lies a misunderstanding."
—S. M. Miller, quoted in M. Rein,
From Policy to Practice, 1985

Introduction

The method presented in this book proceeds by first obtaining a close description of social policy or program implementation and then evaluating its merit according to specified criteria. Six fundamental policy elements are essential to implementation of all social policies. Chapter 3 will consider the first—*goals and objectives*—along with the various forms in which they are expressed. The chapter also will describe the difference between goals and objectives, identify sources and problems in locating statements of program and policy goals and objectives, and review their components and functions. In addition, the way in which goals and objectives differ in the personal social services and the problems of setting them in that context will be considered. The chapter will close with an extensive discussion of the task of evaluating the merit of social policy program and policy goals and objectives through the use of suggested criteria. The discussion in this chapter is intended to set a model for later chapter discussions on other operating characteristics.

We will not discuss "mission statements" here because their utility lies outside the scope of this book. We will consider them here as simply collections of goal statements plus arguments for their virtue. They are, of course, a source for same and a means by which the practical public policy analyst can understand the social problem analysis on which the program or policy is based.

Definitions and Basic Concepts for Analysis of Goals and Objectives

A goal is a statement, in general and abstract terms, of desired qualities in human and social conditions. A goal is always expressed in general and abstract terms. An objective is an equivalent statement but different because it must be expressed in concrete and measurable terms. It is important to grasp the goals and objectives of a program to answer the question: "What is the purpose of this program or policy?" *Thus, goals and objectives are of vital importance because all six of the fundamental elements of the program/ policy under study (e.g., eligibility rules, service-delivery features, etc.) must be judged on the basis of their contribution to its goals or objectives.* The extent to which each element contributes to the achievement of goals and objectives is a measure of the wisdom (or lack thereof) of choosing them as a way of implementing the program. In that way, goals and objectives become the "measure of all things programmatic."

Program goals and objectives are highly variable. For example, one goal of the Low Income Energy Assistance Program (LIEAP) is to protect the health of low-income households via the objective of ensuring they have heat in the wintertime. And commonly the goal of child abuse programs is to protect or prevent the abuse of children too young to protect themselves. It is important to understand that when we describe a goal or an objective we are describing a desired end, not a provided service. The distinction is not complicated; for example, think of a dentist drilling a cavity in your tooth. The drilling is really important, but it would be a strange person who would walk out of the dentist's office and be satisfied if that was all that happened. What you want as an outcome is to have the pain in the tooth go away and not come back another day (well, soon anyway). Avoiding the loss of the tooth and removing the pain might be a couple of other useful objectives. You might think of the goal as increasing your dental health.

In the same way in personal social services, a legitimate outcome statement should not use phrases such as "providing nursing care" or "providing counseling" or even "giving money." As important as those are, they are still only *means to ends*. Outcomes can never be only means to ends; rather they must be statements of outcomes able to "stand on their own," so to speak; be achievements acceptable in their own right. Thus providing nursing care is important in that it leads to greater patient feelings of comfort or morale, avoids surgical infections, detects early signs of danger to health, and so on. Providing counseling is important only if it leads to such things as increased self-regard, self-confidence, relief/decrease of depression, or improved family relationships. This urgent focus on outcomes is an important idea because just providing services without expecting a result means that such a program can never be evaluated against its accomplishments, can never know whether it did any good. *Absent that, programs have no useful way to think about change, to think about how to do things better!*

Here is an example of how the distinction between services and outcomes works in practice. Barrett Foundation is deciding whether to fund the Cherry County Mental Health Service. Its director argues it is successful for the following reasons: It has increased its clientele by 20 percent and the number of treatment hours by 35 percent, and it has opened two new satellite offices in distant counties.

On the basis of these data you must decide whether your organization should fund this operation for another five years at an annual budget of around $900,000. Based on the viewpoint about the importance of goals and objectives expressed earlier, the answer is no, not on these data, because they tell you nothing about program outcomes, program effectiveness. The data speak only about program processes (opening new offices, new staff, providing counseling services, etc.), not program outcomes that would answer the question of whether the services did any good, had any impact. The data speak only about means to ends, not ends themselves. Goals and objectives are not about delivering services (treatment hours, consultation, and the like) but about achieving desired outcomes in regard to the targeted social problem (say, reduced marital or parent–child conflict, increased marital/family satisfaction, reduced negative classroom behaviors of children, etc). If the board of directors doesn't insist on these kind of data it has no rational means by which to make a decision about funding this program nor make program improvements. In an important sense, program outcomes are a public social program's "profit" and basically its justification for being.

Different Types of Goals and Objectives

Long-Term/Short-Term Goals and Objectives

The practical public policy analyst should be alert to the fact that goals and objectives come in a variety of forms. For example, sometimes social programs specify objectives as "long term" or "short term." This specification is useful because it can relate to funding—there may be enough money only for outcomes having short horizons and the program may not last long enough to be concerned about a long horizon. Consider a highly politicized social problem like substance abuse. For a time, a drug education program for grade school children was highly publicized and appealed to the general populace. When these programs were first funded, they were fielded with very short-term goals—to increase children's knowledge about the effects of drugs. Once programs were implemented, change was expected to occur over a matter of weeks. In fact, the program was designed to be delivered and the information learned in a very short period of time because funding not only was limited but also was restricted to a few months' duration. When an intermediate step is crucial to a long-term goal, it is only logical to test for whether the intermediate step is attainable; further dollars await the outcome. The long-term goal here was the reduction in adult, long-term substance abuse, but in that funding environment, the long-term goal was irrelevant from a practical point of view.

Manifest and Latent Goals

A statement about a social policy or program goal is different from sociological statements about the social function served by a particular social program or policy. For example, Piven and Cloward conclude that the primary social function of the U.S. welfare system is to regulate the poor in two ways:[1]

1. To ensure a supply of cheap labor to the economic system
2. To ensure that discontent among the poor does not rise to levels where it becomes a major threat to social order

These are theoretical conclusions about *latent* functions of a social welfare system from the point of view of sociological analysis. Policy or program goal statements are much less global, less inferential, and they are traceable to sources that can be observed directly; they are based on evidence from statements in such visible sources as legislative bills, administrative documents, and judicial decisions.

A *manifest* function is an explicit, stated purpose and so is a goal. Both are discovered through examination of statements in primary documents that contain goals and purposes such as legislation, administrative regulations, and court decisions. But, as sociologists and anthropologists have long pointed out, there are *latent* functions as well, functions that serve unstated purposes. And because they are unstated, *latent* functions are quite different from either goals or objectives, as the reader will see from the following example. One widely discussed latent example is the federal government's Section 8 Housing program that offers substantial rent subsidies to low-income families. The *manifest* goal or objective of this program is to make safe, adequate, and affordable housing available to the poor. Section 8 housing, located in scattered sites outside the inner-city urban ring, is reasonably expected to be an environmental improvement for low-income families and to reduce urban minority populations. As laudable as these goals and objectives are, some policy analysts argue that their *latent* goal is to gradually depopulate housing projects in inner cities so that they can be torn down and redeveloped as luxury apartments and condominiums. This charge is plausible in that one can easily point to housing projects in metropolitan areas that would be prime real estate development sites. Chicago's inner urban ring is one example in which housing projects are being vacated and discussions are being held as to their future. Whereas *latent* goals and objectives are very important *(latent* rather than *manifest* goals sometimes drive program features and implementation), the first-order focus in policy and program analysis is on a description of the stated *(manifest)* goals.

Distinguishing between Goals and Objectives

Goals serve some unique functions not shared with objectives because they are abstract and cover so many different things. That gives practitioners a very "big tent" under which to honor the multitude of ethnic and regional differences among their service consumers. In addition, these abstract goals allow administrators and practitioners to think in common terms about their tasks and to speak easily to their funding sources about their general purposes.

Here is an example from the personal social services to illustrate how many different objectives can be covered under a general goal. This example concerns a program called Literacy, Inc. whose goal is *to increase the command of English among nonnative speakers so that they can create a new life in an unfamiliar country.*

This broad, general goal conveys a clear idea of what the program wishes to accomplish. But notice how this goal could concern several very different objectives:

- To increase reading competence to the sixth-grade level where employment advertisements can be read with comprehension of the job location, work conditions/wages, and required skills
- To increase the ability to understand spoken English at a level where conversation with the average U.S. high school graduate can be conducted to the linguistic satisfaction of both parties
- To increase the ability to read and speak standard English to eliminate any linguistic barrier to passing the GED high school certificate examination

The idea here is that any one of those objectives (or all three together) might be sufficient to satisfy the goal statement of Literacy, Inc. In general a good, well-defined abstraction like a goal statement admits of an almost infinite number of concrete empirical instances. Goal statements have to carve out a defined turf so that some things must be excluded. The wisdom is that a definition that includes everything actually refers to nothing in practice. Statements of objectives are intended to focus on specifics and limit the reach of program efforts.

It is important to note that goals will be constrained by the objectives with which they are associated because the terms of objectives will include quite specific definitions. Notice in the example of the goal previously stated, the phrase "a new life" is very important. In the associated objectives that term could be defined in economic terms (making a livelihood), in socialization terms (conversations with other English speakers), or in educational terms (passing examinations) and each definition would specify a different objective in the previous list. Any of those alternatives constrain the scope of the goal.

Objectives (Not Goals) Must Contain Target Group Specifications and Performance Standards

If objectives are to be of maximal use they must contain *target group specifications*; that is, they must clearly specify who and how many are to be affected or changed, or whose circumstances or surroundings are the target of change efforts. In specifying a target group, the phrase "serving the homeless of the city of Pocatello, Idaho" is not acceptable as it stands because its major term, *homeless*, is not sufficiently specific. Someone could ask, does the word *homeless* include those who are recreational campers, or how about motel guests? On the other hand, it might exclude those who have a roof over their heads but no heat, running water, or toilet facilities. Further, making objectives target group specific is important because it is absolutely necessary for estimating the potential size of the program. Without that there is no way to tell how many staff members and facilities will be needed and thus how much its annual costs will be; in turn there is no way to prepare budgets or think about securing financing. All terms of an objective need to be concrete and specific; for example, "serving the homeless of the city of Pocatello, Idaho—those without permanent, warm, secure, sanitary shelter with running water and toilet facilities." Notice that there could be many definitions of this term (e.g., exclude an age term, include electricity or cooking facilities). The point is not which definitions are right or wrong, rather it is about specificity: Would it allow you to easily recognize the condition of homelessness if you saw it in real life?

Objectives (but not goals) must also contain *performance standards*, that is, statements about the extent of the changes or effects the program is expected to have. A performance standard for a housing program might be something like this:

> [W]ithin five years to secure safe, up-to-standard permanent shelter for one-third of the low-income population of Compton, Mississippi, such shelter is to be inhabited by no more than two persons per room, and has running water, sanitary toilets, and electric outlets in each room.

Certainly, the details can be argued, but the phrases "two persons per room" and "running water" are examples of performance standards. Any housing falling short of those descriptions does not meet this standard of performance and, thus, cannot count as a positive outcome of the program. Another example from the personal social services might be a program for integrating persons who are severely emotionally disturbed into a pattern of community living where the objective is to have each

> person in the program living in a private household shared with at least four other persons, and who takes full responsibility for his/her nutrition, medication, plus has interaction with a nonhouseholder for at least ten hours a week.

In this case, the quoted phrases refer to explicit performance standards for the program. For program consumers for which those standards are not met, that instance does not count as a success for the program.

Most of us would not expect a program with limited resources to serve a total population, but program auditors and evaluators will not make that assumption. Thus, a program objective whose performance standards say it will serve the population of a city means exactly that. If target groups and performance standards aren't specified, goals and objectives will almost always be read to indicate that the program will serve a larger population than is really intended or, for that matter, has adequate resources for. Absent target group specification and a performance standards program, evaluators and those who provide program funds would conclude that the Pocatello, Idaho, homeless shelter mentioned earlier would serve *all* the homeless in Pocatello. If a shelter has accommodations for only ten and there is a demonstrable demand for fifteen, it will almost inevitably be given bad marks because it didn't do what it said it would, never mind after-the-fact arguments that the program didn't really mean what it said.

In sum, it is desirable to constrain objectives and performance standards so that the program is never obligated to provide more service than allowed by the budget resources available. One way (not always ideal) to approach this is to set a percentage of a particular target group: "will serve 30 percent of the homeless" or "will serve an average of eighty teenage homeless persons over a one-year period." Without hard information, performance standards based on local practice wisdom estimates are better than none at all. Needs surveys can provide reasonably reliable guidance for anticipating service demand; any sensible planning would require them. Sadly, funding is seldom available to conduct them.

Why Have Both Goals and Objectives?

Both goals and objectives are needed in social programs and policies because they serve different purposes. Statements about objectives are absolutely essential for two reasons.

1. They give the operational outcome toward which program operations are directed, and no administrator can make decisions about daily issues like constructing budgets, distributing money among various program operations, and hiring and firing without a concrete objective in mind.
2. Programs cannot be evaluated for effectiveness unless there is an objective to serve as a measurable standard against which data from actual achievements can be cast.

Program goals are also necessary in that they provide a crucial link between the more concrete and specific objectives and the public documentary sources (laws, judicial decisions, administrative mandates) that establish the program or policy. Statements in such documents can never be sufficiently specific so that a program or policy can be constructed from them directly. Whatever their source, statements are quintessentially political, the product of political compromise; and political documents can never be truly explicit lest some party takes issue with them. If that happens, it may destroy delicate political, judicial, administrative, or organizational compromises that were necessary to promulgate the policy or program in the first place. Part of the art of politics is to avoid saying what will offend, and in that way both sides believe the issue is settled. As S. M. Miller states, "behind every political agreement there lies a misunderstanding."[2] Thus, program designers must translate these documents into operating programs, and to do that they need to translate the goal in the public document into a statement at a concrete level, that is, a measurable objective. That statement will direct a choice of specific program operations and program provisions that will move events toward the stated general goal as well as allow observations to be made by which program success or failure can be judged.

The following is one example of how goals and objectives function to provide a link between legislative intent and program operations and to assist operations accountability. A large, private, statewide child welfare program is a major subcontractor receiving state and federal funds for in-home services provided to welfare mothers whose children are at risk for abuse or neglect. The source of these federal dollars is the Social Services Block Grant (SSBG), formerly a categorical grant identified also as Title XX of the Social Security Act. Goal III/IV of Title XX speaks of preventing or remediating neglect, abuse, or exploitation of children. Notice that the Social Security legislation itself doesn't speak of anything more specific than this general purpose: no definitions, no mention of how it should be pursued. Often that is the case for enabling legislation. But the private agency program that will administer these funds, likely the departments of child welfare of the several states, will supply a program goal—for example, to preserve, rehabilitate, and/or reunite families.

Then, in order to translate that goal into program activities or interventions, the state or local program will have to specify some "intermediate" objectives that will focus the activities of administrators and practitioners on what to do. They might have chosen the following *intermediate objectives*:

- Mobilize the family's own resources
- Focus on and increase family strengths
- Increase individual behaviors of family members that support family integrity
- Achieve objectives chosen by individual family members

These objectives are crucial because they direct the program's attention to very specific things its staff must/might do to help clients/consumers get the desired outcomes—in this case prevention of the child's outside-the-home placement. To see how concrete outcome objectives are related—as links in a chain—to intermediate objectives, the general goal and the legislative purpose, look at Figure 3.1.

But it is at the level of program implementation, at which people in need (program participants/consumers) come face to face with staff members, that detailed outcome objectives are set forth; that is, those encounters are expected to have the following results:

1. Prevention of the child from being placed outside the household (for 70 percent of the families)
2. Individual program consumers achieve their individual objectives (75 percent of, in aggregate)
3. 80 percent of program consumers will be satisfied with services

This sets out the rough theory that underlies the program: For example, IF we can mobilize resources, increase family strengths, help program participants achieve personal objectives, and so on, THEN we will prevent outside-the-home placement (which is taken to be the rough equivalent of rehabilitating families, which is itself the equivalent of preventing further abuse). It is the IF-THEN sequence that defines the rational process here. The reader may disagree that the statement is rational, of course; and data from program outcome measures may show that the statement is false, but that is part of the point—rational process makes clear what is expected and why, data make clear whether those expectations have come true. Program theory and design are discussed in greater detail in Chapter 6.

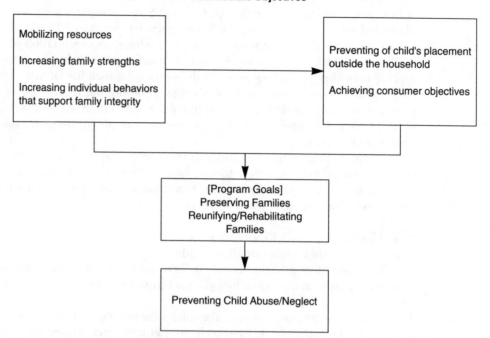

FIGURE 3.1   Linking concrete objectives with abstract goals and legislative purposes.

Setting Goals and Objectives in the Personal Social Services

It is easier to set goals and objectives for a "hard" benefit program (one that delivers goods like housing or food stamps) than it is to set them for personal social services—"soft benefits." The food stamp goal is rather straightforward: to increase nutrition. Notice that the food stamp objective is phrased in ways that shape the buying habits of beneficiaries—thus, junk foods, alcoholic beverages, and tobacco cannot be bought with food stamps.

In the personal social services, there is, or should be, considerable latitude for clients/consumers to shape and set their own objectives. Dedication to practice values like self-determination, maximizing of personal choice, and empowerment would lead in that direction.

Personal social services require much more individualized objectives because they deal with individuals who are so different from one another. There is an unavoidable tension between program/policy goals and objectives and personal social service objectives. Although practitioners would like to think that they are free to help their clients/consumers toward just about any personal objective, it turns out that there are limits on that freedom—in real life, whoever pays the bills has a good deal to say about how the money (and time and effort) is spent.

Client/consumer objectives and the policy or program objectives are often easily tied together at an abstract level. For example, in a program for day care for elderly people whose goal is decreased isolation, one would expect to see very individualized objectives because functional capacities of residents are likely to be quite variable. Objectives like self-control, increased verbal expression, and the like are not difficult to gather under a general objective of increased socialization. But there are other specific, quite legitimate practice objectives that a practitioner might insist be included. Readers might want to think of some as an interesting exercise.

Whether a program's goals and objectives are for all program participants, or are specific to each person can have important consequences. Here is an example showing how highly individualized objectives create an incentive for good personal social services whereas generalized objectives for all clients/consumers do not. Consider residential care centers in which the state pays for client care. If care providers are paid the same for all clients/consumers without respect for their disability or level of care required, there is every motivation for the facility to admit those clients who are *least* disabled. That could lead to a shortage of beds for those more severely disabled who need care the most. One solution is to make home care reimbursement variable and dependent on client/consumer characteristics and level of challenges (code words for special and often difficult behaviors in residential settings). Although creation of a policy and program system that will identify client/consumer characteristics and behavioral challenges is itself no small challenge, it may carry a handsome payoff, as suggested by recent research.[3]

Social Control and Program and Practice Objectives

Finally, the practical public policy analyst should keep in mind that the personal social services often have obvious *social control* objectives. On that account, personal social service goals and objectives should express them explicitly. For example, some organizations (courts and other legal and quasilegal agencies) that probation counselors work for have explicit social control objectives: mental institutions, youth detention centers, and camps are not very different. In fact, mental health clinics often have explicit social control tasks when they work with clients/consumers whose attendance at the clinic is court-mandated, whether for preliminary diagnostic evaluations or for treatment. When that is the case, client objectives should clearly express that. When a client is legally committed to residence at a state mental institution and the problem for which he or she was committed is, say, exhibitionism, then that behavior should be included among others in any statements of treatment objectives. Although it seems obvious, in practice, the principle often is violated in favor of others that ignore the very problem that created the basis for legal commitment. For example, a treatment program that increased self-concept, as desirable as that might be, will not be acceptable if it cannot show findings that such decreases, say, hostile behavior.

Human service and social work practitioners frequently are uncomfortable with social control purposes and they are easy to ignore. To conduct a value-critical analysis of personal social service programs, the analyst should look to see whether the program expresses those explicitly lest this feature be lost from sight. There is nothing intrinsically negative about the idea of social control or using public funds on its behalf. It is, after all, likely to be the reason the program is funded! To be clear on that matter with clients/consumers and organizational personnel is taken as a value position here in the belief that to obfuscate it only leads to serious problems with users/consumers who eventually will encounter it anyhow. Few of them are confused on this matter. Few adoptive parent clients/consumers are confused about the fact that their friendly social worker who is supervising the last few months of their adoption actually can take their child away under certain conditions. Few children who are clients/consumers of social workers and human service workers in mental and penal institutions are confused about the fact that those workers exercise considerable control over whether and when and under what conditions they will be allowed to leave the institution. The value bias at work here opts for honesty and openness with clients/consumers, believing that "putting everything on the table," so to speak, is one of the conditions required for being helpful to people. Sometimes that may prevent the possibility of helping people achieve objectives that require close personal, trusting, nonauthoritative relationships. Nothing is gained and perhaps everything can be lost by avoiding the issue of the existence of the authority factor in relationships when in fact that is the case. Social program goals and objectives should reflect that.

Goals and Objectives Vary According to the Developmental Stage of the Program

In policy or program analysis, it is important to understand the developmental stage of the program at that moment. Social policies and program efforts are much improved when finally implemented if they were routinely pretested in one of two forms: pilots or models. *Models* (sometimes called prototypes) are program designs implemented under the ideal conditions for success. The idea is that if they cannot succeed under these conditions, they can never succeed in real life. Models are very tightly constructed and are not subject to midcourse changes. In contrast, *pilot projects* are the loosest type of demonstration program, whose objectives and interventions are most subject to change. A pilot project searches for unexpected outcomes and the program design is changed on a simple trial-and-error basis "to see what happens" as a result. It is the strategy of choice when not much is known about the social problem of concern. Although this approach is social tinkering in its most blatant form, there is a clear place for it absent good guesses about the nature of a social problem. The main objective of such a program is to gather more knowledge or information about the problem and good interventions.[4]

Methods of Identifying Goals and Objectives

Identifying program goals and objectives is not always a simple matter. There is no one source for the documents that are necessary to draw firm conclusions, even in the case of public social policies or programs. What follows, however, is a routine procedure that ordinarily will result in reasonable conclusions about the goals and objectives of public policies or programs. Note that the procedure does not necessarily need to follow the sequence presented. In fact, the sequence is more or less trivial because conflicting information might be obtained at each step described.

Step 1: Locate the Enabling Legislation

All public social programs are "public," in one way or another, when they are funded from the government treasury. Any treasury expenditure must be authorized by the elected officials constitutionally empowered to do so. Authorizations for expenditures are almost always made in terms of programs under the administrative control of various governmental departments. Programs are set up by what is called *enabling legislation*, acts that usually contain some statement about the purpose or goal of the act and for the program.

Step 2: Locate Legislative History

It is important to gain a deeper perspective on policy goals, purposes, and legislative intent, and the best source for doing so is ordinarily called the "legislative history." *Legislative history* refers to a set of official documents or transcripts of legislative hearings and documents accepted as part of the background material studied by members of the legislative committees that considered the matter at hand and framed the legislation that subsequently was passed into law. Legislative history is more readily available for acts passed by Congress, but it is also available at the state level. Legislative histories can be found in any law school library, statehouse library, or university library public documents department. The privately published *Congressional Quarterly* and the publication of Congress called the *Green Book* (referred to in the following text) also contain legislative histories.

Step 3: Locate Staff and Committee Studies and Reports

Other sources of program goals (including the preamble to the enabling legislation itself) include *staff studies* prepared for use by congressional committees to study issues that may result in new programs or policies and amendments to existing legislation. Staff studies are usually considered reasonably authoritative sources for statements concerning the goal and purposes of public social policy and programs.

Step 4: Check Other "Official" Sources

There are several authoritative sources for statements about the goals and objectives of social programs that entail federal funds or administration. One is the official biannual *Social Security Handbook*, published by the Social Security Administration and housed in all federal document repositories. The *Social Security Handbook* is also available online at the Social Security Administration (SSA) Web site at www.ssa.gov. The National Underwriters Association, a private publisher, also produces annual manuals on Social Security and Medicare. Another major authoritative source for federally funded social programs is the *Green Book*, published at intervals by the Committee on

Ways and Means, U.S. House of Representatives. The *Green Book* provides background material and data on programs within the jurisdiction of the Committee on Ways and Means.[5] It gives exhaustive detail on federally funded social programs as well as legislative history. The *2004 Green Book* can be accessed on the Internet at www.gpoaccess.gov/wmprints/green/2004.html. The U.S. Department of Health and Human Services (DHHS) provides useful information on programs under its administration and can be accessed online at www.hhs.gov. A useful source on federal food programs is the Food Research and Action Center (FRAC), which can be accessed online at www.frac.org. The many Internet sources that provide links to official program Web sites are too numerous to list here; however, a good starting place for the policy analyst is the Finance Project Web site located at www.financeproject.org.

The Government Performance Results Act of 1993 provides for the establishment of strategic planning and performance measurement in the federal government and for other purposes. As a result, each federal agency is required to submit to the Office of Management and Budget and to the Congress a strategic five-year plan for program activities, including a comprehensive mission statement, general goals and objectives (and outcome-related goals and objectives), and other program planning information. These strategic planning documents are an invaluable source of information on goals and objectives to the policy and program analyst. In many cases they can be accessed through federal agency Web sites. Many states (and U.S. territories) and local government entities have followed suit with government performance legislation (or administrative directives) of their own, which offer additional sources of information for social policy and program analysis.

Annual reports issued by state-administered social programs can be revealing sources for statements of current goals and objectives. In some cases they document performance over the past fiscal year in meeting goals and objectives. In the search to document public social program goals and objectives, do not overlook the rich resource of official administrative rules and regulations. Although social program administrators commonly prepare public relations material intended to describe programs and program operations, these releases usually are of little help and often are deliberately vague. Public program operations manuals, on the other hand, are very much public property, although they are not always easy to get (or to use, we might add). For example, the policy manuals for the public agency that operates state foster care and adoption programs routinely list thousands of rules and regulations. The *Federal Register* publishes into the public domain the multitude of rules and regulations and much else that pertains to federal agencies. Buried in these documents are explicit statements about goals and objectives, which, precisely because they are official, can be excellent sources of information on this point.

Locating Sources for Goals and Objectives in State-Administered and Private Social Programs

Social programs that are entirely administered by the state have documentary sources that are somewhat similar to those for federal programs, although exact titles and sources will vary by state. All state legislatures maintain current legislative history sources, and they can be obtained by a simple inquiry directed to the state legislature's library, usually located in the statehouse. In regard to state-administered programs, look for official committee hearings, staff studies, and reports to committees. A simple inquiry to your local state legislator will usually net a short and helpful discussion with an aide about how to locate the documents desired. Checking amendments to bills as originally written will net information on what was *not* intended. A letter to the legislator who introduced the bill may also provide helpful data about intentions and will usually be answered quickly. Social programs in the private sector and those run by local governments, despite their importance to the total social welfare effort of this country, may not have easily accessible official public documentary sources if such programs are not enabled or mainly financed. Therefore, such goals are often fugitive and can be very difficult to identify. Usually, some kind of organizational document is available that supports or mandates the program and, therefore, can serve as legislative history. The most useful sources are face-to-face interviews with program administrators' and staff members' reports. Verbal reports are also quite legitimate sources for goals and objectives. In researching private sources, you may find organizations that have no overall goal-guiding operations; rather, each staff member has personal and professional goals for her or his practice. You may also find organizations that lack overarching goals, whose only goals and objectives are chosen by clients based on their own preferred outcomes. Based on certain assumptions, both cases are legitimate; note, however, that in neither case is a single social program or policy system in place. In effect there could be as many programs or policy systems as there are staff practitioners and clients/consumers. Consider the possibility that there is no public social policy or program at work here and, therefore, nothing to be analyzed. A group of practitioners who don't share objectives or goals is a private practice, not a social program, whatever their good results.

Evaluating Program or Policy System Goals and Objectives: A Value-Critical Approach

Having discovered the goals and objectives of a social program or policy system, how do we take the important next step, judging whether they are "good" goals and objectives? Everything hinges on what standards we'll use to define "good." What makes for a good goal or objective depends on what we most value in the human condition, so it is on the basis of those values that we want to analyze goals and objectives. Doing that is what is called a *value-critical analysis*.

The first step is to declare some fundamental value positions. Value perspectives are implicit in all analytic methods, including this one, and we will set them forth here.

As the reader might expect, *value neutrality is specifically rejected* in a value-critical analysis because, when it comes to statements about the human condition at least, the viewpoint is that very little can be said in a totally objective way—such that it is not rooted in a strong set of value commitments and, thus, inherently subjective. Value neutrality is a seductive ideal, fundamentally misleading because it obscures the inherently value-laden nature of almost all ideas about human affairs. More than a hundred years ago, Max Weber set us straight on this idea, making clear that all social science must be ultimately value oriented and, further, that we can only save ourselves from utter subjectivity by making explicit (and in advance) the value positions that underlie our conclusions. The views of Weber and others like him are widely accepted but not universally, and so readers may disagree here and find themselves in a smaller but still respectable company.

Let us begin by noting that in conducting anything called an "analysis," there must be an a priori commitment to the virtue of logic and rationality as a method of truth seeking. The preference here for rationality and logical consistency yields important things. How else might one have a basis for a belief that any program might actually solve a problem, any problem at all? Generalizing from prior practice experience is exactly one sort of act of rationality in the sense that any logical conclusion involves a thought process of the following kind: "This (new) situation is like a former experience in important ways and because this strategy was successful before, there is a good probability it will work again." Rationality and logic also give us the freedom from the bondage of using *only* prior experience in developing social interventions. Good thing, for as practitioners and social program designers, we are often faced with human conditions that no one has experienced! It is our good fortune that from within the heart of another sort of rationality (hypothetico-deductive reasoning) can come wholly new ideas for better social program designs, designs whose logical chain lets us "see around corners," that is, to have logical expectations for what we have never experienced. And, in that way, rationality provides grounds for believing that a program design might be successful even in advance of the actual trial run. As commonly said—"yes, that makes sense." That is, it seems to meet logical expectations.

In the final analysis, we will argue, it is our North American cultural preference for control and prediction and thus the implicit commitment of our democratic political process that demands a rational basis for public expenditures. Legislative, judicial, and administrative accountability demands it. At the level of ideals, public appropriations, in our North American way of doing things, are not distributed simply by virtue of having faith in the person who will spend them. So, it turns out that the political ideology of our society demands rationality as an instrumental means to just and fair dealings with citizens' money. It creates the necessity to have *advance* grounds for judging that a program will be adequate to answer the social problem of concern, equitable for prospective clients or users/consumers, and efficient in obtaining the most value for money expended. It has other virtues: It can provide a consistent standard for performance and a way of specifying how public social programs or policy systems should operate in order to usefully serve program participants as well as the public and collective good.

In addition to our stress on *rationality and logic*, the reader might already have noticed two other examples of value positions inherent in this policy analysis method: *accountability* and the notion that *product counts*. That means that all social programs, public and private, must be accountable to their relevant funding publics. In the public sector, that means accountability to taxpayers, their elected representatives, and social service consumers. In the private sector, that means accountability to private donors and social service consumers. In its most general sense, accountability simply means that social programs must do what their funding sponsors expect while attending to the satisfaction of program participants. With regard to the former, goals and objectives of a public sector program must reflect its legislative mandates—and so reflect the will of the citizenry whose taxes pay for it. No mystery here: If the legislation and official regulations specify program funding for the purpose of jobs for poor people, then the goals and the objectives of the program system must specify exactly that. *Accountability means that the program must be willing to be evaluated on achieving outcome objectives for specified program participants, whatever else it may or may not do.* Is this the occasion for social control in social programs? Yes, and this is often the case. Although surely it is not always a negative feature, practitioners should always be attentive to that issue and how it might negatively affect the people they serve.

The value position that *product counts* orients the major effort of the program to producing particular results, that is, verifiable outcomes or best results at least cost, whatever else it might do. The perspective here is that social policies and programs are implemented precisely to solve social problems, and their performance in that role is the ultimate measure of their worth. Although these outcomes have the highest priority, note that product is not *all* that matters because there are other matters of priority: A main example is the satisfaction of program participants; another is unanticipated negative side effects of programs and policies.

When we come to personal social services, there are some disconcerting problems with regard to this commitment to "product," this commitment to outcomes that are specified before a single consumer has walked through the front door. Think for a moment about how personal social services are so strongly characterized by individualization and how many involve an empowerment strengths focus or treatment process. When they are directed at mental, social, and/or emotional disorders, those processes often belie specific outcomes or end products on the view that a treatment or empowerment process worth its salt concerns outcomes that go well beyond the scope of the defined social problem. Many human service practitioners prefer outcomes in personal social services to be the prerogative of the consumer/program participant. Personal social services conceived this way do not always appear to serve as a solution to the presenting social problem; for example, they might make it possible for a person to choose a different path for life, where that path might be concerned with some immediate and highly individual personal goal: a good friend, an intimate relationship, better housing, and a reduced anxiety state are all examples. But it may be quite plausible that attaining one of those more immediate objectives will create the conditions for *not* living a life driven by or at the mercy of a social problem such as, say, substance abuse, addiction, or spousal abuse. Experienced practitioners know that for many personal social services, the control of consumers over service outcomes constitutes a highly desirable general and radical freedom on the part of the person. And, further, to the extent that consumers *don't* control outcomes, social services can be characterized as authoritarian and in the service of social control.

But, when *services involve public funds, at some level they must concern the public and not be solely a private interest.* So, does that mean that public social services must always deny consumer control over the direction (outcome) of the helping process? No, but it does require that program designers, managers, and practitioners take it as their task to make clear the connection between consumer control of outcomes and making an impact on a social problem. No mystery here: At a practice level, think of how often it makes sense to engage a service consumer's interest by working on particular issues that are of immediate and pressing relevance, sometimes not those that seem directly related to the defined social problem and the goals and objectives of the program. That is, of course, a characteristic of the strengths approach, now a common intervention strategy for social worker practitioners and social programs.[6] At a policy level, those maneuvers must be related to service outcomes so they create a public understanding of their relationship to the public interest. It is an important policy-level responsibility common to all practitioners.

Now we need to think about how to evaluate the goals and objectives of a policy or program. Are they good ones or not, and why in each case? We will discuss each in regard to their relevance to goals and objectives.

Evaluating the Fit between Goals and Objectives and the Social Problem Analysis

Providing a solution to a social problem is, in our definitions, the main purpose of a social policy or program so the merit of any of its features must be judged by how it fits that purpose. The function of social program goals and objectives is to keep the policy or program going in the desired direction, that is, toward solution (or mitigation) of the social problem. Thus, the fit, goal relevance, and objectives are of premier importance.

Consider for a moment a program of public child care for working parents. Note at the outset how varied the objectives for such child care can be because definitions of the problem to be solved by such programs can vary so widely. Common objectives for preschoolers (for example) include providing educational enrichment (develop preschool skills); providing safe and dependable substitute parent care during work hours; developing early cognitive and emotional creativity; providing nutritionally sound, emotionally stimulating, and health-attentive care. Program features of a multitude of day care settings are recognizable in that list. A neighbor who tends to fewer than three children in her own home but provides no explicit educational or creative stimulation exemplifies day care with a minimum of objectives—safe and dependable care. Alternatively, a local franchise of a national day care chain may focus on educational enrichment and development of cognitive and emotional roots of creativity, as well as program components having to do with nutrition, child health, safe care, and the like.

Imagine how different will be the objectives and organizational policies within these different programs. Behind all that is an implicit social problem analysis. In what follows, you will recognize the four elements of a complete social problem analysis (as described in Chapter 1): (1) problem definition, (2) causation, (3) ideology, and (4) gainers and losers. Thus, the favored definition of the social problem to be dealt with for the neighborhood scenario might be the parent's need to have a dependable person to be in charge of an infant during work hours and to feel at ease about the child's nutrition, physical safety, and health. Although this objective may preoccupy many (if not most) day care parents, that is not to say that other objectives are superfluous. The Montessori school scenario has a much more complex, theoretical, even elegant social problem definition in mind. Perhaps its basic concern might be expressed as the absence of age-appropriate stimulation to the child's cognitive and emotional capacities. Whereas preoccupation with a child's safety and nutrition and the dependability of care may be present, the Montessorri school or parents may demand more.

The point here is that goals and objectives must fit the social problem viewpoint to which the program is intended to be a solution, and so, for each different social problem/policy/program package, goals and objectives are likely to differ conspicuously. Demonstrating this fit is twofold.

First, it is shown by *the equivalence between the terms in the social problem definition and the terms in which the goals and objectives are defined.* Unless this fit can be demonstrated, it is possible that the programmatic solution is irrelevant to the social problem declared to be of interest. Of course, that is a major flaw to the extent that public expenditures are purchasing essentially irrelevant goods or services.

Second, the fit between objectives and the social problem analysis is shown by *the equivalence between the outcome objectives and the independent variables in the causal sequence of the social problem analysis.* Thus, if the social problem analysis contains a causal chain in which the outcome (independent) variable is child abuse, the objectives of the program must relate to child abuse in some way (of course, there can be other objectives as well), but it is important that the same definitions be used. If, as actually occurs sometimes, program designers have developed a set of programmatic interventions targeted not on child neglect but on physical child abuse, then a serious flaw is involved. It is not difficult to make this kind of mistake in a field in which ambiguous definition is commonplace. It might be made because many continue to think of child neglect as simply a lesser version of physical child abuse—despite substantial research evidence to the contrary (concluding that child abusers inflicting serious physical damage are probably a breed apart). It makes no sense at all to contrive and implement an elaborate intervention directed toward a phenomenon that is entirely different from the one intended. The following sections address the second set of evaluation criteria—adequacy, equity, and efficiency.

Evaluating Goals and Objectives against Traditional Economic Criteria: Adequacy, Equity, and Efficiency

Adequacy

This criterion is applied by assuming that the goals and objectives are *actually achieved* and then asking to what extent the social problem will be reduced. In other words, are the goals and objectives adequate to their task? It is a useful question because it might avoid spending scarce money and effort to implement a program when an observant person can tell in advance it won't do the job. Be warned, however, that despite the utter rationality of the question, raising it may not win popularity contests: (1) if a program proposal is the cherished idea of some staff members, raising the question of whether it will actually do its job may be taken as a personal insult and bring a hostile response; (2) no one may expect the program to be effective because the intention is only to satisfy a legislative constituency—and the organization will be embarrassed if that becomes public; and (3) if the intention behind discussing a program proposal is only a media event to show some effort in response to current negative publicity for the organization, the question might embarrass those in command. Readers need to be alert to bringing unwelcome news. "Killing the messenger who brings bad news" is a saying as old as ancient Rome, but experienced practitioners have seen it happen (metaphorically) in modern bureaucratic organizations. The point is not at all to advise against raising issues, only to think before speaking and be willing to brave the consequences.

Traditional economists might want the question of adequacy of goals and objectives answered in terms of how much *reduction in dollar costs of the social problem* is expected. Assuming that the social problem analysis has set forth the relevant dollar costs, then the next question is what savings on those costs should be expected given maximum program success. If the social problem is medical care for the homeless, then some direct dollar costs are such things as emergency medical care for the homeless who are susceptible to physical violence, malnutrition, communicable diseases, and infections associated with lack of ordinary medical care and timely treatment. The appropriate question is whether and to what extent the best possible program outcomes will reduce those (or other) costs. For example, one likely consequence of illiteracy is earning less than minimum wages and probable eligibility for such benefits as food stamps and housing subsidies. *Direct costs* are government expenditures like these, expenditures that would not be spent were the problem eliminated. There are also *indirect costs* (e.g., lost wages means collecting fewer taxes so those working must pay more) and those can be as great as direct costs, though they are more difficult to estimate with precision.

Although there are ways other than dollar cost reduction to make judgments of the adequacy of goals and objectives, "monetizing," that is, rendering outcomes in terms of dollars saved or earned, is probably the easiest way to do this task. The reader should notice that some goals or objectives don't lend themselves very well to dollar signs. That is often true for personal social service programs; think only of programs directed toward grief counseling, for example. It is quite possible to monetize the negative effects of child neglect, as for the medical costs of malnutrition and the extra educational costs of special education for the learning problems of such children when neglect creates developmental lags.

Equity

Equity is complicated, but the basic standard is that citizens must be treated similarly by a social policy or a social program as a matter of fairness or justice. The complication is that there are two kinds of equity: (1) *proportional equity*, in which citizens receive benefits or services that are "in proportion" to their relative need for them, and (2) *absolute equity*, in which citizens receive benefits or services in absolutely equal amounts irrespective of their need. Thus, whether the program goal or objective treats one beneficiary the same as others turns on how equity is defined. Two families whose children receive the same standard course of vaccinations (rubella, DPT, etc.) irrespective of income or their ability to pay is an example of absolute equity. In contrast, an example of proportional equity is when the food stamp program gives a higher benefit to those with lower income (and vice versa). The heart of proportional equity is that although benefits are not equal in dollars for everyone, the benefit given *creates* equal purchasing power for food. Notice that program participants can, in justice, be treated both differently and equitably. Statements of goals and objectives need to be clear as to whether absolute or proportional equity is intended.

Equity cuts other ways as an evaluation criterion for goals and objectives. In specifying particular target subgroups in the statements of objectives, some groups will inevitably get more benefits or services or resources than others. Some statements of objectives might express an affirmative action sentiment: "Transportation services will be provided, first priority, for those sections of the community in which ethnic minorities reside." The equity question here has several dimensions. If the ideological position is that ethnic minorities have been historically and systematically deprived of transportation, then proportional equity might justify the priority service given them in the preceding statement of objectives. On the other hand, if the statement of objectives specifies transportation services operated at the county level of government and specifies that they are to be focused on geographic areas closest to the county seat so they can link up with existing city transportation, the system will expand transportation opportunities for those who live on the city fringe but systematically deprive rural residents. The basic question is not answered solely by judging whether equity exists, but, if inequity exists, whether it is rationally justified as a good fit with the overall social problem analysis.

Efficiency

The efficiency criterion cannot be applied logically to the goals and objectives, basically because the concern of goals and objectives is restricted to *outcome*, whereas the concern of efficiency always lies with *means* to an outcome. The center of the efficiency question is always whether there is a better (least costly, more cost-effective) means to achieve a given outcome. Because goals and objectives must refer to ends and not means, the efficiency criterion is relevant only to program inputs and operations.

Some Evaluation Criteria Unique to Goals and Objectives

Statements of goals and objectives can be evaluated against numerous criteria. We will discuss here only clarity, measurability and manipulability. We will not discuss performance standards because they are entirely specific to the details of program design. For a discussion of performance standards see the section earlier in this chapter titled

"Objectives (not Goals) Must Contain Target Group Specifications and Performance Standards."

Clarity

Goals and objectives can be clear only if terms are well defined; a well-defined term easily distinguishes examples of things to which the term refers from those to which the term is closely related. In other words, meaning of the terms is not left to the imagination. Statements of objectives must be accompanied by definitions for terms whose meanings are uncommon or terms not in general use among the intended public. The following goal statement is unclear because its terms are not subsequently defined and probably are not familiar to most: "The goal of this policy is to raise the level of consciousness about work sharing and its benefits for the unit work group." Note that if the terms *work sharing* and *work group* were defined, the statement might be clear. For example:

> *Work sharing* means splitting one standard forty-hour week of a paid, skilled job into several parts of a workday, each part held by a different employee who works only part-time.
>
> *Work group* refers to a group of people who are employed by and earn wages from the same employer, working in close proximity to each other at the same workplace.

What we have done here is simply to change the goal statement into what we could now call a statement of objective simply by making it concrete and observable.

The second definition holds a number of definitional options: One could loosen the definition (and include more people) by removing the qualifier "working in close proximity to each other." That would increase the number in the work group but, more important, it would scoop up a very different set of people than is referred to in the first definition. The first would likely include people in relationships usually defined as primary; the second would include those usually defined as primary *and* secondary social relationships. It is easy to see how fundamentally arbitrary definitions are. Choices depend on the purpose for the definition: Is the interest actually in primary or secondary relationships? Of course, the phrase "raise the level of consciousness" is more abstruse, but it is still capable of definition. The difficulty is that it could mean so many different things that any one definition probably will seem arbitrary and strange to the ear. That may be true, but that is not a fatal flaw here. A handy idea to remember about definitions is the ancient distinction between genera and specie: One acceptable way of constructing definitions is to have the definitional statement tell the general class (genera) to which the thing defined belongs and then tell the things that make it different from all other members of that class (specie). For example, "raise the level of consciousness" means acquiring "understanding" (genera, the general class of things to which this thing belongs) of why work sharing is a desirable work option (specie, the feature that makes this different from all other kinds of "understandings").

Measurability

Unless statements of objectives are *capable of being measured*, they are of little use in administering or evaluating a program or policy. Remember, it is only objectives, not goals, to which the criterion of measurability applies. Goals are so general as to be immeasurable in principle (as discussed earlier in this chapter). To be measurable means to be quantified, even if only in crude fashion ("none, some, much"). In practice, it seems likely that any term can be measured; all that is required is to give it definitional substance. When definitions are neither given nor carefully constructed, they cannot lead to measurability and that is a serious shortcoming.

Manipulability

Some objectives concern factors that are just not open to change by any conceivable means—literally nonmanipulable. Just to make the point, here is a silly example: "the goal is to develop in military service personnel the capacity to criticize their superiors in the civilian press." The terms in which this goal is expressed refer to factors for which there is no rational basis for expecting change. What would it take to induce a military person to do the one thing that would be most likely to destroy a military career, as the preceding suggests? Probably not anything of which a social program would be capable.

Sometimes arguments about what is plausibly manipulable appeal to the illogic of the ideas as against everyday experience. The more common use of this criterion calls for some kind of evidence from empirical research—historical, experimental—that would give a rational basis for believing that the variables in which objectives are stated are open to influence. For example, it has been clearly shown that a second abuse incident *can* be successfully predicted and objectives thus focused would pass the test presented by this evaluation criterion.[7]

The demand for evidence of manipulability is not overly constraining because it is entirely acceptable to declare a program to be an experiment. The consequence is to loosen the expectation of achievement and to adopt program objectives as *tentative hypotheses* for a pilot program rather than firm outcome expectations. Later in this book an argument will be made that social policies and programs ought to do more of just that kind of thing, given the limited state of our knowledge. Doubtless, the nature of our enterprise is experimental and exploratory.

Good things flow from this attitude. We are more free and, thus, more likely to notice unusual things happening when a program is fielded, things no one expected in advance. And because we are speaking about programs and policies that affect human beings, clarity that a program effort is experimental or exploratory is a necessary condition for alerting program participants to that fact; often, it is a legal obligation. Finally, it is only ethical to be straightforward about such matters in dealing with those who make program and policy funding decisions. Too often, and ultimately to our misfortune, policy and program advocates promise more than they can deliver.

Concern with Outcomes, Not Services Provided

Concern with ends that are outcomes, not just "inputs" or services provided, is another standard that statements of goals and objectives should meet. An example common in social work practice in the personal social services is making studies of the "goodness" or "fitness" of a home for a child in adoptive or foster family care or decisions having to do with which of a child's divorced parents the child should live. It is *not* acceptable to say that the objective of this social program is to "make home studies." Home studies are a means to an end, not an end in themselves. A home study is surely not an activity that could stand on its own and be justified. There is simply no use for home studies unless they are necessary for a decision about a child. It is in this sense that we can say, in a commonsense way, that objectives and goals should be able to stand on their own as justified.

The Analyst's Own Value Perspectives in Evaluating the Merit of Goals and Objectives

At some point, practical public policy analysts will find that their own personal value positions will intrude on their enterprise. Recall a point made earlier that such value intrusions are important sources of bias. So let us use some of your authors' value commitments as examples of how these are likely to show up in judging the merit of social program or policy system goals and objectives. The concept of client/consumer empowerment refers to the idea that the fullest development of human potential takes place in an environment in which it is possible to bring one's choices (empower those choices) into reality; "taking charge of one's life" is a common description. It is, at root, the simple idea that a life can be filled with circumstances that grind into dust the ability to act on the choices one makes: too little money, time, opportunity, training, the moral support of others, skill, vision, energy, health. Valuing client empowerment implies strong medicine, strong constraints on social work and human service policy and practice goals and objectives. For example, in one instance, it might mean that in preference for doing things for people, a practitioner will work toward helping a client/consumer take charge, but it also may mean in another instance that the practitioner will take charge of organizing resources for people who (at that moment) cannot do that by themselves. Making available those resources is a means by which it becomes practically possible for the person helped to take charge. Without direct assistance from a practitioner (or others) in providing resources or access to them, taking charge of one's life in regard to housing and education is unlikely. Without money or training or skills or job opportunities, taking charge of one's work life is often impossible.

Goals and objectives of social programs and policies will be preferred by the authors when they reflect that idea—when they reflect that value commitment. Now think of a shelter program for the homeless, the goal of which is to help its consumers avoid exposure to the elements; contrast it to one that *also* has goals and objectives reflecting empowerment goals, for example, service consumers learning how to do the following:

- Access medical care (empowering service consumers to maximum physical capacity)
- Access housing market facts and resources (empowering service consumers to search out their own housing)
- Access welfare income maintenance benefits plus skills in applying for a job (empowering service consumers to an independent income and all that implies for their ability to make other life choices)
- Support others who have social problems that are similar to their own (empowering them to help others)
- Form political constituencies for the homeless (empowering service consumers to exert political control over their own problems and work for political solutions of housing shortages, for example)

The last program or policy system will be preferred over the others simply because it has empowerment goals and objectives whereas the others do not. Do not be misled— the intent is not to imply that helping homeless people survive is somehow trivial. The issue here is to stress how much better is the solution for the social problem whose goal also seeks to empower the homeless in a way that goes a distance toward assisting people to the point where they can work changes in their own lives and live in circumstances that allow them to pursue the choices they make freely. The fact that it might be preventive is important to us only because it reduces preventable basic human pain, always a value preference for almost anyone involved in delivering human services.

Such value choices can be complicated because they are not benign in every respect or they sometimes impinge on the delivery of best or better services to everyone. That happens because a broad objective (like empowerment) requires so much in the way of additional program services. In a world where finite resources and demand for services exceed availability, doing more for some clients/consumers often means doing less for others. When some get so much that others may get nothing, those with nothing are unlikely to agree that our value choice is a better one. Although we don't believe the preceding choice is always the best, in some instances, we are persuaded it is and here is the best case we can make for it. When a social program does only a little for everyone in need, it may be that a little can be worse (or at least not better) than nothing—that is, its contribution to the solution of the problem is either minuscule or may create even worse problems. Under many conditions, homeless shelter programs can be examples of the potential for that result. It is one thing for a shelter program to provide benefits in the aftermath of community disaster—tornadoes, hurricanes, and earthquakes; it is another when the disasters are personal (or perhaps singularly economic). If a homeless shelter cannot provide enough services or benefits to make it possible to escape from the shelter, it can create a permanent resident population of those who cannot deal with the circumstances that brought them there in the first place; being institutionalized is not far around the corner. Before the advent of psychotropic medication for psychosis, mental institutions were very much in that position. Income maintenance programs like SSI, which has a maximum federal grant of $637 per month in 2008 for a single person, will help people survive but not move beyond that level of existence. The viewpoint in this book is that one aspect of the empowerment idea is that it assumes that people are continuously changing organisms, so that new paths (sometimes, but not always positive and growth-ful) are necessary as environmental conditions, experience, and social circumstances change around us all. The idea is that social programs, policies, and practitioners *ought* to keep that in mind and see their work, their goal, as a continuous effort to enable human potential to come out from under the grind of circumstance—and perhaps even from the outcomes of what we tentatively call not very wise or good choices.

Summary

A goal is a statement, in general and abstract terms, of desired qualities in human and social conditions. Goals are an answer to the question "What is the purpose of this program or policy?" All elements of a program or policy must be judged on the basis of their contribution to the program goals and objectives. The program or policy goals and objectives are the programmatic "measure of all things." When the goals or objectives of a policy or program are described they point to desired ends, not providing services. That is essential because a program or policy system with commitment only to providing service can never be held accountable but could continue service provision indefinitely despite no tangible results. Goals can be manifest (public and explicit) or latent (unstated) and hidden. Whereas a goal is an abstract and general statement of desired outcomes, an objective is a specific, empirical, operational statement about a desired, observable outcome. For any given goal, many different (apparently divergent) objectives can be written. Objectives can also be long term, short term, intermediate, and ultimate.

There are several general types of evaluation criteria the practical public policy analyst should use in judging the merit of goals and objectives: (1) those that concern their fit with the relevant social problem analysis; (2) those from which the meaning of the traditional criteria of equity, adequacy, and efficiency are drawn; (3) those that are specifically relevant to particular policy elements; and (4) those that are the personal value commitments of analysts themselves.

A good fit between the social problem analysis and the goals and objectives of a program or policy system is a matter of demonstrating the similarity between how their terms are defined. A statement of a goal or an objective is clear if its terms are well defined; a well-defined term is one that easily distinguishes actual examples of things to which it refers from those to which it is closely related. Unless statements of objectives are capable of being measured, they are of little use in administering or evaluating a program or policy. The criterion of measurability applies only to objectives, not goals. Many personal social service programs or policy objectives contain intermediate steps (not necessarily ultimate outcomes) in a whole social treatment process. Goals and objectives in the personal social services create special problems because they tend to be highly individualized. The fact is that personal social services can be and often are mandatory and operate with quite obvious social control objectives. Personal social service goals and objectives should express those explicitly where that applies.

EXERCISES

1. Two of your friends are arguing: One says that the reason for high schools in the United States is to keep teenagers out of the labor market for as long as possible so there will be less competition, better pay, and more jobs for adults; the other argues that the school district charter says that the goal of high schools is to teach teenagers the skills they need to get a good job. What does the material in Chapter 3 teach you about goals that would help you sort out that argument? Is one or the other or both right, and why?

2. The Indian Child Welfare Act (P.L.95-608, 95 Stat. 3069) (Sec. 3) says that "it is the policy of this Nation to protect the best interests of Indian children and to promote the stability and security of Indian tribes and families by establishment of minimum Federal standards for the removal of Indian children from families and placement of children in foster or adoptive homes which will reflect the unique values of Indian culture." It also says (Sec. 101[a]) that "in any State court proceeding for foster care placement of or termination of parental rights to an Indian child . . . the court . . . shall transfer such proceeding to the jurisdiction of the tribe (Tribal court) . . . absent objection by either parent or the Indian child's tribe."

Write a one-sentence goal statement and a one-sentence statement of objective from the preceding quotations, using your own words. Then write a short paragraph justifying the difference between the two statements, telling why one is a goal and the other an objective.

NOTES

1. F. F. Piven and R. Cloward, *Regulating the Poor* (New York: Pantheon Books, 1971).
2. M. Rein, *From Policy to Practice* (Armonk, NY: M. E. Sharpe, 1985), p. xii.
3. S. Geron, "Regulating the Behavior of Nursing Homes through Positive Incentives: An Analysis of the Illinois Quality Incentive Program (QUIP)," *The Gerontologist*, 31 (1991): 291–301.
4. J. A. Pechman and P. M. Timpane (eds.), *Work Incentives and Income Guarantees* (Washington, DC: Brookings Institution, 1975).
5. U.S. Congress, Committee on Ways and Means, *2004 Green Book* (Washington, DC: U.S. Government Printing Office, 2004).
6. D. Saleeby, *The Strengths Perspective in Social Work Practice* (New York: Allyn & Bacon, 2005).
7. D. E. Chambers and M. K. Rodwell, "Promises, Promises: Predicting Child Abuse," *Policy Studies Review*, 8(4) (Summer 1989): 749–793.

CHAPTER 4

Who Gets What

The Analysis of Types of Benefits and Services

Introduction

Because there are so many types of benefits and services, sorting them out is, unfortunately, a complicated matter. Here's one approach to it. First, consider social welfare benefits to be any income transfer in a *nonmarket* exchange. That means you count as welfare benefits any money you receive for which you haven't either labored or traded for goods of some kind. It is a common way to define welfare, and done that way, it includes anything from a free school lunch to a government guarantee of a corporate loan. Benefits thus defined can also include nonmaterial things like increased power over organizational decisions, positive discrimination like giving preference to the hiring of special group members such as veterans, as well as "expert services" like we all get from physicians and lawyers. That's because, ultimately, all of the preceding examples translate into cash. In this chapter, we'll be discussing common types everybody refers to as "welfare" benefits and services, but we'll talk about uncommon types as well. Criteria that can be used to judge the merit of benefits and services will be discussed. Finally, examples will be given of benefit packages to illustrate how benefits and services are commonly received in sets as well as singly.

A Classification Scheme for Benefit and Service Types

Practitioners need a clear grasp of the most common social policy benefit and service alternatives. This classification scheme will assume that any of these benefit forms are interchangeable—which may mean positive or negative consequences.[1] A benefit form can only be judged *relative* to the available alternatives, so it might help to see how, in very different ways, each benefit form could be used to solve the same social problem.

Assume that a low-income, working-class family has exhausted its insurance coverage for mental illness. Derek and Drusilla Orkney, both in their mid-thirties, have four children and live in a moderate-size urban area on the eastern seaboard. Derek is a welder in a manufacturing plant, and Drusilla is a server at a neighborhood tavern. The Orkneys' children range from age seven years to eight months. Drusilla is suffering from a recurring psychosis, an illness first diagnosed when she was fifteen. This is her

72

fourth episode. She has delusions of being pregnant with the second Savior, fights with those who frustrate her low tolerance for contradiction, and hallucinates about visitations by the Holy Spirit. When agitated, she paces the floor and pays no attention to her appearance or to others around her. She cannot care for her children now; nor can she work. It is difficult to predict how long she will be unable to function. Derek also fears she will injure the children.

What different types of benefits could remedy or reduce the harm of this situation to the family? Consider Drusilla. Derek wanted a psychiatrist and inpatient psychiatric hospital treatment for Drusilla, what we will call *expert services*. These days, if Drusilla gets those at all, it will most likely be in a community hospital unit, perhaps operated as a part of her local community mental health center. Her hospital care has to be subsidized by public funds because she has exhausted her insurance coverage, and the reason tax money provides the subsidy is likely that the community considers illness a danger to her children—anywhere considered a social problem of importance. But the city or state that provided the funds could have chosen many other types of solutions (or partial solutions). Not likely in reality, but they could have chosen a policy that would simply issue a check to the Orkneys in the amount of the charges on presentation of the hospital bill. That is called a *cash benefit*. Even though the benefit is in the form of a check, the issue defining a cash benefit is how negotiable is the face amount. If it is exchanged for the face amount, it is a cash benefit. In the Orkneys' case, the benefit is both a cash benefit and for expert services.

In a later chapter, readers will be asked to think broadly about who gains and who loses from all forms of benefits and services, but let us here note a feature of cash benefits that is commonly overlooked: Cash welfare benefits also benefit merchants that welfare beneficiaries patronize. *A welfare dollar paid to a merchant (grocery store, clothing store, whatever) by a welfare recipient is the economic equivalent of a dollar the merchant receives from anyone else.* What is meant by that is simply that welfare dollars, like other government dollars, contribute to the economy by providing employment in retail establishments as well as in the wholesale suppliers that manufacture the goods sold by the merchant. It is not true that welfare dollars somehow vanish into the marketplace with no positive economic impact.

The policy options can become much more complex. Suppose that the public policy was to pay private hospitals to provide care for citizens afflicted with illnesses like Drusilla's, but rather than giving the citizens cash, the public treasury gave money directly to the hospital. If this amount of money in this case was directly related to the costs incurred by Drusilla, then this type of benefit is a *credit*. The public treasury *credits* the Orkneys' account at the hospital with a certain amount. Derek will pay the rest of their bill (if the government doesn't pay it all). As in the preceding example, there are two benefit forms here—expert services and a credit. If the public treasury pays the hospital for anticipated costs of the "average patient,"[2] a cost related to a group and not to any one citizen, the benefit looks more like a subsidy (more on this later). *Credits* and *vouchers* are prepayments or postpayments to a purveyor of benefits and services. The difference between a credit and a voucher is that a voucher is a written authorization to receive a benefit or service; the choice of purveyor is left with the consumer or beneficiary.[3] The distinction is important because vouchers retain a good bit of consumer sovereignty. A credit is prearranged in such a way that the benefit or service can be received only by the purveyor chosen by the organization that provided the credit. An example is the "grocery order" given to an applicant from local county or private funds, an "order" that can be redeemed only at particular grocery stores.

There are still other benefit forms that could be used as instruments of public policy. For example, a public policy could adopt a *subsidy* approach to help its citizens gain access to expert services for the treatment of mental illness. In return for a guarantee that the particular facility would serve all or a stated portion of low-income clients/consumers, the state could give hospitals 50 percent of their start-up costs and 70 percent of their net operating costs (or some fixed percentage of each). Even though the state is not directly paying the Orkneys' hospital bills, it is paying them *indirectly* through this institutional subsidy. The hospital may agree to accept the government subsidy as settlement for the account of any low-income patient. Once again, two benefit forms are at work here— expert services and a subsidy. There are a number of public subsidies at work in the United States. Government payments to purchase computers for educational centers; passenger railroad service operations; national, state, and local highway construction; the operation of community mental health centers; many day care centers; and the education of children with developmental disabilities are all examples of public subsidies.

Note especially that what makes the subsidy a distinct benefit form for our purposes is that the intended beneficiary may be several steps removed from receipt of the actual cash transaction. Also note that, as is the case with most other benefit forms, many citizens—other than those for whom the subsidy is directly intended—indirectly and substantially benefit from public subsidies. With respect to government subsidies providing computer networks (CERN, etc.) for universities, students obtain a substantial benefit—they gain marketable computer and research skills they might not otherwise have; the computer industry is a gainer because it sells more machines, given the government subsidy. The Medicaid program, which subsidizes medical expenses for low-income patients, also benefits the hospital industry by picking up costs for services that hospitals cannot deny, services for which they cannot expect to obtain payment from patients. Hospital employees—including social workers—also benefit.

There is a small but useful distinction between market and wholesale subsidies. Those we've discussed so far are *consumer subsidies*, those in which the public treasury supplies monies to provide an indirect benefit to a particular population group so as to serve the national self-interest. The focus of consumer subsidies, their intended purpose, is to benefit consumers, not producers. Consumer food subsidy is a common form of social welfare benefit worldwide. In Britain in past years, the price of bread, cheese, and milk has been subsidized at rates that reduce the price to the consumer some 21 to 40 percent. The government picks up the difference between the price grocers pay to the producers and the price received from consumers. *All consumers*, regardless of income, receive the benefit of this subsidy.

Market subsidies, on the other hand, focus on benefits for producers, not consumers. In a market subsidy, there may be no one who receives goods or cash supplied by the government treasury; nor is there always an identifiable product involved. Some agricultural market subsidies are a good example because the subsidy here is not cash or the availability of a product, but a *guarantee* of a particular price to farmers for specific crops they raise. Under certain conditions, market forces do not generate a price that covers the cost of production for farmers. So, wheat, corn, cotton, peanuts, and tobacco, for example, have a support price, and when market price goes below that, growers will get the difference between the support price set by the government and the market price.[4] Note that the intention of farm support prices is not only to benefit individual producers/farmers (though there is much disagreement over the issue), but also to ensure that the "family farm" remains as a viable unit in the U.S. economy so that those producers/industries that depend heavily on farmers as consumers are assured a strong market for their products (farm machinery, steel, rubber, fertilizer, and such). There are market subsidies in industries other than agriculture, of course. Scarce defense materials (such as uranium and tungsten and even ships) are often in line for government subsidies because of their wide use in the economy and the government's wish to have them available should a defense need arise.

None of the preceding exhausts the benefit forms by which the government could pursue its general policies. It could choose to provide expert services only to those who, because they were unjustly denied in the past, are in very special need. *Positive discrimination* is a benefit form that attempts to restore equity where inequity has prevailed in the past. Applicants for the benefit are not treated identically or equally. They get special treatment now as a way of remedying unequal treatment in the past. Examples include health-related benefits for American Indians through the Indian Health Service (IHS) and Social Security retirement benefits for Japanese Americans who spent a portion of their working-age years in internment camps during World War II.

Affirmative action laws and certain administrative procedures are also examples of positive discrimination, a special benefit made available to three groups—racial and ethnic minorities, persons with disabilities, and women—membership in which is, by public policy, deemed prima facie evidence of past discrimination with regard to employment. These groups are commonly given hiring priority for university faculty and many civil service positions. Clearly, there is little debate about the intent, although widespread public debate in the United States continues on whether the benefit of positive discrimination is a useful and/or effective means by which to right a wrong. *Judicial decisions and state legislatures have recently prohibited many kinds of positive discrimination.*

Three other types of benefits common in the United States are loan guarantees, material goods and commodities, and protective regulation. *Loan guarantees* have been a public policy favorite when the population sector of concern was the middle class or the business community. A common example is the Federal Housing Administration (FHA) Program, which provides federal government guarantees of mortgage loans for private dwellings. If the home owner defaults, the U.S. government will pay off the loan. If no money changes hands, how can the loan guarantee be a benefit? It turns out to be a significant benefit because it will often result in a substantial loan to a homeowner when, without the guarantee, no money would be forthcoming, or sometimes at higher interest rates. As with all other benefit forms, of course, others will benefit nearly as much as the home owner (the primary intended beneficiary): the home builder, the banker, the materials supplier for the home builder, to mention only a few. Loan guarantees are not made to individuals only. The U.S. government has made massive loan guarantees to businesses and whole sectors of industry. The 1990 bailout of the U.S. savings and loan

(S&L) industry is perhaps the most extravagant example. It is clearly the most expensive federal intervention ever, with cost estimates currently running around $230 billion. It makes prior ventures along this line (including investment subsidies to the poor and middle class) pale by comparison. Note especially that these financial guarantees to S&Ls do not necessarily produce a single job or build a single unit of private family housing (arguably a predictable result of other government loan guarantees mentioned in what follows). Nor are main beneficiaries either the poor or the middle class, few of whom are large savings and loan investors. Indeed, S&Ls may once again be a financing resource for middle-class housing, but at the present moment, there is no shortage of such housing or financing. Other forms of corporate welfare, the federal guarantees of loan monies, subsidies aptly called bailouts, were given to large private corporations and cities like New York. Best remembered are those involving Chrysler Corporation and Lockheed Aircraft. Numerous corporations benefited, but without these subsidies both Chrysler and Lockheed would have gone bankrupt and many others would have suffered, including the tens of thousands of workers involved in these industries.

An example of *material goods and commodities* (in-kind benefits) is the distribution of surplus farm products like cheese, flour, and bacon by the federal government. Although little remains of the formerly large Federal Commodities Distribution program, it still operates on Indian reservations. Goods and commodities are as tangible and valuable a benefit as a direct cash grant. *Protective regulation* is a form of protected access to a market. The most familiar examples are public utilities (an electric or natural gas company), and in former years telephone companies and airlines. Protective regulation is a welfare benefit because some regulations virtually guarantee the utility an annual profit; an exclusive franchise to sell a product people believe they cannot live without implies that the company cannot help making money if only it prices its product at more than its anticipated costs, year by year. There are benefits to the public-at-large that result from protective regulation. When utility companies were first formed in the United States, many went bankrupt in the process of trying to meet the intense competition that emerged, so in some cases, the public had no service at all. One of the major justifications for protective regulation rests on preventing a repetition of that history. Airline deregulation, which allows virtually free competition among airlines, has resulted in a mixed bag of disadvantages and advantages: sometimes ultracheap fares but a worrisome reduction in service.

Finally, there is another benefit form that entails no transfer of money: *the delegation of power over decisions*. A typical example is the allocation of board of director positions to persons who are consumers of services or in some way are particularly well suited to represent consumers. This benefit encompasses the right to make decisions that serve the self-interests of the group with which the decision maker is affiliated. Of course, such a benefit is intended to benefit a group, not a particular individual. The issue of how much power is given in such instances and how much is necessary to make the benefit effective (what constitutes token representation and how much representation is required to constitute an effective bloc of power) will be discussed in Chapter 6 on service-delivery systems.

After considering all these various types and forms that government benefits and services can take as ways of responding to social problems, the reader should be mindful that governments don't necessarily *have to* respond with a program to deal with a social problem. In fact, they often don't respond at all! Politicians can make all sorts of responses to public concern about social problems. Sometimes they are simply the substitution of shadow for substance—window dressing hoping to pass for serious effort. A legislator or a public bureaucrat can express lots of indignation about the existence of a social problem, and propose or actually investigate same at almost no political cost whatsoever! It is not the point that legislative investigations or departmental research aren't important, rather that in either case, it can represent *a lack of will* with respect to promoting actual solutions to problems if indignation, exhortation, and research aren't followed by serious proposals.

Summary of Types of Benefits and Services

At least nine major forms of benefits and services are common in the U.S. social welfare system. They may be used singly or in combination; very often a single benefit may represent more than one benefit form. Whereas one form of benefit may appear to be obviously superior, the merit of any particular benefit form ultimately depends on the logic of its connection with details of the social problem analysis and the program or policy goal. The forms of benefit are summarized in Table 4.1.

TABLE 4.1   Major Forms of Benefits and Services

Benefit/Service	Definition
Material goods/commodities	Tangible benefits (e.g., food, shelter, clothing)
Cash	Negotiable currency, exchangeable without loss in value
Expert services	Skilled, knowledgeable performances by credentialed professionals
Positive discrimination	Benefits directed to protected groups to redress past inequities
Credits/vouchers	Prepayments or postpayments to purveyors of benefits and/or services. A *credit* can be used by a beneficiary only at purveyor(s) chosen by the organization providing the credit. A *voucher* can be used at purveyor(s) chosen by beneficiary.
Subsidies	Payments made to a third party (e.g., federal funds to private hospitals)
Government guarantees	Government promise to repay loan in event signatory defaults
Protective regulation	Grants of exclusive or near-exclusive right to a certain market as a result of lack of competition
Power over decisions	Right to make decisions that serve self-interests of a particular group with which decision maker is affiliated

Multiple and Interrelated Benefits

It would be a mistake to leave the reader with the conclusion that most social policies and social programs pursue their objectives through single benefit or service strategies. Although there are instances of that, it is not the general case, especially in relation to programs that intend to deal with the social problem of poverty. It is common for citizens to think of programs like Social Security or even unemployment security as providing only a single benefit, but in fact eligibility for one benefit form often automatically qualifies a person for multiple benefits. The fact of interrelated benefit packages certainly makes the analysis of social policy with respect to benefit forms, in particular, a lively and complex venture. It is not surprising that programs and policies should have more than a single kind of benefit; after all, we have already seen that multiple goals or objectives are commonplace. Where that is the case and where such goals are diverse it would be expected that different benefit types and thus multiple benefits would occur.

The U.S. Unemployment Insurance (UI) program is an example of a benefit that generates multiple benefits: eligible, involuntarily unemployed workers might receive both a cash payment, services from the state vocational and rehabilitation service, and referral to employers searching for workers. The purpose of rehabilitation services is to retrain the employee and to provide trained and ready-to-work employees for employers. Maintaining the stability of a large workforce for the economic enterprise of the country as well as for relief of unemployment is a goal of the UI program. The Temporary Assistance to Needy Families (TANF) program is another example of a highly complex package of benefits and services. It is difficult to elaborate because of interstate variation, but the list that follows characterizes the most general case: a cash benefit, a medical card, child support enforcement, special food allowance for infants and pregnant mothers, vocational training, family planning services, and so forth. Notice that elements in this benefit package are mostly compulsory: child support enforcement, job searches, and/or vocational training are compulsory. In the past, "benefits" were sometimes used punitively against clients: sterilization, family planning, and abortion. Furthermore, some program policies automatically disqualify a recipient from benefits from another program. We will discuss those complex examples in Chapter 8, which deals with program and policy interrelationships.

Criteria for Evaluating the Merit of Benefit and Service Types

Stigmatization, Cost-Effectiveness, Substitutability, Target Efficiency, and Trade-Offs

Whenever there is a benefit to be given in remedy of a specific tangible need, it can be given in the form of cash or it can be given it in the form of directly consumable articles (e.g., food or clothing). The question is: "Which form is best, why, and from what point of view?" Almost all U.S. public benefits available in income maintenance programs could be given in kind. The issue touches on more than income-related benefits. Think for a moment about the delivery of medical care benefits and services. A cash approach would give dollars directly to families in need, that amount equivalent to whatever was the price of the necessary medical care. This benefit is most commonly given not in the form of cash, but in the form of a credit or voucher.

Such examples serve to illustrate how the evaluation criteria apply to this general question. From the consumer's point of view, the major difference is the degree to which a choice can be exercised with regard to the goods or services delivered—the evaluation criterion we earlier called *consumer sovereignty*. From the benefit giver's point of view, the major difference is the ability to exercise control over the nature of the article and the way it is consumed—the evaluation criterion we earlier called *target efficiency*. If a family needs cheese and you give them $5 to buy it, the family can decide whom to buy it from, when to make the purchase, under what conditions, and at what price—an example of maximum consumer sovereignty. If you give the family a letter telling the cheese store to give the family $5 worth of cheddar and to add it to your bill, the choices that can be made by the family are thereby limited. But notice that from the point of view of the benefit giver (the person who is paying for the cheese), it may be important to restrict the choices. For example, the benefit giver may get a special price from the cheese dealer if a great deal of cheese is purchased this way because our cheese dealer can purchase more economically if he can count on volume sales. Not only that, the merchant knows that no advertising expense is incurred. Thus, the benefit giver is able to help more hungry people because cheese can be purchased for less in an in-kind, rather than a cash, benefit form. Under this condition (but *only* this condition), giving the benefit in an in-kind form satisfies the evaluation criterion of cost-effectiveness—the benefit is delivered at a cost that is effectively the lowest relative to the other forms and means of delivery.

Note that it is also true that the benefit goes directly for the specific social problem of concern—hunger. This is an example of the evaluation criterion called target efficiency, a virtue here because the efficiency involved makes it possible to benefit more hungry people. There is not much else to do with cheese except eat it, though a genuinely imaginative person might use it to catch mice, or sell it to a neighbor at a cut-rate price, or trade it for another commodity. And, of course, there is a well-known street trade in food stamps.

Here are the arguments against the preceding conclusions. With regard to the lower expense of in-kind benefits, they say, it is not entirely clear whether economies of scale work in a way that inevitably yields a lower unit cost than cash (and, thus, generate a cost-effective benefit form). A person can take the view that the only way to establish a true cost is through an exchange in a free market, even a cheese market. How can the benefit giver really know that the price charged by the cheese merchant was the best price on that day for that amount of cheese of that particular kind? Whereas the price quoted to the in-kind benefit giver may have been the best price the benefit giver could have obtained that day, suppose there was a cheese crisis the day following; if the family had cash with which to deal, they might have obtained twice as much cheese for half the price. On the other hand, the cheese merchant may have had bad luck selling his Swiss that week and would've sold twice as much to the family for half the price. (Of course, it might also have worked in exactly the opposite direction.) The same argument raises an objection to an extension of social control via the purchase of cheese. The cost to the family is a lack of consumer autonomy, and that makes them even more dependent and less able to cope with the stresses of life. After all, this argument goes, independence and self-reliance are built on experience in such small matters as deciding whether to buy cheddar, Swiss, or mozzarella. Notice how important are the details, for it is on them that the ultimate conclusion depends.

Notice the *trade-offs* operating here between the various evaluation criteria. A trade-off occurs when the policy system has to suffer some disadvantage in order to get another advantage. In general, benefits delivered in the form of cash increase consumer sovereignty and reduce target efficiency. Another example of trade-offs is with regard to programs to reduce poverty. When such programs create low unemployment (a virtue), economists believe that they will invariably increase inflation (a vice) as more employed workers become consumers with money to spend. Although considered by economists to be a side effect—and certainly it is in the sense that it was not intended—it is undeniably an important effect on the lives of most people.

Somewhat more serious is the argument that the price of in-kind benefits is *stigmatization*. When the consumption or acquisition of benefits is public, certain kinds of items become associated with "being on welfare," and negative attributions are made to those so identified. Disparaging comments are made to women who spend food stamps or Women, Infants, and Children (WIC) vouchers in grocery stores (a mild form of in-kind benefit). According to Terkel, local welfare agencies bought certain kinds of shoes and dresses during the depression, and those who wore them were sure to inspire negative comments from others.[5]

Some of these objections to in-kind benefit forms do not apply in all instances; it is surely not the case that all noncash forms stigmatize recipients—not all consumption or delivery of the article or good is public. For example, one way to avoid public consumption or delivery of foodstuffs in a noncash form is to use a subsidy method that was common in England. If the U.S. government wished to increase the nutritional level of its low-income citizens, it could subsidize the price of a popular food to the point where it could become the least expensive, most nutritious food available (e.g., bread or milk products). The public treasury could subsidize the bakers or grocers, perhaps 40 cents a loaf; every month, those vendors would tote up how many loaves they sold and submit a bill to the public treasury. In return, they would agree to sell bread for half the former price, maybe 35 cents a loaf. Thus, the consumer gets bread at a reduction and the baker or grocer still makes a profit. Would the consumption of bread increase? Very likely. Would consumers be stigmatized for buying bread? Not very likely, because everyone pays the same price. Would the benefit go only to those who "really" need it? No, because there would be considerable "seepage" to those not in low-income brackets (again, a question about the target efficiency criterion). Would this form of the benefit be more cost-effective than cash? That question can be answered only through the empirical study of increased nutrition as a result of the increased use of the subsidized foodstuffs. The increase in nutrition resulting from the cash-benefit strategy would also have to be studied and the net results of the two compared.

Note that the cost of achieving the nutritional goal is the cost of the subsidy for the foodstuffs actually bought by the poor; the cost of the destigmatization of the in-kind strategy is exactly the cost of subsidizing the foodstuffs bought by the nonpoor. Thus, in this case, the exact cost of the trade-off can be specified. Those who strongly support cash benefits argue that it clearly has an advantage along the lines of ensuring consumer sovereignty by means of which receivers maintain control over when, what, and how things are bought. From the consumer's point of view, that autonomy is a major issue.

The Political and Public Administration Viewpoint

How does all this look from the benefit giver's view, the perspective of the legislature, and the public program manager? Politicians and bureaucrats have their own prefer-ences for benefit forms, as well as evaluation criteria of their own.

It's only natural to expect that public administrators will value a benefit form that is simple rather than complicated to administer. It would seem preferable to administer a fairly simple program delivering a partial cash subsidy to the elderly to pay part of their winter heating bill rather than administer an in-kind commodity program for the same purpose—one in which the benefit would be gas or oil or electricity (or cow chips for that matter), which the government owned and would deliver directly to consumers. Think of the problems of storage, delivery, services, and all the rest. A cash benefit places the responsibility on the beneficiary for obtaining the product needed and, thus, avoids the administrative complexities. Or consider a program that delivers services for severely mentally ill children. Such a program may involve such complexities as administering income or asset tests to a wide variety of income levels (e.g., to determine whether to charge for hospitalization); coordinating the program activities of a wide variety of professionals; facing high costs per case and treatment strategies of uncertain and sometimes controversial validity to consumers potentially capable of deviant and antisocial behavior. On the other hand, the public policy may choose to deliver this benefit in a form that simply subsidizes the costs of such services in the private sector by the consumer. In this case, the public administrator looks to the cost issues and struggles with determining whether charges are fair and whether services were actually delivered, but certainly that is less complex than taking respon-sibility for their actual delivery. The form taken by the benefit is determining here. Material, hard benefits are obviously simpler to administer than personal social ser-vices, which are often intangible and often controversial as to their effectiveness. It is quite likely that less complex practices also entail *low administrative cost*, another eval-uation criterion of preference to public administrators and political figures who must account to the public in such matters.

Another evaluation criterion common to public administration and the political context is the extent of *adaptability across different kinds of users*. A subsidy (equivalent to cash) is obviously quite adaptable to different kinds of users: those who heat with gas versus electricity; those who live in apartments versus their own homes; those who live in rural areas versus central cities. An in-kind benefit may not be so adaptable across the diverse users in those examples. *Political risk* is also an evaluation criterion in this context; for example, the level of public visibility of the benefit form may be an issue here. The cash-equivalent subsidy for the winter heating program for the low-income elderly is quite invisible in that such programs can be handled via the U.S. mail. Note, however, that even if benefit receipt were visible, in this case it might be a political advantage rather than a liability; the viewpoint in our society is that the low-income elderly are surely "deserving poor," and that a politician who helps them projects the image of a social and moral conscience—good political images, no doubt. Contrast the level of political risk via the high public visibility of a program that generates benefits in the form of psychiatric services for severely mentally ill children. Because such children are capable of social deviance, they can be highly visible to a sensitive public and if the benefits (no matter how great or obvious the need for them) are delivered to a population group that is considered deviant, the political risk is high. It is widely believed among social historians that the popularity of mental institutions as a benefit form for people who are severely mentally ill or shelters for homeless individuals are, in the first instance, appealing to politicians and public administrators simply because such institutions effectively reduce the visibility to the public (hence the political risk) of the targeted social problem and the people who are subject to it.[6]

Finally, another evaluation criterion, *potential for failure to reduce or soften the impact of the social problem*, should attract the attention of the reader. There are few social programs that have an unmitigated record of success. New programs should actually be thought of as experimental ventures and should be proposed to decision makers as exactly that. Too many unkept promises, and too many disappointments on the part of those who fund programs create an enduring pessimism that will come to haunt social program providers in the future. This evaluation criterion points to that issue; surely, before politically astute legislators make a public commitment in support of a social program, they make calculations of their potential for failure. Those who seek funding should be prepared to make statements about the probability for success of their program design. Furthermore, they should also be prepared to make proposals as clear experiments on ideas that have no history. Experimental failures are not a moral mistake; program failures, for which success has been widely advertised, are immense political mistakes.

Criteria for Evaluating the Merit of Benefit Types: Consumer Sovereignty, Coercion, and Intrusiveness

This section considers an important evaluation criterion for the authors: *consumer sovereignty*. One argument for its generally positive effects is that it allows for making choices—a strengths approach. The cash benefit expended contributes to the support of the general public economy in ways that in-kind benefits cannot. Cash benefits support ordinary businesses and ordinary employers and employees. In-kind benefits, if they are to achieve their major advantages of economy of scale and expense reduction do not do so because they must enter a special market—certainly not the same retail market corridor used by the ordinary citizen/consumer. Support of that market bypasses many free markets, and in a way, that costs jobs. Cash benefits remain faithful to a cash market system; cash benefits ensure that "the consumer is king." The point is that, in contrast to in-kind benefits, cash benefits have capacity for welfare-expenditure reductions just because when welfare recipients spend welfare dollars, those dollars create some employment whereas in-kind benefits do not. One wouldn't expect that free-market advocates would prefer a welfare benefit form that takes welfare beneficiaries *out of the free market* in the ways outlined before.

Still, there are those who seriously advocate for in-kind benefits. Alva Myrdal, the 1983 Nobel Prize winner in economics, is an example. Most of the arguments discussed before can be read in greater detail in her classic work.[7] However, Myrdal makes two other points we have not covered previously and are worth noting because they concern cogent arguments about their limitations. The first is that the issue of consumer choice is not very relevant when it comes to benefits targeted primarily toward children; children seldom exercise much consumer choice in poor families. The second is that in-kind benefits cannot be seriously preferred where family income is not adequate in the first place. In the last analysis, Myrdal comes out for restricting in-kind benefits to secondary needs, nonbasic food, shelter, and clothing. With that view, then, it would seem that the kinds of benefits Myrdal really advocates as appropriate for in-kind forms are items such as medical care, education, perhaps clothing, and surely expert services.

The issue of *substitutability* of goods, also important to Myrdal, refers to the possibility that a public policy or program the intent of which is to increase food purchases, for example, may not do so because more food is *not* purchased. Instead, the family uses food stamps to purchase the same amount of food they would have bought ordinarily; the money released by the availability of food stamps can then be used to buy other commodities of choice; the net gain, then, is not necessarily in food items. For example, the socially conforming family may use the extra purchasing power to buy books or more vegetables for the children. The less socially conforming may use it to buy illegal drugs, clothes, or a good time. Substitutability is an important idea because it shows how the in-kind benefit, when it concerns items that are vitally necessary for survival, may not always be an effective way of controlling the consumption pattern, amount, or kind of benefit received. The same argument might be made with respect to the provision of vouchers for medical care, physician prescriptions, and credit for child care or work clothing, for example. Substitutability is probably a criterion that has wide relevance to the evaluation of the merit of benefit forms, whatever those benefit forms might be.

Consumer sovereignty is a virtue because it works against coerciveness and intrusiveness of government in the lives and private affairs of citizen-recipients of public benefits. *Coerciveness and intrusiveness into private lives* should be conceded as an important criteria for evaluating benefit and service types. It is important for readers to remember that intrusiveness into private affairs can violate a citizen's right to privacy—which itself derives from constitutional provisions. Being a recipient of public benefits doesn't change that. Obviously, some types of benefits and services are worse offenders than others in this respect. The greatest potential for this offense is when beneficiaries are dependent on public benefits for their very physical survival. That would direct us to means-tested programs like TANF, food stamps, or SSI for persons who are disabled or elderly. Their means tests must be repeated at intervals in order for the program administrators to carry out their responsibility to see that beneficiaries are still actually eligible: for example, beneficiaries may be living a shared life with a household member who is working and earning but not be reporting it as household income. Notice that reporting it requires revelation of the beneficiaries' personal relationships, where that would ordinarily be considered "private affairs" were the person not a welfare beneficiary. One of the reasons means tests are objectionable is that they cannot easily avoid this kind of intrusiveness. But notice, in contrast, programs like Social Security Retirement and Disability, which are usually means tested but only at the level of individuals, not households. There is no need to be concerned about who else is sharing a household, a bed, or an income as in TANF or food stamps.

Aid to Families with Dependent Children (AFDC), in particular, had a history of notorious intrusiveness. The best example is the public welfare staff/county prosecutor "night-riders" in Newburgh, New York, who routinely stationed themselves outside recipients' dwellings after dark to see who came and went. It was a county-administered program at that time and the local policy concerned what was called the "man-in-the-house" rule: Any recipient who had a "man-in-the-house" (anytime after dark presumably) lost her benefits (illegally as it turned out). The point is that the eligibility rule has to do with who shares a household income, *not* with who sleeps together. Besides being a violation of citizens' privacy rights, knowing that there was a "man in the house" doesn't necessarily tell you anything about household income sharing, though recipients were disentitled just on that basis. The reader shouldn't conclude that this is an argument against administrative rules; rather, it is an argument about how such rules should be applied with due respect for their legality. And it is advice to practitioners to be alert to abuses of that kind.

Of course, the reader must realize that there are social programs whose very nature it is to intrude into private affairs, the obvious example being families whose children are being severely physically abused. Notice that the issue there is social control but of a kind that *is legally sanctioned*. Although that cannot justify just any kind of intrusion or coercion, it is an important distinction because when the intrusion has occurred by court order, it also means there is a way of remedying abuses through the court system and the legally required defense attorney. In contrast, administrative, extrajudicial coercion, and privacy intrusions occur buried in organizational privacy, without clear and ready remedies.

Criteria for Evaluating the Fit of the Benefit/ Service Type to the Social Problem Analysis

Whatever the type of benefit, the basic question is whether it fits the social problem analysis, that is, fits compatibly with the definition of the problem. One way to approach this question of fit is to look at what the problem definition implies as the most prominent needs of the people who have the problem and ask whether the benefit the program delivers is relevant to any of them. If it is not, then the benefits are clearly off target and irrelevant to the social problem. They may even be desirable yet not a relevant benefit. Think of an after-school recreational program for children who are disruptive in classrooms. As desirable as this recreational program might be (perhaps it provides after-school hours supervision for working parents when no adult is at home), if the program cannot make a case for some linkage with classroom behavior, then the program fails the fitness test. Notice that you might create a fit by a design for the recreational program that tailors itself to outcomes that are relevant to decreasing disruptive classroom behavior in some way. That is, of course, exactly the point: If the tailoring is strong, the program activities would likely be much more specific than just simply "recreational"— recall that the definition of recreation is "doing what you want, when you want."

The policy and program analyst should also look at the social problem theory and, in particular the social *program* theory. Note that program theory will specify some set of factors as a preferred outcome and describe how to set in motion a chain of events (or processes) to obtain just that outcome. And besides, there must be a plausible and logical argument as to why this benefit would be expected to have that result. That is what "fit of the benefit/service type" is all about. If that argument is not there or the outcome is unrelated to the social problem, then there is no fit.

There are some historical examples of bad consequences as a result of this lack of fit with the social problem analysis. In the 1970s, federal payments to states for foster home care were raised to 100 percent of state costs. There was an entirely innocent motive on the part of the U.S. Congress: States complained that they didn't have funds to provide all the foster home care they needed to protect children from abuse and neglect. The legislation and the federal dollars appropriated made cost-free foster home care available to states. The benefit/service was a bad fit to the social problem of concern. The social problem wasn't just the lack of foster home care—couldn't be, because foster home care is never more than a means to some other end. In this case the "bad thing" that identifies the social problem was the neglect and abuse of children. Clearly, foster care protects children from immediate harm, but it doesn't by itself change anything for next year or the year after that. As it happened, within the year, there were massive increases in the numbers of children removed from their homes and placed in public foster home care facilities. It would appear that cost-free foster care created large-scale overuse of this service.[8] Not only that, many believe that cost-free foster home care funding was a major factor in children continuing in long-term foster care, "stuck" there for interminable periods. That phenomenon came to be called *foster care drift*, a phrase referring to children who neither return to their own homes nor are placed in permanent adoption. Foster care drift has bad consequences: Many children in foster care for long periods literally lose their place in families because families are living, organic things, changing with age/stage development of their members and adapting to the surrounding social and economic circumstances. *The program of cost-free foster home care actually created a whole new social problem*—foster care drift—an outcome that should be kept in mind when initiating new social programs.

It is a great temptation for legislators, policy makers, and social practitioners alike to believe that a personal social service can (somehow) substitute for a necessary material need. It is almost always a mistake to believe that job training can provide a livelihood when the economy itself is not at that moment providing jobs for that particular person, to believe that various "counselings" can help a mother find a way to deal with an aggressive child acting out when she has to work two jobs and twelve hours a day in order to feed and provide shelter for her family. That is not to say that personal social services are never effective; rather, they can only be effective for people who are at least minimally fed, housed, and clothed. It would seem to be obvious, but the history of the provision of social welfare benefits in the United States shows that important and very costly mistakes can be made in that regard. In legislating the 1962 amendments to the Social Security Act, social workers and other human service proponents convinced Congress that personal social services should be institutionalized as a major strategy against the problem of poverty. It wasn't exactly a new idea—the emergency relief legislation of the depression era in the early 1930s had provided for special units of social workers to be available for "difficult cases" on an individualistic basis to those who were poor and/or had personal problems. Prior to that time, private charitable agencies as far back as the Charity Organization Societies (COSs) of the mid-1800s included social workers as part of a system to tailor cash assistance to individual characteristics and to plan and implement service and benefit delivery. In its 1962 amendments, the Social Security Act provided the first federal statutory instance in the United States for the general provision of personal social services to families on relief. According to Morris, at the same time Congress increased the federal dollar match (to state funds) to 75 percent for this purpose as if to underscore their commitment to the "rehabilitation" of the poor via personal social services.[9] This effectively put into practice the idea that services were an inextricable part, if not the major strategy, for a solution to the problem of poverty. The social problem viewpoint there was that the cause of poverty was an interaction between lack of material resources and some personal attribute (attitude, cultural approach to work) and was amenable to change by a service strategy: family, group, and individual counseling; job and parent training; referral agencies; and service coordination, which avoided duplication of services. Indeed, the very name of the federal agency responsible for basic income maintenance programs (e.g., AFDC) was changed to the Family Services Administration (FSA).[10]

Congress was convinced to increase appropriations by hundreds of millions of dollars for services and the training of personal social service workers on behalf of those ideas. Federal expenditures for personal social services increased from $194 million in 1963 to a billion and a half dollars by 1972.[11] Not surprisingly, services weren't successful in reducing poverty. The money was directed at what was perceived to be the shortcomings of individuals rather than the shortcomings of the economic system. The mistake was to think that these services could somehow substitute for the problems of an economy that created most of the poverty in the first place.

The English historian Barbara Wootten puts it this way: "It is always easier to put up a clinic than tear down a slum . . . we prefer today to analyze the infected individual rather than . . . the infection from the environment."[12]

But it isn't that difficult to take all this history into account and then recreate a social problem analysis based on a broader economic and social system viewpoint.

If one did, the implication would be reasonably clear that the most obvious cause of poverty is lack of money and the most obvious remedy is via material benefits: cash and/or adequately paid, full-time jobs. History shows that such jobs can be increased by a wide range of governmental public policies including (but not limited to) the following:

- "Trickle-down" policies that give tax cuts to employers and investors to invest in new industrial plants and equipment to create new jobs (very slow but steady in producing effects and with sizable benefits to the wealthy)
- Governmental policies to place new orders to private business for military equipment, roads, bridges, and hydroelectric power dams in employment-distressed regions (quicker effects for the middle class but expensive and controversially cost-effective for the poor)
- Projects directly administered by the federal and state government to construct public buildings, roads and bridges, and national park facilities like the Works Progress Administration (WPA) and the Tennessee Valley Authority (TVA) during the 1930's depression (quickest for the poor but controversially cost-effective for the product produced and sometimes politically controversial in the United States, though not in Europe)

And, of course, there is an incident in world history that, although not so intended, dramatically demonstrates the effectiveness of public policy remedying poverty by hard benefits like money or food or the access to opportunity for the ordinary jobs that produce income. In the 1800s, Great Britain, stubbornly ignoring the relationship among crime, poverty, and general economic distress, decided to solve its problem of an immense overload of civil prisoners by shipping them off to their colonies in Australia and New Zealand—out of sight, out of mind, out of trouble. No one believed that these colonial societies would be successful. As hindsight shows, successful modern social and economic structures were built on a populace of outcasts and convicted criminals. The desire to work and the ability to compete and survive are shown by this example *not* to have been lacking among them. The economic and social development of these countries is the premier example of the importance of having available sufficient economic opportunity created by public social utilities when the private sector cannot provide it. Given abundant land made available by explicit public policy in the form of subsidies, land grants, transportation, and settlement, a society made up of outcasts created a hardworking, ordered, socially conforming, and economically productive life.[13] The mistake in the British approach to its social problem of crime was an ideological error in their understanding of the problem of criminal behavior—the problem was thought to be about moral lack, not of economic opportunity. However, when given a labor market that provided opportunity, these early Australian and New Zealand settlers took advantage of its benefits and turned them to their own self-interest. Personal social services were not required. One might say that the lesson to be learned from this history is that it takes very dramatic, hard-benefit–oriented mechanisms (jobs and money) to produce a major impact on serious national poverty and crime and no personal social service strategy—training, rehabilitation, job search sophistication, however well financed or conceived—can substitute for it. Will there be some who don't work however many jobs are available? Of course there will be, because no social program or policy is ever perfect. The question is which strategy is most effective.

Criteria for Evaluating the Merit of Benefit Forms: Adequacy, Equity, and Efficiency

We have already considered adequacy and efficiency in the earlier section on the fit of the benefit form with the social problem analysis. But there are moments when *equity* has a special relevance to the choice of benefit type. Educational vouchers, it turns out, provide a good example. Here is the argument. Suppose that instead of providing neighborhood schools for children, a school district decides to issue educational vouchers. When presented to a private school, the school district will guarantee payment of a child's tuition costs from tax funds. Commonly, educational vouchers pay tuition costs up to the dollar per pupil costs in the local school district—some places that could amount to, say, $5,000 per year per child, not an insignificant sum of money. Those who object to this form of educational benefit argue that for most private schools, the tuition is always more than the voucher will provide, so that only those families with greater-than-average income who can make up the difference can take advantage of them. And, if a significant number of parents choose vouchers and private schools, the number of citizens who support public schools will not only diminish but also actively oppose their improvement because they are paying double educational costs. Indeed, with fewer pupils, per pupil costs rise, and at some point, these cost increases mean less will be provided for public school students. Some voucher opponents argue that ultimately vouchers mean that public schools are only for those of less-than-average income and will not have enough support from taxpayers to avoid serious deterioration in teaching staff and curriculum offerings, not to mention buildings and facilities.

That is, of course, a consequence that is seriously inequitable because it falls primarily on low-income citizens who are least able to accommodate to it. The issue here is not that vouchers are inevitably inequitable, only that where it creates inequities, the voucher policy design must have features that eliminate it. Vouchers can have some important positive qualities, particularly the increase in what we have earlier called consumer sovereignty—parents can exercise free choice over what kind of school their children attend. The *trade-off* is between that free choice and the inequity in the form of lower-class schooling it visits on children who remain in public schools. There are a number of ways of reducing the inequity. Most of the solutions turn on different ways of equalizing educational costs so that all parents have the opportunity to send their children to private schools: for example, private schools could be prevented from charging more than the local district per pupil costs, the school district could subsidize private schools at a higher rate than their own per pupil cost, and so on. Note that all the previous discussion avoids other important issues in public payments to private schools, notably the issue of church–state separation.

Summary

Nine types of benefits and services were presented for use in the analysis of social programs and policy provisions: material goods and commodities, cash, expert services, positive discrimination, credits/vouchers, market/wholesale subsidies, government loan guarantees, protective regulation, and power over decisions. Criteria for evaluating the merit of benefits and services were presented: fit with the social problem analysis, fit with the program design, potential for stigmatization, target efficiency, cost-effectiveness, consumer sovereignty, substitutability, and trade-offs, among others. Interrelationships between benefits and benefit packages accruing from more than a single program will be the sole concern in a subsequent chapter of this book.

EXERCISES

1. Review the exercises in Chapter 3. Now think of a way the government could provide emergency substitute care for children without a government agency recruiting and selecting foster homes.

2. Write a paragraph expressing some conclusions you have drawn about whether the alternative benefit forms you have proposed in answering Exercise 1 do better or worse on the four evaluation criteria for forms of benefit discussed in the chapter.

NOTES

1. M. Howlett, "Policy Instruments, Policy Styles and Policy Implementation: National Approaches to Theories of Instrument Choice," *Policy Studies Journal*, 19(2) (1991): 1–21.
2. Of course, the U.S. Medicare system had reached that point by 1990 and now finances hospitalization under a diagnosis-related group (DRG) system in which the same (average cost) payment is made for patients whose diagnosed medical conditions lie in the same DRG.
3. A. Burwick and G. Kirby, *Using Vouchers to Deliver Social Services: Learning from the Goals, Uses, and Key Elements of Existing Federal Voucher Programs*, Mathematica Policy Research, March 30, 2007, www.mathematica-mpr.com/publications/pdfs/voucherdeliver.pdf.
4. Of course, sometimes the U.S. government has worked out agricultural subsidies in ways that require direct federal ownership and handling of grain: for example, there have been times when the federal government would actively take ownership of wheat, corn, rice, and soybeans and store them for years in its own granaries located across the country. It would do this as a way of artificially creating low supply (acting to "corner the market" and, thus, control prices), to increase demand and, therefore, increase prices paid to farmers for what grain they either retained or grew the next year. That is still a market subsidy because its purpose is directed toward producers, not consumers. This is only a different mechanism for working it out.
5. S. Terkel, *Working* (New York: Avon, 1992).
6. L. Stone, "Madness," *New York Review of Books*, July 10, 1988, pp. 8–12.
7. A. Myrdal, *Nation and Family* (Cambridge, MA: MIT Press, 1968).
8. A. Kadushin, *Child Welfare* (New York: Macmillan, 1986).
9. Robert Morris, *Social Policy of the American State* (New York: Harper and Row, 1979), p. 120.
10. Ibid., p. 121.
11. P. Mott, *Meeting Human Needs, a Social and Political History of Title XX* (Columbus, OH: National Conference on Social Welfare, 1976).
12. B. Wootten, *Social Science and Social Pathology* (London: Allen and Unwin, 1959), p. 329.
13. M. A. Jones, *The History of the Australian Welfare State* (Sydney: Allen and Unwin, 1988).

5 Who Gets What, How Much, and Under What Conditions

Analysis of Eligibility Rules

"That's not a regular rule, you invented it just now," said Alice. "Yes, and that is the oldest rule in the book," said the King.

—Lewis Carroll, *Alice in Wonderland*

Introduction

Fifty years ago, textbooks on economics referred to air and water as examples of "free goods." So far have we come from that more plentiful time that it is now difficult to cite any example of a free good: free in the sense that it is neither rationed, regulated, nor priced. Because no social welfare benefit is a free good, rules and regulations allocating such benefits abound. Such rules and regulations are not dispensable. As long as the demand exceeds the supply of benefits and services, some rule or principle must be used as a guide for deciding who gets the benefit or service and who does not.

Social workers and other human service practitioners need to understand eligibility rules because they work daily within the context of these guidelines and use them at all levels of complexity. For example, the practitioner may need to seek exceptions from those rules to meet a client's/consumer's special need or need to understand the eligibility rule to decide whether to advise a rejected client/consumer to seek an administrative hearing on the issue. As an agency representative, the practitioner needs to understand the details of the rule so the applicant has the same chance to receive a benefit as every other citizen.

Practitioners must also live with the fact that they are in the business of denying as well as qualifying clients/consumers for benefits—a hard fact of life that is a consequence of scarce resources. In an earlier chapter, the argument was made that finite resources are one reason social policies had to be invented; in an important sense social policies are the vehicle by which social resources, services, and benefits are rationed when there isn't enough for everybody under every condition. So, as long as there are insufficient resources for every conceivable social need, every time a benefit or service is given to one client/consumer, it takes away the opportunity to give it to another one in need.

Eligibility rules are the most important vehicle for rationing benefits and services. On the positive side, they seek to target resources on those who need them or those who need them most. If they are off-targeted and go to clients who don't need them then, at some point in time, someone who does need them will go without.

It is a mistake for practitioners to think they can just "work harder" to deliver services to clients/consumers so that *no one* will go without. Practitioners' time is also a scarce and expensive resource, every bit as scarce and expensive as cash. It is tempting to think that a way around this problem is to deliver services via a "first-come, first-served" eligibility rule. Although that rule has qualities of "rough justice" that are somehow appealing, the justice involved is probably illusory. Think of how a first-come, first-served rule gives a not necessarily merited advantage to those who *by chance* hear of the rule or the service first; there is no particular justice in that. At some point, those who implement that rule will run out of resources, so that denying clients/ consumers has only been postponed. First-come, first-served is not inherently a bad eligibility rule, but it has no great virtue either—why shouldn't it be preferable to give preference to those who are, on some basis, most needy? Indeed, practitioners may even be responsible for constructing such rules at some time later in their career and at that moment there is at stake a professional responsibility for good service to clients/consumers. When a policy does not meet the needs of clients/consumers adequately, neither the exercise of simplistic eligibility rules nor a large dose of moral indignation will suffice to discharge professional responsibility. Practitioners are responsible for advocating their clients'/consumers' needs even to their own administrative superiors as well as to their colleagues in other agencies who have resources that clients/consumers need. Furthermore, practitioners are responsible for joining with others in pursuing legislative or judicial advocacy as a remedy.

Types of Eligibility Rules

The decentralized disarray of the U.S. welfare system creates literally hundreds of public and private programs that offer welfare services and benefits. Each has a somewhat different set of rules for determining who gets what, how much, and under which conditions. Faced with this bewildering variety, we need to reduce its complexity by some kind of scheme that makes it more understandable. The purpose of the following scheme is to group together eligibility rules so that we can talk about types of eligibility rules without the trouble of weighty discussions about lightweight differences. Many schemes serve this purpose—none perfect—so we will borrow heavily from one that seems well suited to the purpose. It was devised by Richard Titmuss, a student of social policy in the British tradition of Beatrice Webb, Beveridge, and others.[1] Titmuss was humble about this analytic scheme: "This represents little more than an elementary and partial structural map which can assist in the understanding of the welfare complex today."[2]

- Prior contributions
- Administrative rule
- Private contracts
- Professional discretion
- Administrative discretion
- Judicial decision
- Means testing (needs minus assets and/or income)
- Attachment to the workforce
- Eligibility inclusion and exclusion

Eligibility Rules Based on Prior Contributions

Eligibility for many important social welfare benefits is established by rules about how much prior contributions have been made to the system that will pay the benefit later. A prominent example is benefits paid by the U.S. Social Security system: retirement income for workers and survivors (OASI), disability income for workers and dependents (SSDI), and payments for medical care services (Medicare) for both disabled and retired persons. The basic ideas behind the prior contribution method of establishing entitlement are the same principles that lie behind all private insurance schemes: (1) payment in advance provides for the future and (2) protection against the economic consequences of personal disasters is best achieved by spreading the risk among a large group of people.

Exactly how much prior contribution is required varies with the age at which benefit is drawn and the type of benefit in question, but some *prior contribution* is always necessary. In general forty quarters of coverage (minimally ten years) are required, although for disability benefits it is twenty quarters in the ten years prior to determination of disability, with special insured status for persons who are disabled before age thirty-one. The prior contribution of which we are speaking comes from the worker and the employer and in matching amounts, calculated by a complicated formula and expressed as a percentage of workers' wages written into legislation. As of 2008, a tax rate of 7.65 percent (15.30 percent for self-employed) is paid on wages for Social Security and Medicare. The Social Security portion (OASDI) is 6.20 percent on earnings up to $102,000, which goes into the Social Security Trust Funds. The Medicare portion (HI) is 1.45 percent on all earnings, which goes into the Medicare Trust Fund. It is from those trust funds that retirement, Medicare, and disability benefits will later be paid. Note that some citizens receive Social Security benefits not because they made prior contributions but were dependents of those who did: spouses, children, and other legal dependents of contributing wage earners.

In 2007 Congress provided a new benefit for those already receiving Medicare via their Social Security Disability or Retirement benefits: "Part D, Medicare," which provides for physician-prescribed pharmaceuticals. The eligibility rules are only partly based on prior contributions because it is a coentitlement with OASI or DI.

Beneficiaries select Part D pharmacy coverage by signing on with one of more than sixty approved insurance companies that will pay for medications via a complicated system that involves some payment by the recipient and some by the company. In general, it has been very helpful to low-income elderly persons and individuals with disabilities (who pay very small copayments) as well as those with huge pharmacy bills. It is profitable for providers. In this legislation Congress chose not to address the astronomical rise in retail pharmacy costs and their burden on the public purse.

Unemployment Insurance (UI) represents another program in which eligibility rules are based on prior contributions. In order to be eligible for benefits, an unemployed worker must have worked in covered employment for a period of time specified in *state law* for eligibility (in most states, the first four out of the last five completed calendar quarters). The insurance is funded by a tax on wages paid by employers[3] in covered employment, and funds are credited to each state's unemployment insurance trust fund (maintained by the federal government). Note that a person who has not yet worked (no prior contribution made on his or her behalf) is not considered unemployed by UI eligibility standards and, thus, not eligible for unemployment cash benefits. A new work record must be established by an unemployed worker who has exhausted benefits (an average of twenty-six weeks) before any additional unemployment cash benefits can be received.

Eligibility by Administrative Rule and Regulation

Although eligibility rules for public social programs may be laid out in some detail in the law, seldom are they sufficiently detailed so that no administrative interpretations need be made. Thus, we will call these *administrative rules* made to clarify the law. This is an advantage to client/beneficiaries because it gives social workers and other human service staff members a means by which to administer the benefit or service program evenhandedly and reliably, so that people similarly situated are given similar benefits. On the other hand, administrative rules restrict the freedom of staff members to use their discretion, that is, to judge need for the benefit or service in individual circumstances. There are some eligibility rules that are almost fully spelled out in the law, and the food stamp program is probably the best example. Almost all of the details necessary to determine whether a citizen is entitled to food stamps are built into the law. The exact amount of assets, as well as income, is specified by family size in the text of the act, along with definitions of what constitutes a household. Consequently, no discretion is needed in determining whether (for example) a live-in friend of either sex should be included in determining household size. The administrative rules for the TANF (Temporary Assistance for Needy Families) program, on the other hand, are so numerous and concern so many different topics that they are bound into ponderous manuals. These administrative tomes not only include the state and federal statutes relevant to the program but also (mainly) they address how those laws are to be interpreted. One reason for the complexity of eligibility rules in the TANF program is they are means-tested, meaning that eligibility is established by a test of whether a person's assets and income are greater than some official standard of need for a given family size. Apart from all the administrative rules that concern how to count assets and income, the TANF program has to be built on numerous administrative rules that tell the staff who sign the eligibility documents how to interpret the law. For example, should a child's paper route income be counted as family income or should Aunt Lily's inherited piano count as an asset? It is in the character of administrative rules that they can be modified over time; if they are devised by administrators, they can also be changed by administrators. Therefore, it is important to know whether a certain entitlement rule originates with judicial decision, administrative rule, or individual staff discretion, for on that fact depends the probability for change—staff decisions certainly are changed more easily than are formal ("manualized") rules or statutes. Furthermore, as you might imagine, the method, resources, and time used to effect changes differ for each rule source. Chapter 6 will discuss the details of administrative appeal hearings that are required by law for all social programs established under the Social Security Act and for many programs that receive federal funds.

Eligibility by Private Contract

Strange as it may seem, it is possible to become entitled to a public benefit through the provisions of *private contracts*. The workers' compensation system is constructed this way.[4] In every state, employers are required to purchase insurance policies from private insurance companies (or a state insurance fund) to pay to workers for income and medical costs to replace what is lost through work injury. There is nothing optional about the law, and employers are subject to substantial fines for noncompliance. In this case, the benefit form is a cash payment plus a voucher for medical expenses.

Another source of entitlement to public benefits in which private contracts are involved is purchase-of-service contracting (POSC). In the past decade, more and more welfare services—counseling, special education, day care, and foster care, and adoption—are delivered by private contractors. In the case of purchased services of various kinds, the state actually pays the bill (or some of it) directly to the private purveyor of the contracted service. Because the state is the purchaser of services, the state can insert conditions into the contract concerning who can obtain the service, for how long, and under what circumstances.[5] Not only state and federal governments subcontract for services, but private charitable organizations do so as well. For example, private hospitals contract out to private profit-making corporations the operation of psychiatric units—Humana Inc. operates many such units nationwide. Another example is a midwestern private social agency that operates a "high-tech" foster care program for its state. This program serves children who are severely emotionally disturbed who cannot be cared for in the ordinary family foster home setting. In both these examples, the entitlement rules embedded in the private contract determine who is eligible for services.

A hotly contested issue is the matter of relinquishing public-sector responsibility for eligibility determination to a private contractor. Some social programs (e.g., welfare-to-work) provide states considerable flexibility in allowing private contractors to process eligibility. So far, elected officials in favor of privatizing the Food Stamp Program have been unsuccessful in attempts to turn over eligibility determination to private contractors. Further discussion is to be found in Chapter 7.

Eligibility by Professional Discretion

One of the most widely used sources of entitlement is the *professional discretion* of individual practitioners. A common and concrete example is eligibility for medical benefits, which is always contingent on the discretion of the physician (or physician surrogate). Almost every licensed profession controls part of the entitlement to some social welfare benefit: dental care for TANF children is entitled in part by the judgment of dentists; legal advocacy for low-income people is entitled in part by the judgment of lawyers and judges; foster care for children is entitled in part by social workers. In each case, the entitling professional whose judgment is necessary is presumed to have some expertise about the matter. Social work and human service practitioners must keep in mind that such discretion can be challenged in an administrative or judicial hearing, and when such discretion seems prejudicial to their clients, practitioners have a professional obligation to help their clients challenge it. Sometimes professional discretion is the leading evidence that severs children from parents, as in child physical abuse, sexual abuse, or neglect cases: physicians, clinical psychologists, and social workers are commonly used. No doubt those opinions are important and often accurate, but social workers and human service workers should be wary of a blanket assumption about the validity of those very difficult judgments.

Eligibility by Administrative Discretion

Another kind of discretion that serves as a source of eligibility for social welfare benefits is *administrative discretion.* A common example of this is the policy in some states and counties that allows a county welfare worker to distribute small amounts of cash and credits for food, housing, and utilities to poor people who apply. This kind of policy is characteristic of the General Assistance programs (less than half the states and U.S. territories have them). General Assistance is financed by the local government and is usually oriented toward short-term emergencies. The staff member must account for the funds only in the fiscal sense; administrative judgment is seldom called to account, and there is little systematic effort to document its accuracy. However, there are more important examples of administrative discretion. It is indeed widespread and the source of such extensive power throughout modern public organizations that, according to Michael Lipsky, there may be serious questions as to whether "street level bureaucrats" or the chief executive *actually control* the organizational operations.[6] All general organizational policies and administrative rules must be interpreted and applied to individual situations, so it is important to understand that such significant personal judgment on the part of the staff member is always involved. For example, a state patrol officer sees a person stopped at the side of a highway applying a newspaper to the rear end of a five-year-old child. In a hairbreadth, the officer is dutybound to make a serious decision about whether to stop and make inquiries. His decision is essentially administrative because it comes out of the role he fills as protector of persons. Later, he may have to make an even more serious decision. Was what he saw simply a child who had tried the parent's patience and was being disciplined within acceptable bounds? Or was it a cruel physical attack that will leave black-and-blue bruises or break the skin of a child too young to defend himself? The discretion entailed here concerns interpretation of the state child abuse statute. Does this instance, and the data selected to report it, constitute an example of what the statute delineates? The statute will not reveal to the patrolman what rules he should use for its interpretation; it will not say he should always define this as abuse. Nor will it always protect the officer from consequences if the parent claims illegal detainment or false arrest. The same situation is faced by the social worker and the physician while examining a child at a hospital emergency room. Here, however, it is *professional* discretion that is being asked for. Their task is to render a professional opinion about the matter, and they are prepared by training and experience and specifically empowered by law to make that judgment. The difference between professional and administrative discretion is the source of authority of each: Professionals exercise discretion because of the authority of their professional preparation and training, whereas administrators exercise discretion because they are appointed by the law or their superiors to do so.

There are important examples of administrative discretion gone amok, so social work and human service professionals should be aware that administrative discretion—as important and humane as it can be—also can be used in ways that work to the detriment of their client's/consumer's welfare. Few cases are so flagrant as the massive disentitlement of the chronically mentally ill from Social Security Disability benefits during the early 1980's Reagan administration. Although it is not a common case, it is useful to summarize briefly here to illustrate this point. At that time, the Social Security Administration (SSA), ostensibly concerned about the rising costs of the Social Security Disability system, began a systematic effort to reduce approved benefit claims of chronically mentally ill individuals. Some 150,000 beneficiaries had their benefits canceled during those few years. Not only were people with mental illness disadvantaged; there are documented cases of rejected applicants with severe, disabling cardiac conditions who died from their conditions in the waiting rooms of Social Security offices.

The mechanisms by which this was accomplished included changes in the standards used for mental disabilities and attempts to impose a quota on SSA hearing judges for benefit denials—judges were expected to hand down a constantly increasing number of benefit denials. If the quota was not met, they were subject to considerable harassment: reassignment or mandatory attendance at lengthy "educational seminars," for example. The Association of Social Security Administrative Law judges appealed these measures on the grounds that they constituted unlawful interference in the fair-hearing appeals system which is legally independent of administrative authority. The association won on those grounds, after showing that indeed there were systematic, illegal, plainly political attempts to influence the outcomes of the fair-hearing system. In subsequent court cases, rising to the level of the U.S. Supreme Court, sizable proportions of the benefit denials were declared illegal and restored. It is clear from the data available that beneficiaries with disabilities who persevered in challenging the administrative decisions of the SSA increased their chances of a favorable decision to nearly 80 percent. The higher the federal appeals court rendering the decision, the more likely was a decision against the SSA.[7] Only through the efforts of both legal advocates and social work and human service advocates were these reversals accomplished. This example should give heart to practitioners that advocacy can succeed and, when conditions warrant, should be a part of their daily work.

Practitioners who advocate in these matters should understand that the most important issue in these cases was whether the SSA had *followed its own rules* in denying disability claims. That is the standard required by administrative law, and it is the most common ground for appeals. The law requires that when specific criteria are established for public benefits, the agency must adhere to them and *apply them equitably* among applicants. If rules change, the changes must be made public and published in certain ways. In a concrete way, administrative rules are the "rules of the road," and justice requires that citizens know about them so that they can equitably pursue claims to which they may be entitled. On that account many (though not all) rules of due process apply: due notice, opportunity to know the grounds for denial, opportunity to present testimony in a fair hearing, and the like. (Some of these rules will be discussed in Chapter 6.)

Eligibility by Judicial Decision

Judicial decisions are important sources of eligibility, virtually ruling applicants in or out of program benefits and services. After a program has been in operation over a period of time, it is very likely that a contention will arise about whether the enabling legislation or whether an administrative rule or discretionary judgment was faithful to the spirit and intention of the law under which the program or policy was established. Appeals to the judiciary for clarification of the law are routine and in the end they can become as important as the legislation or administrative rules themselves. Sometimes judicial rulings prevent administrative rules from excluding people from benefits. An example is the 1969 ruling of the U.S. Supreme Court on the constitutionality of what were then called "residence requirements." Under residency rules in effect at the time, citizens of a state had to establish permanent residency over a specified number of days, weeks, months, or years (usually one year for the old AFDC program) as a condition of entitlement. (Residency is an ancient eligibility requirement going as far back as the Elizabethan poor laws in England.) In 1969, the U.S. Supreme Court held that such requirements were unconstitutional infringements on citizens' (labor's) right of free movement between states.[8] The same applies to TANF, the program that replaced AFDC.

Some judicial rulings operate not only to prevent exclusion from a program but also to positively assert eligibility where none existed before. In one of the most familiar, *Brown v. Board of Education* (1954),[9] the U.S. Supreme Court ruled that all children are entitled to an equal opportunity for education, regardless of race. It was truly a landmark decision and marks the beginning of an era of efforts to establish civil rights, benefits, and services. Paternity determinations serve as a source of judicial entitlement to the child support payments by nonsupporting fathers. The human leukocyte antigen (HLA) test will rule out, with 99.9 percent accuracy, whether a given individual is the father of a particular child. Almost all courts accept use of the

HLA test in paternity cases.[10] Another kind of judicial ruling that represents a source of eligibility is somewhat unusual, but it occurs in the process of the judicial review of all children in temporary foster care and is now required by law in most states.[11] Begun in New York State in 1971, that state's court review statute provides that for eighteen months, the court will review cases of all children in involuntary placement and determine whether they shall be discharged to their biological families, continued in foster care, freed for adoptive placement, or placed in an adoptive home. In essence, this is a decision by a judge as to whether a child is entitled to parental care, adoptive placement, or foster home services.

Eligibility by Means Testing

One of the best-known and most widely used of all eligibility rules is a *means test:* Income and assets are totaled to see whether they are less than some standard for what a person is believed to need. If the assets and/or income exceed this standard, then no benefit is given; if assets and/or income are less than that standard, the person is given a benefit in such an amount that total assets and income are equal to the standard. The central idea is that when assets and income are up to the standard, the person "ought" to have enough to meet his or her needs.

Despite its apparent simplicity, the whole idea turns out to have enormous complications. For example, there is the issue of what to consider as income. Some means tests concern both assets and wages (SSI and TANF), whereas others concern wages alone (workers' compensation). Benefit amounts and types of beneficiaries turn out to be very different depending on which version of the means test is used.[12] Note the world of difference in terms of administrative complexity between income only versus income and assets with regard to the test. Income is usually a matter of record (often public) and is often in the form of cash; therefore, it can be immediately valued. Assets are usually held privately and, because they are seldom a matter of record, determining their valuation is often problematic. Then there is the question of how to establish a standard of need against which to cast income and/or assets. Even determining what minimum nutritional need is can be very controversial; the same goes for minimum need for housing, clothing, and on it goes. As a result of the difficulty of arriving at a consensus on these issues, a different standard of minimum need applies in almost every state. Means-tested eligibility procedures also vary with respect to whose income and assets are being considered when the means test is calculated. For some programs, focus is on individuals (e.g., SSI) or on families (TANF); in others, it is on workers (workers' compensation); in still others, it is on households "who purchase food together irrespective of blood relationship" (food stamps); and in still others, focus is on blood-related families (Title XX; Child-Support-Parent Location services). Table 5.1 summarizes some of the wide variability that can be found in concrete, selected social programs with respect to means-testing policy. Means are tested along three major dimensions: (1) type of resource counted (wages and/or assets), (2) concept underlying needs, and (3) beneficiary unit (child, household, worker, and such). These dimensions are useful in knowing what to look for in analyzing means tests as entitlement rules.

TABLE 5.1 Variability in Means-Testing Procedures for Selected Social Programs

Program	Type of $ Counted		Concept Underlying Idea of "Need"	Beneficiary Unit of Concern
	Wages	*Assets*		
TANF[a]	Almost all	Almost all	Absolute minimum subsistence	Child
Food Stamp	Almost all	Almost all	Nutritional adequacy; income less than 125% of poverty line	Household: those who buy food together
WIC	Almost all	Almost all	Nutritional adequacy; income at or less than 185% of poverty line	Pregnant or postpartum women, infants, and children up to age 5
SSI[a]	Wages above $65 a month and half the amount over $65	Assets over $2,000 in general	Absolute minimum subsistence	Individual

[a] Varies by state, but these are the best general rules.

Establishing Attachment to the Workforce

When social welfare programs are aimed at the primary workforce, that is, the working populace, it is of crucial importance to determine eligibility by a means that will qualify *only* those who are part of the workforce. This is done by setting a minimum to be contributed (via wage deduction at a workplace) that will entitle a person to benefit. Note that in many programs that require prior contribution for eligibility, not just *any* prior contribution will do; it must be a particular minimum amount, over a specific time, that counts for eligibility. The U.S. Unemployment Insurance (UI) program is a major example of this mechanism of entitlement. The goal of the UI program is to benefit those who have some significant work history—the program does not now intend, nor has it ever intended, to benefit those working part-time, only in casual employment, or only for insignificant wages. Although specific rules vary state by state, UI typically requires the worker to have received wages for at least six months and to have received at least $200 in wages during each prior three-month period. The purpose of such eligibility requirements is to establish that the worker has some significant attachment to the workforce. The Social Security Retirement and the Disability Insurance (DI) program has a similar policy built into prior contribution policies, but workers' compensation is not concerned with limiting coverage to those with attachment to the workforce. If a worker is injured on the first day of the first job ever, and the employer carries workers' compensation insurance, that worker is eligible for benefits appropriate to the injury as provided by law.

Eligibility Inclusion and Exclusion

Eligibility standards generally have the effect of expanding or delimiting a safety net for poor and disadvantaged persons. Historically, for many social programs eligibility rules have been eased over time to cover more people within the safety net. Examples can be found in the social insurance programs (e.g., extending Social Security benefits to workers' dependents, to individuals whose religious commitments involve taking a vow of poverty, and minimal retirement benefits for individuals who have worked at very low wages over a lifetime). With public assistance programs, an example of expanding the safety net can be found in raising the means test level of income relative to poverty—say from 100 percent above the poverty level to 150 percent above for eligibility. By the same token, eligibility rules have been used to cut back social programs by decreasing numbers who can receive benefits or services. An example is when the old AFDC entitlement program was converted to the time-limited TANF program. Finally, we can observe eligibility rules that have the effect of clearly excluding individuals or groups: Nazi war criminals are denied Social Security benefits; someone who is a fugitive felon or is incarcerated cannot receive SSI or DI; and a large number of immigrants considered noncitizens of the United States cannot collect benefits. It is with the latter group that growing social policy controversies can be found.

Access to public benefits for immigrant noncitizens is a complex matter because there are many different categories of immigrants, exclusions, and rules that apply to specific social policies/programs.[13] The federal effort to exclude social program eligibility for illegal immigrants (aliens) can be seen especially in the welfare reform legislation—the Personal Responsibility and Work Opportunity Reconciliation Act (PRWORA, P.L. 104-193)—passed by Congress in 1996. Section 431 of the law identifies aliens "qualified" for eligibility to means-tested public benefits to include (1) legal permanent residents—those with "green cards"; (2) refugees and persons granted asylum; (3) entrants from Cuba and Haiti; (4) certain battered spouses or children; and (5) victims of trafficking and their dependents. Most other immigrants are considered "not qualified," though eligibility may be possible for some aliens who entered the country before August 22, 1996. Furthermore, even qualified aliens are denied federal means-tested public benefits for their first five years in the United States.[14]

States have also passed measures to deny access to public benefits/services for undocumented immigrants. One of the most publicized state initiatives was California's Proposition 187, passed in 1994. The proposition denied undocumented immigrants access to schools (including higher education), hospitals, and other public services. Although Proposition 187 was found to be unconstitutional in federal court, the initiative signaled the level of dissatisfaction over the current state of illegal immigration.[15] In the absence of federal action to pass a workable guest worker or amnesty provision for illegal immigrants, states continue to pass laws to restrict eligibility for illegal noncitizens, even to pose "criminal prosecution" to private-sector charities that offer the remaining safety net for many undocumented immigrants and their families. One such law is Oklahoma's HB 1804 which took effect in November 2007. The law makes it a felony to "aid, assist, or transport any undocumented person in Oklahoma."[16]

In reaction, religious leaders in that state made a "pledge of resistance" to the oppressive features of this law.[17]

It is unknown how many undocumented immigrants (noncitizens) are in the United States, though a reasonable estimate for 2005 places the number at 10 million.[18] It is also estimated that approximately 5 million children have at least one undocumented parent.[19] There is a popular image that undocumented immigrants have migrated illegally to the United States in order to take advantage of social welfare benefits, but the overwhelming evidence is that they came here in search of better lives for themselves and their families. Overall, they work hard, contribute significantly to our workforce and economy, pay taxes, and obey their civic duties while in this country.

Criteria for Evaluating the Merit of Eligibility Rules

Fit with the Social Problem Analysis

Correspondence between Eligibility Rules and the Target Specifications of the Social Problem Analysis. For a program or policy to be a coherent solution to a social problem, those who receive the program's benefits and/or services must be included within the group whom the social problem analysis identifies as having the problem. Recall from Chapter 1 on social problem analysis the necessity of social problem definition containing "concrete observable signs by which the existence of the problem can be known." *Those concrete indicators, subtypes, and quantifications are main sources from which entitlement and eligibility rules must be drawn.* Eligibility rules that don't correspond to those indicators will off-target the program benefits and services. If poverty is defined as annual cash income less than $120,794 (threshold for 2007) for a family of four, then at least one of the eligibility rules must restrict the benefits of a cash assistance program to those with that level of income. If inability to attain a university-level education for their children is defined as one problem for families with annual incomes less than $20,000, then the same stricture applies to eligibility for student aid. If the social problem of providing income support for people who are physically and mentally disabled is defined as applying to those with a verified disability and proven inability to work for the next six months, then indeed the eligibility rules are about verifiable standards for determining disability and the inability to work for that period of time. The quantifications embedded in the social problem definition are the basis for the target specifications that must be a part of well-formed goals and objectives and it is to those that eligibility rules must be relevant.

A central question is whether the entitlement rules expand or reduce the agency's ability to bring its program to those who are affected by the social problem. Recall that definitions in the social problem analysis can always be changed to widen *target specifications* and, thus, provide an improved answer to that question. Note, however, that doing so may have serious consequences. First, an enlarged target specification of those who have the problem might create large increases in program costs. Second, a narrower target specification might very well change the causal factors on which a program design should focus and, thus, the whole program design. The reader should not interpret this as advice against changing a social problem viewpoint; rather, it is to alert the unwary. With experience, viewpoints on social problems become more sophisticated and hopefully better program designs emerge.

Correspondence between the Eligibility Rules and the Ideology of the Social Problem Analysis.   Eligibility rules do more than just reflect target specifications; they also reflect general ideological positions that underlie or are associated with the viewpoints from which a social problem is defined. An example is commitment to the work ethic, an idea that refers to the common belief that work is inherently virtuous and that the virtue of a citizen is related to work effort and work product. English poor laws required work tests as a condition for eligibility; that is, one way a person proved he or she was poor was to be willing to accept placement in a nineteenth-century workhouse. The modern U.S. equivalent is the requirement that unemployed food stamp recipients be registered for work referrals at their local state employment agency. That requirement is itself a condition of eligibility and, thus, an eligibility rule. It reflects an ideological commitment to the idea that citizens should expect to work for their own bread and that, if they don't, they should have to show that no work is available or that they are unable to do the work that is available. The "relatives-responsibility" policy is another instance of eligibility ideology. England's Elizabethan poor laws, as well as U.S. social policy through about the 1950s, provided relief for the poor but were constrained by the common ideological commitment to the idea that families were always primarily responsible for their members. Thus, the underlying practical understanding of the social problem of poverty was that three descending generations in the family group— grandparents, their adult children, and their children's children—must be poor before any individual member was deemed poor. The eligibility rules for the expenditure of public funds for the poor reflected that ideology: Parents were financially responsible for the relief of the poverty of their children, and children were responsible for the relief of the poverty of their own parents.

Good entitlement rules for personal social services must have an ideological fit with the relevant social problem analysis. For example, in the field of mental health, there is an interesting split between ideological positions: One implies that severe and chronic psychosis is a problem of greatest concern, and the other implies that prevention of mental health problems is the premier priority. Thus, for the eligibility rules to be consistent with ideology here, the former would give priority to those with psychotic behaviors, whereas the latter would give priority to those considered to have high potential for the development of mental health problems (however those problems are defined). Of course, that applies only under conditions when resources are insufficient to provide services for both, but that is almost always the case for social policy and program systems. For a different example, consider child protective services. If the ideological position implies that children should never be considered to be a cause of their sexual abuse by an adult, then the rule that entitles them to protection by state intervention should also entitle them to remain in their own homes while the adult perpetrator is required to leave. That is not universally followed as a matter of public policy on child protection.

Criteria Specific to Eligibility Rules

Stigmatization. Side effects of some eligibility rules may have such serious consequences that they outweigh benefits received. Some argue that these side effects are intentional. Two of the most widely discussed side effects of eligibility rules are stigmatization and alienation. To be *stigmatized* means to be marked as having lesser value, to bear the burden of public disapproval. There are many meanings of *alienation,* but here the term refers to the subjective sense of being estranged from the mainstream of the society in which one dwells. How is it that an eligibility rule or mechanism can produce such strong negative social effects? Both alienation and stigmatization are serious side effects that are believed to be associated with many consequences (suicide, social deviance, tendency toward serious crime, and chemical addiction).

To understand how eligibility rules can produce these strong side effects, think for a moment of what is entailed in an application for a means-tested public assistance program like SSI or TANF. (Recall that TANF offers both cash benefits for all citizens whose income is less than some "official" needs standard *and* personal social services designed to do such things as increase parenting effectiveness, offer children foster care, and help single parents get jobs.) Basically, the application requires a person to lay bare the details of her or his financial and work history in order to document income and assets. Thus, it requires a person to reveal all details about when jobs were left (for whatever reason), when spouses or children were abandoned—without regard for unflattering details. The application requires a person to say some or all of the following: "I'm broke. I can't keep a job. I left my last job because I had to go to jail (or the mental hospital). I couldn't be enough of a success in school to get the credentials so people would hire me. My parents, relatives, and spouse have all left me and don't care enough about me to help out." Revealing such details to a stranger cannot help but make the strongest constitution quiver in the telling. The ordeal is self-stigmatizing because the teller can no longer hide what may be humiliating facts—at least one other person knows. The more a person believes he or she is regarded negatively, the more likely he or she will accept the stigma as real. The stigmatization that appears to result from eligibility rules associated with the TANF or the old AFDC program is widely discussed in the literature.[20]

It is important to observe that not all entitlement rules are associated with this kind of stigmatization. Few elderly individuals feel stigmatized by the application process guided by the eligibility rules of the Social Security Retirement or Disability program. Nor do people feel stigmatized by the means tests involved in the application for student loans (BEOG [Basic Economic Opportunity Grant] or NDSL [National Direct Student Loan]) or, for that matter, the means test inherent in payment of income tax. Two factors distinguish a means test involving an application for TANF from a means test involving a loan for attending college or university and illustrate how stigmatization occurs. (1) The reason for application for TANF (say) is most likely to be something that must be apologized for or explained. In contrast, the reason for applying for a BEOG or NDSL loan is almost never the occasion for an apology or explanation; to the contrary, it is likely to be occasion for congratulation or recognition that a person is about to embark on a path of high social regard—going to college. The same applies to the instance of the means test entailed in paying taxes: The very fact that a person struggles over filling out forms and takes a long time at it suggests a person who has considerable assets and income.

The *worst* consequence of the means tests involved in a BEOG loan application is that a person would have to look elsewhere for funds or delay going to school for a year. Contrariwise, the *best* consequence of the means test for TANF or the old AFDC is that a person will receive a poverty level income and medical card.

Some years ago, George Hoshino suggested that, in a phrase of Gilbert and Specht, the means test did not have to be mean-spirited.[21] Hoshino suggests that one of the main reasons for the negative effects of the means test as a way of determining eligibility is that it places great stress on determining unique individual needs when all that is really required is to determine average need for categories of family size, age, and so on. Verification of assets is a process filled with arbitrary and specious judgments of the market value of mundane goods. As any experienced social worker knows, the administrative cost of such determinations far outweighs the relatively small misplaced benefit that might be given were the verification of the value of highly personal assets simply ignored. It was a considerable step forward when the means test for the food stamp program cleverly avoided these pitfalls and determined need on exactly the basis Hoshino suggested in earlier years—that of some concept of average need (for food, in this case) and by "average" deductions for major items like cars, houses, and insurance policies. Although there may be an applicant who has a house full of expensive new furniture and who might not declare it when applying for food stamps, this would probably not characterize the majority of food stamp applicants. The administrative cost of tracking down that odd exception outweighs any saving that might result.

Off-Targeted Benefits. Another criterion for judging eligibility rules and their associated procedures is the extent to which benefits are directed to population groups who are not the main object of the program. One example from the early 1980s concerned the NDSL funds for college and university students in the United States. NDSL loan funds were very attractive to students in those years because their interest rates were far below the existing market rate of around 7 percent. The difference between the interest rate on the loan (some as low as 3 percent) and prevailing high interest rates in 1981 on such things as long-term savings accounts (12 to 17 percent) was so much that some students who already had sufficient school funds took out an NDSL loan simply to make a little money by banking it at a higher interest rate. The net profit on this no-effort enterprise would have been the difference between the dollar yield of the two interest rates, that is, $1,700 − $300, or $1,400 total. Easy money!

There aren't many examples of porous eligibility rules as outrageous as that and, in fact, that gaping wound in the design of this eligibility rule was closed by raising interest rates on loans to competitive levels. But eligibility rules such as this should be judged negatively because the off-targeting is significant and has no obvious impact on the social problem. In fact, it represents off-targeting of the worst kind in that it takes away money for income transfers from those who are most clearly in need of them, and the profit for those who took advantage of the opportunity was and probably still is being paid for by taxpayers like you and me. It is important, nevertheless, to notice that some instances of off-targeting are intentional and not always a bad thing.

In fact, some social policies are operationalized in ways that purposely produce "seepage" of benefits to nonmembers of the target group. Perhaps the best example of off-targeting intended to produce positive results is the Social Security Retirement program (OASI). As noted earlier, the program is nonstigmatizing because its designer ensured that nearly *the whole population would receive benefits* (nearly all were entitled because they contributed as workers). In the usual case, social programs that are universal cannot stigmatize or alienate because it joins citizens to their peers rather than identifying them as "apart" or "less worthy." In fact, the actual cost of "destigmatizing" this (or any) program is precisely the cost of the off-targeting. Though the total cost is not relatively large, OASI does off-target benefits; those over normal retirement age (sixty-six in 2008) can earn *unlimited* income and still receive full retirement benefits.

There are other ways to avoid stigmatization besides universalizing eligibility. Here is an example of one that failed becoming law in the 1970s by only a single vote. Its virtues are that it does avoid stigmatization, has simple eligibility rules, can be administered without constructing yet another bureaucracy, and is probably more fair than other alternatives because most administrative discretion is removed from the eligibility process. This proposal would abolish all existing cash and cash-equivalent programs (TANF, food stamp, SSI, and UI programs) and replace them with a cash benefit that will provide a minimum subsistence standard of living for those who, *for whatever reason*, do not have a minimum amount of income and/or assets. The program would use the regular IRS administrative procedure for collecting income tax as a means of distributing benefits to the poor, a system generally called a negative income tax (NIT). Originally called the Family Assistance Program (FAP), the program was first sponsored in Congress in 1974 by the conservative Republican Nixon administration (called "Nixon's Good Deed" by some). The basic idea is that every three months, people would file an income tax statement. If their total income and assets were less than some designated poverty line, they would receive a monthly amount over the next three months that, when added to their past three-months' income, would equal the poverty line for their household size. When income exceeded the poverty line, that household would incur a tax liability and be required to pay the government additional tax dollars. This scheme was neither clearly universal nor clearly selective. In fact, the system carefully selects and benefits most those in greatest need, even though all citizens can potentially benefit and the system is nonstigmatizing in that there is almost no public revelation of benefit receipt. The Nixon administration scheme was automatic in that it was operated by the IRS and had a built-in work-incentive feature. If there was no earned income, the family of four would get a standard base payment, a fixed dollar amount, say $10,000. Families could work and still keep part of the base payment. For example, the first $10,000 of earned income is excluded from consideration and doesn't affect the base payment at all. But, the next $10,000 of earned income reduces the base payment by $5,000 because for each earned dollar above $10,000 the base payment is reduced by 50 cents. The base payment is reduced even more, 75 cents per each dollar earned, for earned income above $20,000. More and more of the base payment is taken away as earnings climb so the benefit is finally zero. Still, most earned dollars by low-income families will continue to add something to the family coffers and thus constitute a work incentive. A point is reached where finally the base payment is totally wiped out by the reductions for earned income.

In contrast to the negative income tax program, which targets benefits heavily on those presumed to be most in need, there is a program called Children's Allowances. It is semiuniversal because it benefits every household having children irrespective of their level of need. Some form of Children's Allowances operates in nearly every country in the Western industrial world except the United States (including countries such as Germany, France, and Ireland). Canada has had a Children's Allowance since the 1930s and Great Britain since 1945. Although benefits are usually small, they are a significant addition to family finances for poor people. Proponents often argue that it targets benefits directly on children and their needs in ways that other (more or less) universal programs don't in that benefits are paid directly to mothers. The Canadian Children's Allowance programs, called Canada Child Tax Benefit (CCTB) and National Child Benefit Supplement (NCBS), are administered by its federal tax agency. They are means tested, thus are not universal but selective programs focused on low-income families. Benefits for a family of two children in 2007 were about $525 per month (U.S.–Canadian exchange rates are now approximately equal), with substantial gradual reductions for annual income above $23,000 for the NCBS portion and further gradual reductions for annual income above $37,800 for the CCTB portion. The benefits are eliminated for both programs at around $43,000.[22] Finally, note that the NIT idea must always involve some kind of means and asset test. It is the presence of this feature in NIT and the lack of it in Children's Allowance that always generates controversy over whether there is strong off-targeting in any Children's Allowance scheme. An additional point of vulnerability for Children's Allowance proposals is that the benefits must be very low per family or else the cost is overwhelming. Simple arithmetic will show that a payment of $100 per week per child in a nation with 50 million children would cost $260 billion per year—more than the cost of the U.S. defense budget in peacetime. Though child advocates would not find that unseemly, no doubt it would be an unacceptable division of the pie to the advocates for other constituent groups, like the American Association of Retired Persons (AARP) or AIDS advocates. It is important to note that Children's Allowance schemes are not inherently bad proposals, but they are neither cheap nor insignificant in that their redistributive qualities would require a radically different national consensus in the United States about the importance of children and the justice of large-scale income redistribution programs.

Trade-Offs in Evaluating Eligibility Rules

So, if off-targeting has both good and bad effects, how is the practical public policy analyst to judge between them? It is an important question and doesn't yield to a simple answer. Let us use the concept of trade-off to characterize what we will be considering here. It is not an exotic idea; rather it is one we all use in working out our everyday lives. We all learn that getting one good thing sometimes means having to endure some bad things. Usually, we choose so that the good outweighs the bad—but not always: If I have only enough money to buy badly needed new household appliances—perhaps a refrigerator, a washer-dryer, and a stove, but I also need a better used car, the choice is not so simple. Here is the trade-off: If I buy the appliances, I buy freedom from having to go to the laundromat, enjoyment of a new stove, ability to store food longer and, therefore, shop less often. In return, I have to endure an unreliable car that spends weeks in the repair shop, which forces me to depend on friends or public transportation. So, how does the ordinary person living an ordinary life make that decision? The answer ultimately depends on the relationship to what one values and disvalues—in a word, preferences. Now let us consider what those value/preferences might be and how a person might go about making decisions based on them.

The most obvious decision rule rests on a preference for getting the best value for the money. Taking into consideration only the most obvious costs and savings, one might add up the costs and savings of choosing (in this example) to buy appliances. But I must also add in the expected cost for car repairs and the extra public transportation costs. A notable feature of the best-value-for-money standard is that it can depend on whether I want to make it work for the long or short term. With every passing year I lose some money in public transportation costs; not buying the better car costs money, and when my appliances begin to need repair I will go deeper into the hole. The point is that in the long run I might be better off, dollarwise, in choosing the better used car; but in the short run, I am better off choosing the appliances. Still, that doesn't take into account those preferences that are more difficult on which to put a dollar value—my preference for saving time and trouble by having a dependable automobile. Best-value-for-money is an obvious standard for choice, but it won't sort out whether I would prefer the convenience of a reliable car compared with the convenience of new appliances. Choosing among trade-offs that involve social programs is no different in principle—whereas costs are important, they are not always (and in all ways) the crucial issue.

When we think about public benefits, trade-offs are ultimately cost *and* value issues: Is the public interest better served by exercising a preference for avoiding stigma and increasing costs (as in Children's Allowance or NIT) or by exercising a preference for lower costs (e.g., in which case, the monies saved can be spent on reducing other social problems) at the expense of creating stigma for beneficiaries (as in the means-tested TANF program)? There are many other examples of trade-offs; in fact, almost all policy and program choices involve trade-offs of one kind or another, and because they ultimately are settled on value/preference grounds, it is one additional reason a value-critical perspective is essential for the practitioner. Two concepts are used to examine some types of trade-offs: vertical equity and horizontal equity. *Vertical equity* refers to the extent to which resources are allocated to those with the most severe need— the kind of close target efficiency spoken of earlier in this and other chapters. *Horizontal equity* refers to the extent to which resources are allocated to *all* those in need.[23] The point here is that, given scarce resources, there is almost always a trade-off between vertical equity and horizontal equity—the difficult (sometimes tragic) choice between meeting a little of the need of *all* those afflicted or adequately meeting the need of those in *most serious* difficulties. There is no consensus on the value/principles on which that decision can or should be made. Other important criteria for evaluating eligibility rules involve trade-offs and are discussed in what follows.

Overwhelming Costs, Overutilization, and Underutilization

Bad eligibility rules can create severe *overutilization* and, thus, serious cost overruns. Medicare is a leading (and interesting) example in that cost containment is a major problem for Medicare. The entitlement for Medicare is universal for U.S. citizens age sixty-five and over who are entitled to OASI benefits (forty quarters of insurance coverage, minimum of ten years) and for those with fewer quarters of coverage if they pay Part A premiums. Medical care for older people is an expensive business because they need more care and they constitute a rising proportion of the U.S. population. Not only that, but both absolute and relative costs of medical care have risen exorbitantly over the past decade as technology improves and corporate pharmacy profit increases.

For example, such procedures as bypass operations for heart disease are now routine. Kidney dialysis is at present included as an acceptable medical procedure for Medicaid beneficiaries. The problem is even more complex because the long-term health benefits for both are debatable for older persons: Is adding a few years onto the life of a post-sixty-five-year-old citizen the best expenditure in view of the pressing health needs of children and working adults in the United States? Recall that all policy systems operate under a condition of finite resources, so that every dollar spent for kidney dialysis and heart bypass procedures is a dollar that cannot be spent on disease prevention for children: The United States still does not make routine immunizations for smallpox, diphtheria, and typhoid available to its children, even though many Third World countries do so. The value-critical policy analyst must search for the value stance from which this policy choice is made. Universal entitlement to medical procedures is filled with great ethical issues, vexing and ambiguous in the extreme. As a nation, we seem unable to face these issues squarely. The consequence is that when it comes to the choice of which medical procedures will be universally provided for the people, it may be determined by which drug or medical supply or hospital corporation lobbies Congress most persuasively. There is nothing inherently right or wrong with profit making. Profit-making and markets are imprecise tools, often blunt and cruel when it comes to determining choices of who lives or dies; sometimes that is decided by where the money goes for scarce research and care. But where should the first priority lie: AIDS, Alzheimer's disease, developmental disabilities, chronic mental illness, or neonatal intensive care—newborns less than one pound ten ounces? Here are some facts about neonatal care of very early neonates, born less than thirty-two weeks: About half will live; a fourth of them will have major neurological problems. Only 2 percent of births occur this early, but these account for half of all the congenital brain injuries. Costs involve months of hospital care and years of services and can be astronomical in total. This example shows how public policy has avoided the basic value issue: Because there are insufficient funds for every problem, *on what value premises shall medical care, indeed life and death, be rationed?*

Some eligibility rules create *underutilization*; that is, program benefits are not taken up by the people for whom they are intended. There are several important examples of underutilization in the United States, some more serious than others. One that perhaps is less serious is the low take-up rate of the Low Income Energy Assistance Program (LIEAP), a federally financed program initiated by the Carter administration with the object of subsidizing increased energy costs among the low-income population. The entitlement program rules rested heavily on a reasonably flexible and nonstigmatizing income test, but the public was poorly informed about the program even though in many states the LIEAP benefit was certainly more than a trivial amount.

One more serious example of underutilization of a public benefit program is the SSI program offering, which gives cash income maintenance benefits for which a means-tested entitlement rule is in place. The take-up rates for this program run between 55 and 60 percent.[24] Although this underutilization is not totally an eligibility rule problem, there are suspicious signs: SSI is a program for which persons who are elderly or disabled qualify and, for complex reasons, much of the underutilization concerns those with disabilities. Note first that application cannot be made until a year after the disablement occurred. The eligibility rules have a very complicated procedure, which appears to qualify only those completely and totally disabled for long periods; also, it was originally designed for physical, not mental, disabilities. For example, it ordinarily disqualifies those who can work only some of the time, which, of course, applies especially to those disabled for reasons of mental illnesses like psychosis, bipolar disorder, or schizophrenia. Reestablishing benefits takes as long and is as complex and demanding as the original application—seldom less than several months and often more than a year. Also, it is well known among the disabled population that the outcome of application is unpredictable at best. It is reasonable to expect that rational people will hesitate before committing themselves to pursuing such benefits, especially when they involve heavy expenses in time, legal fees, long-term doggedness in documenting medical treatment and diagnosis, and not trivial monetary sums for a population that has no discretionary income. People with mental illness are not the largest proportion of the homeless, but they are a significant group. Homelessness, sometimes a consequence of long delays in gaining eligibility, creates public costs, an illustration of the point that underutilization doesn't automatically create cost savings in tax dollars, because of, for example, jail stays, emergency medical care, and street violence.

Overutilization and underutilization criteria have special applications in the personal social services. A leading example of eligibility rules that create unintentional underutilization are programs for older Caucasian and minority children who, otherwise available for permanent adoption, nevertheless remained in foster care for lack of parent/applicants. Until the 1980s, child-placing agencies that had adoptable minority children in their custody in fact contributed to their problems by holding to certain eligibility requirements: for example, requiring separate bedrooms for children, typical middle-class income levels, a nonworking adoptive mother for infants, and/or formal in-office interviews held in a distinctively white middle-class office environment. Such eligibility rules actively disentitled working-class and minority and ethnic parent/applicants from consideration in two ways. First, working-class and minority status can mean absence of average incomes and many working mothers; therefore, if an eligibility rule is based on average income or the presence of a nonworking mother, it disentitles many minority and working-class applicants and single parents except those with incomes above the average compared with their own racial group. Such a rule offends against the *equity* criterion because it systematically disentitles based on social class status that has nothing to do with any feature of the social problem the program is intended to solve.

Second, some people from minority and ethnic groups have limited experience in making formal applications—in fact, the whole idea of applying for children and having their parental and social competence judged is an experience outside the realm of their cultural expectations. For most such groups, not only is taking responsibility for others' children not unusual—whether children from their own families or otherwise—but also it is usually negotiated in face-to-face encounters and in familiar surroundings with little or no expectation that motives are under scrutiny. Whereas there is good reason for adoption agencies to be concerned about applicants' motives for parenting, any good eligibility rule will take cultural practices into account and not run hard against them. Agencies have dealt with this by featuring initial contacts in the applicants' home, church (or other religious site), or lodge; sometimes these contacts have been initiated by friends or acquaintances. In that way, the whole encounter in adopting a child occurs in the context of a familiar social network where the agency staff member, although a stranger, is at least vouched for by someone already trusted.

Here is another extreme example, this one from the eligibility rules apparently in use some years ago by some public Central American child-placing agencies: Part of the application process involves psychological testing via such measures as the Minnesota Multiphasic Personality Inventory (MMPI). Firsthand interview data suggest that the results of such tests have serious implications for adoption placement decisions.[25] In fact, a requirement for MMPI screening is listed in the administrative documents of one Central American public adoption agency. Screening is an issue because local Central American adoption agencies commonly have in their custody a number of local children of color (e.g., indigenous native people and Caribbean blacks), including infants and preschoolers, children whose only hope for kinship associations of their own are non-Indian (most frequently Latino) families. Those agencies report that adoption by local non-Indian citizens is uncommon. Psychological screening of this kind as an eligibility rule creates underutilization because it is so alien to the applicants' experience (leaving aside the cogent argument about its cultural transferability to a Central American culture or the doubtfulness of its ability to predict good parents or even to screen out individuals who are mentally distressed). That alien nature of psychological testing discourages scarce applicants. And news about agency experiences spreads widely in minority communities by word of mouth, especially among potential adoptive applicants, which further discourages applications.

These considerations probably apply equally well to other personal social services such as mental health and counseling services where their delivery takes place in formal clinics and office buildings. That is one reason why, years ago, street workers and outreach programs were invented—to create access to services when they could be encountered in the everyday and familiar lives of the people for whom they were intended, rather than limiting formal application to unfamiliar, hard-to-get-to office settings. In small communities, it can be stigmatizing to enter a building known to be the community mental health center. Certainly, that applies to more controversial birth control and/or abortion locations.

Clearly, eligibility rules for insurance-covered services can be sources of under- and overutilization. Insurance companies find eligibility rules for mental health services to be problematic, not least because for mental and emotional illnesses or problems, the need for treatment and what constitutes adequate treatment are debatable in the field—debatable in a way that appendicitis or diabetes or athlete's foot for that matter is not. Insurance companies need to ask where is the clear and definable point at which a patient is not helped by further office visits for the purpose of increasing self-awareness, self-concept, or personal insight. As might be expected, insurers don't find underutilization a problem, but if eligibility rules for insurance coverage aren't on target, underutilization can lead to tragic results.

The general solution insurance companies have resorted to is to place arbitrary dollar or time limits on mental health and/or counseling service—$1,000 a year for outpatient services or fifteen days of inpatient services is not an unusual standard. Costs are an issue and insurance companies have a telling point, one that the psychotherapy industry has yet to answer, coincidentally, because the insurance principle requires ability to forecast use (via some actuarial design) in constructing rate schedules for prepaid insurance premiums for health coverage.

On the other hand, the health insurance industry is not noted for its leadership in this regard either; between the two, sizable underutilization and overutilization continue because of the arbitrary nature of the caps placed on mental health and counseling services.

Work Disincentives, Incentives, and Eligibility Rules

Almost all agree that eligibility rules should be evaluated against their potential for *work disincentives*. The argument about whether cash benefits in social welfare income maintenance programs cause people to choose benefits over work for wages is several hundred years old. A major concern during the Speenhamland experiment in England in 1795, it is presently a concern of U.S. economists and politicians as they attempt to reduce welfare costs.[26] Both economic theory and common sense would seem to indicate that cash benefits from the public treasury could strongly reduce work effort on the part of the ordinary citizen—why would people work if they didn't have to? Both the question and the answer are complex issues that for years have eluded practical resolution and scientific experiment. Who, after all, would give money to someone just to see whether he or she would continue to work, work less, or not work at all?

In fact, that experiment has taken place. The economic theory behind the income guarantee experiments runs a little like this:

> One person can view time as being divided among three activities: working for wages, working at home, and enjoying leisure time, depending on relative opportunities and rewards. The reward for market work is money income, which ultimately is used to buy goods and services. One of the goods that people may "purchase" is leisure, but each person pays a different price, one equal to his or her wage rate. Economists theorize that the amount of nonworking time "bought" by a person depends on two factors: (1) the wages that must be foregone and (2) the amount of nonwage income that is available to the person. As a person's wages rise, leisure (non-work) time becomes more expensive. So, besides the question of whether public benefits cause less work effort, two other questions arise: (1) whether if there *is* less work effort, it is due to the fact that leisure time becomes more expensive as income rises, causing people to regard increasing leisure costs as "expenditures" or (2) whether with more income, people value increased income less and are willing to substitute leisure for work.

These questions have vexed discussions of welfare reform for many years. The U.S. Office of Economic Opportunity (OEO) undertook a series of large-scale experiments beginning in New Jersey in 1968 and extended in the 1970s in Iowa, North Carolina, Colorado, and Washington state. These experiments, all long term (five years for the most part), were carefully designed and instrumented, and strong attempts were made—not always successfully—to insulate them from external contaminating influences. It wasn't a perfect experiment but then no experiment in the real world (outside a laboratory) ever is. And real-world research has arguable advantages over small-scale simulations that, for example, might ask people to imagine their response to questions if they were low income and offered the choice between work or staying at home. We will focus here on the Seattle-Denver Income Maintenance Experiment (SIMDIME) because it was the last in this series and provides the best data. It had the largest sample among all the experiments, in that it included around 5,000 one- and two-parent families of black, white, and Hispanic ethnic origin. In SIMDIME, the families were assigned either to one of several experimental groups receiving cash assistance payments at various levels or to one of a control group of families who received no experimental payments but continued to receive whatever benefits they were eligible for under current governmental programs. Hours of work of experimental families were compared with hours of work of the control-group families during the course of the experiment. First, the results showed no significant difference between responses by racial or ethnic background, holding all other characteristics constant. Next, *some decrease in work effort was shown when people got an income guarantee, but the difference was small.* The report has this to say about the results:[27]

> The results for husbands show, for example, that if a family's preprogram annual income was $4,000, a cash benefit that raised income by $1,000 would cause the husband to work about an hour less per week... the effects on a wife in a family with the same income would cause her to work two hours per week less.... However, since wives usually have lower wage rates than their husbands, a given benefit reduction rate usually would have a smaller dollar effect on the wife's net wage than on the husband's.

Table 5.2 presents the results of the effect of the income guarantee on work effort for all four work-incentive experiments. Although some of the wives' reduction in work hours appears large, observe that the authors interpret this as a relatively small-scale response. "Since wives in poor families usually work relatively few hours to begin with, the large percentage change in their labor supply effort amounts to relatively small numbers of hours."[28] The net result, as stated before, is that a $1,000 increase in the family's income "causes" the wife in a poor family to work only two hours less per week. So what should be our conclusion about the work disincentives of social welfare programs offering cash benefits like this one? A conservative conclusion, faithful to the facts the experiment reveals, would be that the effect is there but is very slight, probably insignificant to most people. The experimenters believe that the results from all four of the experiments show a "striking similarity," particularly considering that the experiments provided different sets of benefit levels and benefit reduction rates, that they took place in states with widely differing tax and transfer systems, and that different criteria were used to select the four samples.[29]

One result of the guaranteed income experiment should not go unnoticed: There was a marked increase in the proportion of marriage dissolution under the impact of an income guarantee. It was about the same for whites as for blacks but noticeably greater for Latinos.[30] One important consequence here is that if a national income guarantee program were put in effect, the proportion of female-headed, single-parent families might increase substantially, particularly for whites and Latinos. Remarriage rates for blacks under conditions of income guarantee is sufficiently

TABLE 5.2   Estimated Percentage Reductions in Work Hours in Four Income Maintenance Experiments

Control/Experimental Group Differences as a Percentage Control Mean[a]

	New Jersey (White Only)	Rural Wage Earners	Gary, Indiana	Seattle-Denver
Husbands	6%	1%	7%	6%
Wives	31	27	17	17
Total	13	13	8	9
Female heads	b	b	2	12

[a] These estimates are weighted averages of the response in hours worked by different study groups. Because of the technical problems in estimating the response of black and Spanish-speaking groups in the New Jersey experiment, estimates reported here for New Jersey are for whites only. Recent reanalysis of the New Jersey data provides evidence that the response of these groups is similar to that of whites. Total responses (and base hours) include only husbands and wives in the Gary and Seattle-Denver experiments; in the other experiments they include other family members as well.

[b] None included in the experiment.

Source: The Seattle-Denver Income Maintenance Experiment: Midexperimental Labor Supply Results and a Generalization to the National Population (Stanford, CA: Stanford Research Institute and Mathematic Policy Research, 1978), Table 2, p. 64. Reprinted by permission.

high, so it would not affect the proportion of single-parent families among that subpopulation.

Subsequent to policy debates and the income guarantee experiment in the 1970s, interest in this major social policy shift for income maintenance programming diminished. Instead, welfare reform has been focused more on adding work incentives (or simply requiring work as an eligibility requirement) for existing social programs. A prime example is the Personal Responsibility and Work Opportunity Reconciliation Act of 1996 (PRWORA). A central theme of PRWORA is the goal of moving welfare client/consumers into the labor market. A popular slogan associated with this welfare reform policy is, in fact, "welfare to workfare." PRWORA added a provision that working-age adult food stamp beneficiaries are required to sign up for work in order to receive benefits. Particularly clear is the message of the TANF program. TANF caretakers are given a time limit (five years or less) of cash assistance, and are encouraged or required to meet established work experience standards. A brochure from one state welfare department sends the message in the following:

> You can earn your own money, choose what you want to do and take charge of your own life. You may never need to come in here again—but we're here to help you if you do. We will provide day care for your children under age 13 while you are in approved TANF work activities. We may also pay you a Participation Allowance to help with transportation and other expenses. You may be able to get an Earned Income Tax Credit from the federal government if you are working or have worked recently. This money will not count against your TANF grant. After you have a job and are earning enough that your TANF case is closed, you may continue to receive help with child care, medical assistance and food stamps.[31]

In the years since its inception, there have been dramatic reductions in the number of families receiving assistance from the TANF program: Whereas nearly 86 percent of eligible families were receiving assistance when the TANF program began in 1996, by 2002 that had decreased to only 48 percent. Employment rates among single mothers jumped from 10 to 20 percent. Child poverty fell about 20 percent between the mid-1990s through 2005. What was it about TANF that made the difference? It is important to understand that some of these important changes occurred during a *very strong labor market* (rising wages and increasing jobs); historically, recipient rates in welfare programs generally rise and fall during such periods. Some (but not all) of these effects can be attributed to that. The research indicates there are other factors behind these changes and they tell us something important about work incentives—it is crucial to *make work pay off* for recipients. For example, in the old AFDC program benefits were reduced dollar-for-dollar by earnings, or by income from other benefits like the Earned Income Tax Credit (EITC). Under the TANF program such provisions were removed and it clearly made work pay for recipients. In addition, the provisions that *help single working mothers pay for child care* appears to be crucial. Research also shows that some provisions outside of TANF such as increases in Medicaid and State Children's Health Insurance Program (SCHIP) provisions *enabled mothers to go to work and leave welfare without losing medical care for their children.* Another important item is that legislation associated with the welfare reform movement *enhanced child-support enforcement* for single mothers; collection rates doubled, the number of contributing fathers went up 20 percent, and collection totals increased by over 80 percent.[32]

However, there are some discouraging work-incentive issues with the TANF program. A serious one is that no provision for inflation was built into the federal financing of TANF; that may mean that benefits have already lost 22 percent since the program began and as benefits erode, so do work incentives.[33] States have much latitude in how they spend federal TANF funds and, sadly, some have used this discretion to cut subsidies to child care, definitely not a good idea as it works against the "work pays" idea of TANF. Finally, although "TANF has indeed reduced welfare recipiency it hasn't lifted a large number of female-headed families out of poverty.... Average earnings of welfare leavers under TANF (were) only around $12,000 per year in the late 1990s."[34] And, it is also of concern that an in-depth study in one large community showed that a large share of those staying "long term" on TANF benefits had serious physical and/or mental health problems that limited their ability to hold a job, low cognitive abilities, and/or basic literacy. For those individuals the TANF requirement that ends benefits at five years may work a significant hardship because the program was probably not designed with them in mind.[35]

Another measure has the manifest purpose of transitioning people with disabilities into the labor market. The Ticket to Work and Work Incentive Improvement Act of 1999 is designed to encourage individuals with severe disabilities and chronic conditions who are receiving SSI and SSDI to enter the labor market. Historically, this population has been discouraged from seeking employment for fear of losing eligibility for disability benefits and/or health care benefits. The Ticket to Work provision of this legislation was implemented in 2002 with mail-out tickets encouraging voluntary involvement of SSI and SSDI beneficiaries to contact employment networks that could assist in developing individual work plans and placement for appropriate employment. Among others, a major incentive provision is a feature allowing states and U.S. territories the option to give SSI and SSDI beneficiaries the opportunity to earn more and keep Medicaid coverage at little or no cost. This incentive feature, called the "Medicaid buy-in" option, allows states to extend Medicaid coverage to persons who are disabled and working whose income would have prevented them from qualifying for the program. Whereas it is too early for full evaluation of results of Ticket to Work, the program has encountered serious difficulties in implementation of its rather original, somewhat complicated program design. Participation rates are particularly troubling at less than 1 percent overall, varying by state and beneficiary characteristics.[36]

Procreational Incentives, Marital Instability, and Generational Dependency

Other criteria for evaluating eligibility rules, especially cash-benefit programs, are the extent to which they provide incentives for procreation, marital breakup, and/or the dependency of the children of families who receive public benefits.

The possibility that citizens conceive children in order to become eligible for, or to increase, welfare benefits surfaces regularly as a matter of public and political discussion. For some the issue is that when benefit eligibility is tied to the number of children in families it is possible that it serves as a significant *childbearing incentive.* The latter issue is usually argued from a social problem viewpoint that is ideologically committed to the notion that work is a highly valued instrumental activity and that citizens have a predominant propensity *not* to choose work if there is an available alternative—no matter how grim. It is certainly possible to conceive of a person who would endure the physical discomforts of bearing children as the preferred alternative to working, but even if the standard of living it afforded was considerably less than a poverty line existence, such a choice is neither economically nor socially rational. What are the costs of bearing and rearing a child, when measured against the welfare benefit gain? Where such calculation is made, few would find it to her advantage to bear children just to obtain an increase in benefits. A "family cap" rule is used in most states to deny increased cash assistance to women who have another child while on TANF. Where additional assistance is given, it is less than the costs incurred in adding a child to the family.

Surely, there will always be a few people who make irrational choices that work against their own economic self-interest, but to rebut such an argument we only need assume that the ordinary person acts in ways that will be of most economic benefit to herself or himself. Furthermore, there is every reason to believe that the average poor person, well acquainted with the realities of life at the poverty level, does that in serious matters of everyday life.

Persuasive evidence *against* the notion that financial incentives stimulate childbearing is found in the results of programs in countries that need to *increase* population rapidly: Attempts to do so are made through social welfare programs that grant benefits, often sizable, to citizens who bear children. The most massive of such programs was the French attempt to raise their birthrate in a population decimated by World War I when France lost half its male population. Both Sweden, Russia, and more recently Canada have made similar attempts for similar purposes. All these programs have been *entirely unsuccessful.* It is worthwhile noting that in Third World countries as standards of living and wage rates rise, along with increased literacy and educational attainment of women, birthrates go down rather dramatically, irrespective of the availability of birth control.

In summary, does the fact of eligibility for welfare benefits serve as an incentive to procreation? Given the evidence reviewed before, it is very unlikely that there is any such effect in a population or even any of its subgroups, though there may be some marginal and individual instances. There is, of course, no wisdom in forming large-scale public policy around small marginal effects. We are left with the conclusion that increasing benefits with family size does not create an incentive to further childbearing.

Another widely discussed issue is whether public benefits like the old AFDC (now TANF) create *marital instability:* Do families split if income support programs are available? Nancy Murdrick studied that issue directly through data on when AFDC applications occurred relative to the marital split and observed differences between high- and low-income families with respect to the same issue. Study results are clear. The data show that most AFDC applications occurred nearly two years after the split. Murdrick concludes that the AFDC application is a response to the consequences of the split, not a premeditated outcome. Nor does it matter whether the applicants had an above-average or below-average income prior to their split.[37] Findings from the 2005 Gennetian and Knox long-term study (using a random assignment design) show "no overall effect (of welfare recipiency) on marital stability but contrasting effects on certain subgroups... (and) that it actually lowered the divorce rate among families who were already receiving welfare when they entered the study."[38] Perhaps some couples do split up just to qualify for welfare benefits, but the number is not apparently large.

Yet another problem said to be a consequence of eligibility for public welfare benefits is that, generally speaking, citizens who now receive public benefits were reared in families who depended on public benefits and that this current generation will produce children who also will live at the expense of public benefit. In its most rational form, this argument over *generational dependency* (as it is sometimes called) asserts that social and personal identity is crucial in determining the choices made about work and "getting by." It assumes that a child who grows up in a family in which there are no models of working to make a living will simply follow the pattern set by adults, so he or she will search out the welfare option. In its more unsympathetic form, the argument asserts strong antisocial, deviant motives to both parents and children in poor economic circumstances. In order to make this argument plausible, it would seem necessary to assume that generational dependency must involve primarily those children whose families spent long periods as welfare beneficiaries, because the learning of role models and the socialization process referred to is never a short-term matter. No current explanation or approach to socialization suggests otherwise. If that is the case, the data from the Michigan Panel Study of Income Dynamics bear strongly on the plausibility of the generational dependency argument. This study, which has few challenges to its methodology or conclusions, shows clearly that only 12 percent of all welfare beneficiaries had received benefits for as long as four years, cumulatively. The authors conclude that there is little support for the existence of a sizable welfare class, that the most characteristic welfare recipient receives public benefits for about two years in succession and then may move on and off benefits for two considerably shorter periods of time later in their lives.[39] If there is no large number of persons who spend long years on welfare benefits, it seems unlikely that the necessary conditions are available in which the mechanisms that are said to create generational dependency can work. Of course, this only shows that if generational dependency exists at all, it is a small-scale problem.

More recent research has generally supported those conclusions, for example the Duclos, Fortin, and Rouleau study in Canada that finds no strong effect but still "cannot reject the generational dependency hypothesis."[40] A Swedish study shows stronger effects but, as the author notes, that might be expected because the Swedish welfare system is intended to support low-income families in a way that may not make it easy to compare it with the selective U.S. system.[41] One study by Rank and Cheng does draw explicit conclusions about how large and important the generational welfare dependency effect is. Based on a nationally representative sample of 13,017 households, the authors find that

- "only one of ten current recipients grew up in a household that frequently used welfare programs"; and
- "only one of twenty recipients who are now using welfare frequently, also grew up in a household that frequently used welfare."

Given this (and other) data this study also concludes that intergenerational welfare use "has very little to do with welfare per se; rather it has to do with economic class." Children from welfare families generally come from lower-income families where parents are limited financially and their adult children are economically more vulnerable, thus have a greater likelihood of their turning to welfare at some point. In summary, the research over forty years seems to show that, yes, there are some welfare children who grow up to be welfare mothers but the number does not appear to be as large as popular media concern would indicate, perhaps, as shown by the Rank and Cheng study, on the order of one in twenty or 5 percent.[42]

Opportunities for Political Interference via Weak Eligibility Rules

At one level there is every reason to believe that political influence is one route to the entitlement to public benefits for individuals and groups—of course, social programs are a vehicle by which political interests are (and should be) expressed. But once the program or policy is implemented, it becomes bad social policy for citizens, or groups of them, to be either eligible or not simply because of political influence that circumvents the legislative or judicial processes that keep social policy as an expression of the will of the people in a democracy. Equity is the value issue here. Citizens in a democracy should have equal access to public benefits, and that access should not depend on whom one knows or doesn't know. Nor should it depend on the desire of the executive branch of government to shape a social program in ways that it couldn't achieve through the regular channels of the legislative or judicial process. There is an unusual modern example of the latter, which we will briefly review for its value in illustrating the great danger posed by eligibility rules that are vague and uncertain in administration. Well-formed eligibility rules are not valuable just for their tidiness, but also that they might avoid political intervention in the operations of social programs, an intervention of a particularly vicious sort for vulnerable people. This example, from the mid-1980s, concerns the Social Security Disability Insurance (DI) program.

Probably the premier policy problem of a social program for people with disabilities is to construct a useful and stable definition of *disablement*, and the DI program is no exception. Robert Ball, chief actuary for the Social Security Administration for many years, reports that the slippery DI definition of disability allowed opposing biases to be used within one rather short period of time.[43] The reason for its "slipperiness" is that it leaves one part of the eligibility rule to medical and *administrative discretion*—the determination of whether a disability exists in fact. Thus, administrators and physicians were left to liberal interpretation of medical facts. One has only to look at the sizable proportion of initial application decisions that were reversed and "re-reversed" at every stage of reconsideration and appeal to realize that what is technically called "interjudge reliability" was a hallmark lack in this eligibility process.[44] Over a ten- to twelve-year period beginning in the 1970s, reversal rates on disability denial appeals rose to nearly two-thirds of all appeals; in regard to mental disabilities, reversal rates reached as high as 91 percent of all appealed denials of benefit applications.[45]

In explanation, Robert Ball noted that in the early years of the program, "I can assure you gentlemen, that the general attitude . . . [was] wanting to pay claims."[46] To the point, it is notable that in this climate, even though Congress expressly forbade the Social Security Administration (SSA) from reversing the findings of state disability determination units, it did so regularly (to the advantage of applicants).[47] However, under the prodding of a Congress worried about rising program costs and a presidential administration looking with disfavor on most welfare benefits, SSA began by a variety of means to administer a very different definition of the term *disability*. Clearly, SSA was able to turn the DI system around simply by the strength of its own ability to reinterpret the definition of disability and change some of its procedural mechanisms: In five years, DI benefit allowance rates were cut in half, terminations increased, and total costs slowed significantly. "[D]isability examiners have become more conservative in the way in which they interpret and apply standards [for DI awards]."[48]

Despite the significant changes that had already occurred, with the 1981 inauguration of President Reagan, who had made explicit campaign promises to reduce the size of entitlement programs, not only were new applicants under fire, but people with disabilities who already received benefits were affected as well. Unprecedented terminations of thousands of DI beneficiaries took place between 1980 and 1985: 71,500 in 1980; 98,800 in 1981; and 121,400 in the first five months of 1982—with 360,000 expected to be terminated in 1984.[49] "In the 1960s, the loose and ambiguous definition of disability could not constrain a [Democratic, neo–New Deal] political administration determined to *expand* the program any more successfully than in the 1980s it could constrain a [Republican, conservative] political administration determined to *reduce* the size and costs of the DI program."[50] Now another highly placed Social Security administrator could say, mimicking Robert Ball's earlier statement, "I can assure you gentlemen, the general attitude [in the Social Security Administration] is to deny, deny, deny."[51] Intelligent programs cannot be administered under such conditions of radical political changes in programs. Beneficiaries with serious disabilities have had reason to expect that they could count on their benefit income in one year, only to learn a few years later that despite no change in their condition, benefits will be withdrawn. Worse, they learned a few more years later that many if not most terminations were illegal in the first place, so that if they reapply there is good chance that their benefits will be reinstated (*Minnesota v. Schweiker*, 1983; Social Security Regulations no. 83-15, 16, 17s, 1986). On such grounds as outlined before, it is clear that this policy system was in ragged disarray.

The definitional ambiguity of disability with which the DI has (and still does) operate has been used by parties of opposing political persuasions to expand and contract the program at will. Note that it is possible to increase substantially the clarity and reliability of medical disability determinations, as Mashaw (and Nagi before him) have clearly shown, by fairly simple attention to definitional clarity, plus well-known modern research findings on making clinical judgments. It is also clear that there is every reason to expect further political adventures into the Social Security system absent the correction of this policy problem. "If the same policy weaknesses that made possible the political intrusions into this social program are still in place when the next liberal administration comes into office, it will simply use the very same weaknesses to restore the system to its former condition."[52] Such a political scenario would continue into infinity, a prospect that is not in the best interests of the country or its citizens with disabilities.

This example teaches two key lessons: First, it highlights for us from Mashaw the conclusion that there is nothing inherently wrong with using expert judgments as a basis for eligibility rules. Second, it shows that some conditions are necessary to keep the process on track and functioning. Social researchers have learned of those requirements: define very carefully the thing to be judged, train and orient judges to apply only that definition within a specific procedural context, and indoctrinate new judges into that system, a few at a time. This process is not inexpensive, but almost any trained researcher can achieve a 90 percent agreement with almost any set of judges making even complicated judgments. Costs will surely be less than the direct administrative costs of disentitling and reentitling beneficiaries with disabilities time and time again.

Summary

This chapter presented concepts to assist the practitioner in understanding the variability among common eligibility rules and procedures. The following types of eligibility rules were discussed:

- Prior contribution
- Administrative rule
- Private contracts
- Professional discretion
- Administrative discretion
- Judicial decision
- Means testing
- Attachment to the workforce
- Eligibility inclusion and exclusion

Whereas the ultimate test of the merits of any particular eligibility rule is its fit with the social problem conception that underlies the program or policy under consideration, special problems are likely to be created by eligibility rules. The practical analyst should examine the available data and the general workings of the policy or program to search for evidence of the following special problems:

- Stigma and alienation
- Off-targeting of benefits
- Overwhelming costs

- Overutilization and underutilization
- Political interference
- Negative incentives and disincentives (work, procreation, marriage, and so on)

The presence of any of these special problems works against the achievement of a functional policy and programs—against adequacy, equity, and efficiency.

EXERCISES

1. What is the difference between the eligibility rule known as administrative discretion and the one known as administrative rule?

2. What are the consequences of basing eligibility for social welfare benefits solely on the type of entitlement called "attachment to the workforce"?

3. There are three branches of U.S. government: legislative, executive, and judicial. What role does each play in establishing the eligibility rules for TANF benefits? What may each branch do to affect eligibility rules once the TANF program is established? (Remember, no state is required to have a TANF program.)

4. What is the major difference between professional discretion and administrative discretion as methods of determining eligibility for social welfare benefits or services?

NOTES

1. The scheme concerns only "selective" eligibility rules. However, this book will not consider the traditional selective versus universal distinction in regard to (among other things) eligibility rules, siding with Titmuss in his belief that its utility for the practical policy analyst is only marginal. There are almost no universal programs in the United States.

2. R. Titmuss, "Welfare State and Welfare Society," in *Commitment to Welfare* (London: Allen and Unwin, 1968), pp. 130–134.

3. In three states minimal employee contributions are also required.

4. Only in the United States is the workers' compensation system operated as a private enterprise.

5. L. Gates et al., "Performance-Based Contracting (POSC): Turning Vocational Policy into Jobs," *Administration and Policy in Mental Health*, 31(3) (2004): 219–240.

6. N. M. Riccucci, *How Management Matters: Street Level Bureaucrats and Welfare Reform* (Washington, DC: Georgetown University Press, 2005); N. M. Riccucci, "Ethical Responsibility of Street Level Bureaucrats Under Welfare Reform," *Public Integrity*, 19(2) (2007); M. Lipsky, *Street Level Bureaucracy: Dilemmas of the Individual in Public Services* (New York: Russell Sage Foundation, 1980).

7. D. E. Chambers, "The Reagan Administration's Welfare Retrenchment Policy: Terminating Social Security Benefits for the Disabled," *Policy Studies Review*, 5 (2) (1985): 207–215.

8. M. E. Arthur, "Claims to Benefits as Property Interests," *University of Maryland Law Review* (Spring 2006): 783.

9. *Brown v. Board of Education*, 347 U.S. 483 (1954).

10. M. Cauncian and D. Meyer, "Fathers of Children Receiving Welfare; Can They Provide Child Support?" *Social Service Review*, 78(2) (2004): 179.

11. U.S. Congress, Committee on Ways and Means, Statement of Bill Stanton, Director, Dependent Children's Services Division, Administrative Office of the Courts, Phoenix, Arizona, and

President, National Association of Foster Care Reviewers, Washington, DC, January 28, 2004, http://waysandmeans.house.gov/hearings.asp?formmode=view&id=1132.

12. TANF beneficiaries live below the poverty line and seldom work at jobs paying more than minimum wage, whereas workers' compensation beneficiaries almost always earn average wages or above and do at least semiskilled work.

13. T. Broder, *Overview of Immigrant Eligibility for Federal Programs*, National Immigration Law Center, July 2007, www.nilc.org/immspbs/special/overview_immeligfedprograms_2007-07.pdf.

14. U.S. Department of Health and Human Services, Office of the Assistant Secretary for Planning and Evaluation, *Summary of Immigrant Eligibility Restrictions under Current Law*, October 4, 2004, http://aspe.hhs.gov/hsp/immigration/restrictions-sum.htm.

15. S. Jonas and C. Tactaquin, "Latino Immigrant Rights in the Shadow of the National Security State: Responses to Domestic Preemptive Strikes," *Social Justice*, 31(1–2) (2004): 13.

16. D. Blatt, "Interpreting HB 1804: A Guide to Understanding Oklahoma's New State Immigration Bill," *Issue Brief*, Public Policy, Community Action Project, August 20, 2007, www.okpolicy.org.

17. House Bill 1804—Pledge of Resistance, Catholic Archdiocese of Oklahoma City, October 26, 2007, www.catharchdioceseokc.org/alert.htm.

18. J. S. Passel, *The Size and Characteristics of the Unauthorized Migrant Population in the U.S.: Estimates Based on the March 2005 Current Population Survey* (Washington, DC: Pew Hispanic Center, 2006).

19. National Council of La Raza, *Paying the Price: The Impact of Immigration Raids on America's Children* (Washington, DC: Urban Institute, 2007), p. 1.

20. S. K. Schneider and W. G. Jacoby, "Reconsidering the Linkages Between Public Assistance and Public Opinion in the American Welfare State," *British Journal of Policy Science*, 37(3) (2007): 562–563.

21. G. Hoshino, "Simplifying the Means Test," *Social Work* (July 1965): 98–103.

22. "Canadian Child Tax Benefit Program," (CCTB) 2007-07-26. www.cra-arc.gc.ca/benefits/cctb/faq_qualifying-e.html" J. Bradshaw and N. Finch, *A Comparison, of Child Benefit Packages in 22 Countries*, Department for Work and Pensions Research Report No. 174 (Leeds: Corporate Document Services, 2002).

23. S. Danziger and K. Portnoy, *The Distributional Impacts of Public Policies* (New York: St. Martin's Press, 1988), p. 124.

24. L. Schmidt and P. Sevak, "AFDC, SSI and Welfare Reform: Caseload Reduction versus Caseload Shifting," *Journal of Human Resources*, 39(3) (2004): 792–812; J. Curs, "What Other Programs Can Teach Us," *American Journal of Public Health*, 93(1) (2003): 68–74

25. Data from personal interviews with local public and private child-placing staff and administrators while conducting research on the exportation of Central American children to Europe and the United States.

26. In 1795 the English town council of Speenhamland solved its poverty problem by providing bread to needy persons, which provoked public outcry that it would destroy all incentive to work.

27. *The Seattle-Denver Income Maintenance Experiment: Midexperimental Labor Supply Results and a Generalization to the National Population* (Stanford, CA: Stanford Research Institute and Mathematica Policy Research, 1978), p. viii.

28. Ibid., pp. 11–12.

29. Ibid., pp. 12–14.

30. M. T. Hannan, N. B. Tuma, and L. P. Groeneveld, "Income and Marital Evidence from the Income Maintenance Experiment," *American Journal of Sociology* (May 1977): 1200–1201.

31. Oklahoma Department of Human Services, Family Support Services Division—TANF Section, *TANF Work: The Future Is Yours. . . .* (brochure No. 93-10). (Oklahoma City, OK: Author, 2000).

32. S. Parrott and A. Sherman, *TANF at 10: Program Results Are More Mixed than Often Understood*, Center on Budget and Policy Priorities, August 17, 2006, pp. 1, 3–5, www.cbpp.org/8-17-06tanf.pdf.

33. Ibid., p. 11.

34. D. Besharov and P. Germains, "Welfare Reform: Four Years Later," *Public Interest* (Summer 2000): 17.

35. Parrott and Sherman, "TANF at 10," p. 10.

36. P. Wehren and G. Revell, "Lessons Learned from the Provisional Findings of Employment Services for the MR/DD Programs," *Journal of Disability Studies*, 16(3) (Fall 2005): 84.

37. N. Murdrick, "Use of AFDC by Previously High and Low Income Households," *Social Service Review*, 52(1) (1978): 110.

38. L. A. Gennetian and V. Knox, "The Effects of a Minnesota Welfare Program on Marital Stability, Six Years Later," *Population Research and Policy Review*, 23(5/6): 567.

39. J. N. Morgan et al., *Five Thousand American Families: Patterns of Economic Progress*, vol. 1. (Ann Arbor, MI: Institute for Social Research, 1974), pp. 1–9.

40. J. Duclos, B. Fortin, and M. Rouleau, *"Economic Analysis of Intergenerational Reliance on Social Assistance"* (unpublished manuscript, McMasters University, Hamilton, Ontario, Canada, May 2000).

41. S. Stenberg, "Inheritance of Welfare Recipiency," *Journal of Marriage and Family*, 62(1) (2000): 228–239.

42. M. R. Rank and L. Cheng, "Welfare Use Across Generations," *Journal of Marriage and Family*, 57(3) (1995): 682–683.

43. M. Derthick, *Policy Making for Social Security* (Washington, DC: Brookings Institution, 1979).

44. Chambers, "The Reagan Administration," p. 4.

45. U.S. Congress, Senate Subcommittee on Oversight of Government Management of the Senate Committee on Governmental Affairs, "SSDI Reviews: The Role of the Administrative Law Judge," Hearing Report, 98th Congress, 1st Session (June 8, 1983), Appendix, memo from Carl Fritz to Louis Hays, Chief of the Appeals Division of the Social Security Administration.

46. Derthick, *Policy Making*, p. 310.

47. D. Goldsborough et al., "The Social Security Administration: An Interdisciplinary Study of Disability Evaluation" (Washington, DC: George Washington University Law Center, 1963), mimeographed, pp. 98–100.

48. M. Lando, A. Farley, and M. Brown, "Recent Trends in the SSDI Program," *Social Security Bulletin*, 5(2) (August 1982): 50.

49. J. Mashaw, *Bureaucratic Justice* (New Haven, CT: Yale University Press, 1983).

50. Chambers, "The Reagan Administration," p. 7.

51. Mashaw, *Bureaucratic Justice*, p. 37.

52. Chambers, "The Reagan Administration," p. 15.

6 Analysis of Service-Delivery Systems and Social Policy and Program Design

He who would do good to another must do it in minute particulars. General good is the plea of the scoundrel, hypocrite, and flatterer.

—William Blake, 1784

Introduction

This chapter concerns designing and delivering social services. First, the heart of the matter, the social program or policy design, will be considered. Readers need to learn how to develop program designs out of program theory, so that will occupy an important place here. Types of service-delivery organizations will be examined so that readers can readily recognize them in the field. The chapter ends with a discussion of evaluation criteria for judging the merit of service-delivery programs and organizations.

Social Policy and Program Design

In the most fundamental sense, providing a solution to a social problem is the main reason-for-being that a social program or social policy can claim. And the only legitimate purpose of an administrative or service-delivery system is to provide the means by which that solution can be implemented. Let's call that solution the *policy or program* design (for the sake of simplicity, hereafter referred to as a *program design*). The program design consists of sets of carefully defined program activities that the staff or the implementing organization intends to deliver or undertake on behalf of its consumers/beneficiaries. These activities are the heart of the social program; however, the program has many other parts because programmed activities must have a context—it is like a theater production that must have an actual location, a stage or set and a cast, among other things. So it is for a social program: It must have a geographic location (a neighborhood street corner, a center, or office, but it could be a tavern as well); it must have a cast (practitioners and program participants), it must have costumers/makeup artists/lighting folks (program consultants), and it must have such creative and administrative staff as producers/directors (clinical supervisors, program directors, and the like). But the heart of the "drama" is the practitioner/consumer cast and the program design, a sort of script to which all the organizational actors play. We'll call that script the *program specification*. Figures 6.1, 6.2, and 6.3 show, respectively, an example of a common (program) theory concerning the physical abuse of a young child, a program design, and a program specification based on the theory.

The word *theory* is being used loosely to mean only a rough-and-ready sketch of a sequence of activities performed to make a difference and achieve the desired outcome(s). The logic of these connections (i.e., how and why certain activities are sequenced) is not given here, but if it were, it would set out basic premises about the events described and the reason they are connected to the desired outcomes. These rough-and-ready sketches are the fundamental ideas that highlight the cause-and-effect relations that are presumed to lead to the stated outcome that represents—wholly or in part—a social problem solution. An advantage for the policy analyst can be gained for programs that already have a *logic model* identifying the logical links between program design, assumptions, and desired outcomes.[1]

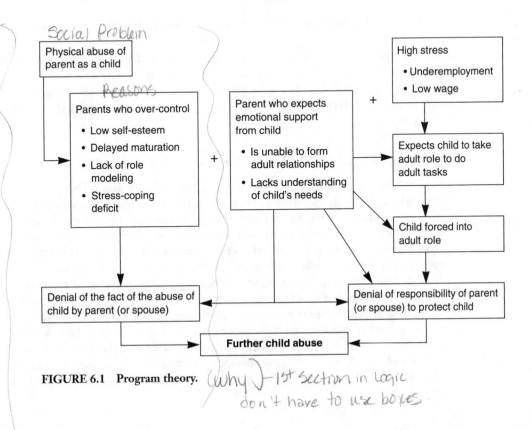

FIGURE 6.1 Program theory.

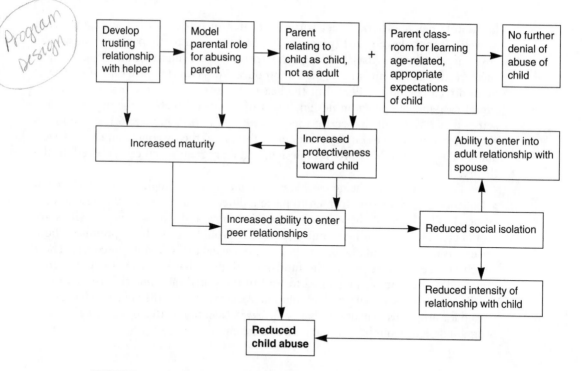

Program Design

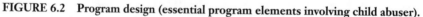

FIGURE 6.2   **Program design (essential program elements involving child abuser).**

The presence of a clear and credible program theory and program design is an important evaluation criterion, one by which the merit of a program of service delivery should be judged. Note that we will stress this aspect of service-delivery and administrative systems rather than the direct administration of such systems, a topic that is beyond the scope of this book.

Program Theory (The Logic Model)

Program theory is important for obvious and nonobvious reasons. First, it is the source from which the program activities are drawn; absent a program theory, program activities can amount to random choices or at best, assorted and uncoordinated "good ideas." If we care about the people who suffer from social problems, then it seems only right that we care enough to design a sensible and coordinated set of activities we have reason to believe will make a difference and then see to its implementation.

Second, for nonobvious reasons, program design is essential for managers in order to assess the quality of program implementation. Otherwise, how would a manager know what activities to observe? For example, it is not difficult to observe *whether* the program has credentialed staff, files reports, or pays bills. But the heart of quality assessment is whether program activities were in fact implemented in a way that makes it plausible that it will achieve its stated outcome(s). That assessment is of more than passing interest to program managers because it is essential to management

I. **Program theory**

(the selected variable)

Parent expects child to take on adult roles and tasks

↳ Parent expects emotional support from child and the child to be responsible for adult tasks and roles

II. **Program design**

(intended to decrease the effect of the preceding "selected variable")

(a) Teaching the parent age-appropriate expectations of children

    1. teaching *not* expecting adult roles/tasks from child

    2. teaching *not* expecting emotional support from child

(b) Practitioners model doing these age-appropriate expectations with the child (in the parent's presence)

(c) parent model doing these age-appropriate expectations with the child in practitioner's presence

III. **Program specification** (example)

(a) Content to be taught and learned by parent

    Age-appropriate behaviors: What to expect of a child:

        being held/crying/demand for affection

    1. self-feeding

    2. toilet training

    3. bedtimes and naps

    4. dressing

    5. caring for siblings and other children

    6. staying close to home

    7. getting ready for school

    8. helping with housework and meal preparation

    9. ability of child to "be a best friend"

(b) Educational processes must include:

    1. Video demonstration of age-appropriate expectations

    2. Discussion of content by peer parents in group

    3. Parents role-playing the expectations with peer tutor

    4. One-on-one opportunity for discussion of special problems with practitioner

FIGURE 6.3 **Program specification.**

decisions about personnel, organizational change, allocation of program resources, and the like.

Third, and perhaps even more important, outcome data showing success are useless unless one knows whether the program was implemented successfully. Put simply, just because the program activities occurred prior to the positive outcome is not sufficient reason to think that the program caused the outcome. It is possible that any number of other factors about clients and external conditions were responsible. Recall here the standard distinction between correlation and causation: Correlation is not sufficient reason to attribute causation. The scientific standard for attributing causation is control over factors that the experimenter hypothesizes will produce change, control in the sense of ability to consciously manipulate them, put them in place in conjunction with things to be changed. That, as well as other things, is what implementing a program design achieves.[2]

Fourth, a good program theory will contain statements that are essential to high-level planners whose role is to decide when and where else such a program might be successful. Good program theory speaks about the *conditions* required in order for it to achieve the desired outcomes. That is important because the kind of theory social programs use is generally very specific, perhaps even local—dealing as it does with the particulars of problems, people, and cultures. The specification of those conditions is an important function of program theory. Notice in Figure 6.1 that one of the factors is "high stress (underemployment/low wages)," which is an example of a factor so important that failure to attend to it in the program design may result in failure to reduce child abuse, the desired outcome. It is difficult to specify all such conditions because very often we simply don't know enough to do so. Our theories soften in the face of hard unyielding realities of the everyday life of program users and program personnel. For example, even the most clever and devoted case manager or social work practitioner working with people who are chronically mentally ill cannot do his or her main job—acquiring resources for clients—if (as is too often the case) basic housing, public income support, and essential medical care are simply unavailable to this population. This instance is, of course, just another example of how services are no substitute for food, shelter, and medicine. It is critical to understand those as basic conditions for successful outcomes for a case-management program. Good programs can be dismissed as bad theory when they don't show positive outcomes, when in fact the conditions for positive outcomes were never present. Good intervention ideas are too scarce to let that happen.

Chapter 1 referred to causal chains in a social problem analysis. We should take some pains to distinguish causal chains from program theory. Understanding the causes of social problems does not necessarily guarantee knowing enough to do anything about them—the factors that created the problems may be beyond reach of ordinary programmatic interventions. That is particularly true of the "soft" benefits of personal social services (though it also can be true of "hard" benefit programs). For example, no act of intervention will restore the loss one suffers from the death of a family member. Nor can anyone identify the exact factor that creates most chronic mental illnesses. Knowing so little about such imponderables means that the program objective may be simply remedial—taking the hardest edges off the consequences. In that case, that *is* what program theory should be about. Just on this account, theoretical causes of social problems may differ notably from the causal sequences in the social problem analysis. That difference will also be the case when social program or policy objectives are intended to deal only with a partial aspect of the social problem (e.g., the stresses and reactions of family members to an alcoholic parent or spouse).

Finally, the idea of multiple causation is important in understanding why causal sequences at the social problem level may be different from those at the program design/intervention level. Multiple causation holds that there may be more than a single cause (or a single causal sequence) for any given human problem. Thus, *it is quite possible to assist people with problems other than by working just to reverse the same factors that were causal in the first place.* It is a fortunate idea because—again—the historical roots of certain social and personal problems are beyond our interventions; we can no more restore dead family members to life than we can go back and undo personal tragedies, cataclysmic weather, or catastrophic economic events. Note that the route *into* poverty is not necessarily the way out. Note that the route back to a solid and sustaining marriage is not necessarily to redo the past, but rather to help a relationship reestablish itself on an entirely different basis—changes in role descriptions, occupations, preoccupations, and the ways of the loving heart. The good program designer and the wise and witty interventionist understand that human beings have wings as well as roots, as the saying goes.

Program Specification

Now let's turn to the details of *program specification*. When the practitioner or program designer turns to the problem of playing out the theory in the real world, he or she quickly discovers that program theory cannot be directly implemented because it is, by nature, entirely an abstraction. The problem is how to make the thing concrete, how to choose concrete instances of those theoretical ideas. Doing that is not so mysterious, an ordinary thing, something most of us do every day. What do we do when we keep locking ourselves out of the house because we left the keys inside? We develop a sort of minitheory about why it happens using some observations, facts, and some logic. For example, we recall that we always leave the key ring in the coat last worn (fact) and forget to take them out the next day (fact). The idea that springs to mind (program theory) is simply to put them away in a place where we'll see them the next time we want to leave the house. Or we remember that there's only one key for three roommates (fact) and the last one to leave has to put the key under the outside doormat; then (we theorize) if everybody had their own key, I could put mine on my own key ring, which I recall as a fact that I've never locked inside the house. Problem solved?

Oops, no, not quite. Notice that the idea "everybody has their own key" doesn't make keys appear like magic, rather they have *to be made*. And that is the idea of program specification—it instructs a person, very concretely, what has to be done to make good outcomes result. So, the program specification here looks like this: (1) take the key to the locksmith, (2) get the keys made, (3) pay for them, (4) test them out to see if these duplicates actually work, and (5) distribute them to the roommates. Unless each of those steps are completed, no solution to the problem is obtained! Could there be other program specifications? Sure—throw away all the keys to make sure nobody locks the door...ever! But that may involve some not-so-pleasant consequences— some program specifications (and theories) are better than others.

Here is an example of how a program specification is drawn from a real social program theory. First, in the program theory diagram in Figure 6.1, the reader will notice a variable called "Parent who expects emotional support from child" (center box). Notice that there is an arrow indicating a consequence of this, which is that a parent "Lacks understanding of child's needs." The program design in the lower part of the figure selects this last variable with the idea that reversing it will, ultimately, go some way to prevent further abuse of a child. The designer expects to reverse it by including a parenting classroom for "parents to learn age-appropriate expectations of a child," one of which is that children cannot be expected to be a major source of emotional support for their own parents. The idea is that this expectation can be reversed by "learning" some basic, straightforward things like this about child development. Ultimately, this program design anticipates that if parents view their children as just children, not adults, it will engage their "natural" drive to protect them, rather than look to them as adults capable of giving emotional support.

If the objective is parental learning, the program specification, the program activities here, must be about teaching abusing parents age-appropriate expectations: Thus, it might include, at least, (1) content about age-appropriate expectations and (2) specific educational processes dedicated to mastering that content (e.g., group and individual classroom exercises, readings, group discussions providing opportunity for parents to learn the content). Notice that this will require yet another theory—this time explaining how parents learn new things. The specification must be sufficiently detailed so that a practitioner will know what to do and an observer can tell by looking whether that is what is happening in program activities.

Program design and program specification are essential to managers for monitoring the quality of program operations. Program design answers the question of *what to observe* (monitor) in order to know whether "things are going right." A clear program design and specification show what program activities are important for a manager to keep track of. The heart of what she or he is observing lies in whether those activities were implemented according to specification. In the foregoing example, the issue would be whether the specified content about age-appropriate expectations was *actually* presented to program participants. And were class exercises and discussions *actually* taking place, whatever else was also happening? The reason the manager needs to be concerned is that if it is not happening, there is no reason to expect positive outcomes. That's bad for program participants and, ultimately, bad for the service-delivery organization. Some bright reader may think: "What if positive outcomes happen even if a program design isn't actually implemented to specification?" Good question. Here are some answers. "Spontaneous remissions"? Not likely. Either something was happening in the lives of these parents that no one is taking account of *or* practitioners were doing something right that needs to be identified and learned from, and it might be replicated in whole or in part for the benefit of others. Good programs take care to do that.

Some practitioners might be offended by the idea of program specification, believing it would take the natural flow, the intuitive interchange, out of the helping process. But that's not the idea here. Program specification is not an exact script for practitioners, only a minimum description of practice activities that sets out helping processes that *have* to be done. Along the way, practitioners and program participants discover a way to relate to each other so that people can actually benefit from the program. Nothing is automatic. It isn't that program specifications prescribe boundaries for the helping adventure as much as they identify places that have to be visited. The paths followed in wandering through the geography of a helping encounter is a matter of the art of conducting a helping relationship. The stage-play metaphor may still be helpful: Although no actor invents her own script, she is the *central figure* who delivers the message to the audience. Because she is free to interpret within her performance, she gives the script its meaning—and it is to the interaction between actor and the audience that any drama, helping or otherwise, owes its life and its vitality.

Some Different Types of Administration and Delivery of Social Service Programs, Benefits, and Services

Neither love, money, nor good intention alone is sufficient to get benefits and services to masses of people who need them. Some kind of organizational system is necessary to deliver the benefits or services that bridge the gap between problem and solution. In its original sense, to describe something as bureaucratic was to call it thoughtful in pursuing logical, effective, and efficient means to specific ends, of people working together in a set of defined roles when clear divisions of labor and authority enhanced the effectiveness and dispatch with which responsibilities were accomplished. That is still an ideal for organizations, certainly those we are concerned with here. Let us now consider some different types of organizations and their particular problems.

Centralized Service-Delivery Systems

Authority is always important in centralized organizations, and it is *always* clear where authority resides. The organization is pyramidal, with the highest authority at the peak, usually residing in a single chief executive officer (CEO). That office will include *support staff* who have specialized duties: for example an information systems staff responsible for routine data gathering and care of its computer systems, a legal staff, someone responsible for buildings, and, of course, accounting. The *line staff* are administrative officers (e.g., program directors and supervisors) who carry out the CEO's directives having been delegated his or her authority over all other personnel and actions in the lower-level departments and offices of the organization. Hence, it is easy to show the lines of authority in an organizational chart, which reveals who is responsible to whom, who carries what responsibilities, and how one office or department is distinguished from another.

In contrast, some organizations are decentralized, where different departments and offices are under *only* the authority of the CEO and report directly to her or him—*no* supervisors or department heads. In a large organization, that can mean that each department has greater freedom to develop its own ways of operating, ways that may be different from other departments; of course, in a small organization, such decentralization might only mean that a CEO has more chance for close supervision of operations. In a large organization, the number of layers of authority between any department and the CEO can be (but isn't always) a measure of how much freedom each unit has in designing its own operations. The number of authority layers is equivalent to the number of administrators, including the CEO, who must authorize an action the administrator or staff member wants to take.

But note, at some point, an organization becomes so large that an informal local organizational autonomy sets in. There is some size at which no CEO (or even lower-level administrators) can personally monitor organizational operations; hence, given a sufficiently large size, lower-level departments are shielded from close oversight and thereby gain a measure of informal autonomy. Like little colonial outposts of the

1800s, far removed from the capital of the empire, they begin to set their own style and rules—often (but not always) for the better. And it is not only size but geographic separation that can produce this result; statewide social service programs, for example, as in geographically large U.S. states with large rural areas scattered widely throughout a number of county or city local offices, gradually work out their own styles. On this account, organizational charts should be viewed with some suspicion because they show the planned state of affairs, seldom up-to-date in any case and ordinarily not reflecting how things actually work.

Local administrators and staff can and do exploit this freedom to the advantage of program consumers. Personal social service practitioners and programs should exploit it because they perform individualized services for consumers. It's not a subversive suggestion, rather a perfectly straightforward matter. Some services are simple enough for a state office to design and plan in the abstract. But, if services are for abused or neglected children or the homeless, a "one-size-fits-all" set of administrative procedures is unlikely to meet program participants' needs. Readers should notice that the perspective here favors decentralized administration for personal social service programs and centralized administration for programs delivering hard benefits like school meal programs, housing subsidies, and food stamps.

Centralization has other common problems. One is the time it takes for a centralized organization to make decisions. Unless authority is clearly delegated and the conditions for making decisions at levels lower than that of the top executive are clear to everyone, decisions, even simple, obvious ones, will often be time-consuming when passed on to a higher executive level.

Most important, because a centralized organization has many executive or supervisory layers, there is, necessarily, a large distance between clients/program consumers and administrative decision makers. That is a problem because those who plan the organizational future and make large-scale decisions about services can be far removed from the way the organization deals with program participants and consumers. In this sense, it is fair to say that although centralization increases formal accountability within organizations ("easily identifies who is at fault"), it also decreases accountability to those it serves. Rapp points out that this kind of organizational structure "reinforces the tendency to maximum nonresponsiveness to clients and their welfare." And he makes clear that the focus in centralized organizations is on control over operations, most usually on the basis of what the organization needs (reporting and data gathering, adherence to policy rules, and so on), rather than what its consumers or program participants need.[3]

Client-Centered Management and "Inverted Hierarchy" Service-Delivery Systems

Social service–delivery organizations, especially public social services, can be notoriously unsatisfying places in which to work. Staff who work directly with clients are often overburdened beyond belief, pay is low, and organizational support is often absent in the extreme. And, in an important way, centralization is one of the reasons for those problems. But it is only the most obvious reason. *The main problem in centralized organizations is that the organization is centered on its own structure and survival and has little time or energy to be client-/consumer-centered, much less to care for its practitioner staff.*

Rapp and Poertner have designed an alternative to the traditional, centralized service-delivery agency and called it "inverted hierarchy."[4] They believe it will deliver better social services precisely because the driving metaphor is client-/consumer-centered. Rapp and Poertner, like all good paradigm breakers, stand the idea of centralized structure/authority on its head: at the top of the organizational hierarchy in place of CEOs and administrators are clients/consumers and direct service workers—all other personnel in the organization are (chartwise) below and in service of them. The task of management is not to control but to assist those who are most directly in contact with people in need. Rather than focus on control and monitoring direct service workers, managers' main function in this type of organization is to provide organizational help in four ways:

1. Making clear what is to be done and expectations for those doing it: literal modeling by managers of the idea of client-/consumer-centeredness, helping workers reframe client/consumer situations, clarifying service plans, and so on
2. Providing the tools to do the job (resources, adequate time, and equipment)
3. Removing obstacles and constraints: large caseloads, less paperwork, meetings, office noise, and so on
4. Creating "a reward-based environment" in which successes of direct service workers are made noticeable and responded to positively by those around them so that the organization becomes a place for work that is satisfying, full of pride, and pleasurable[5]

This client-/consumer-centered management goes well beyond its historical roots in this field; the principle is "managers venerating people called clients." It refers to specific managerial behaviors:

1. Managers must have frequent, friendly, and respectful contact with clients/ consumers.
2. Managers must assume client/consumer advocacy as their task.[6]

When Rapp and Poertner speak of managers' responsibility to "create" organizational focus, they mean a focus on clients/consumers and client/consumer outcomes plus "an obsession with achieving (them)."[7]

Federated Service-Delivery Organizations

Federations are two or more organizations that agree to cooperate and coordinate their services and/or financing in certain specified ways. For example, several nonprofit day care programs may agree to have one of them take responsibility for advertising services and receiving and processing applications. In return, other programs may take responsibility for food service and another for building maintenance, and yet another for on-site nursing services, and so on. Recreational programs such as the YWCA, YMCA, and Boys Club may agree to focus services only on specific neighborhoods so that they cover a whole community without duplication. The hoped-for effect of federation is to serve the total need (or at least a greater proportion) and serve it in a way that avoids duplication of effort while making efficient use of available resources. Note that in federations, no program necessarily gives up any authority over its internal program operations *except* about what agreements specify. And, of course, federation is voluntary, so no program makes a commitment it cannot revoke after the terms of the agreement have been completed. Most federation agreements specify time periods. Tucker has described five types of interagency federative and cooperative efforts:[8]

- Loaning staff to another organization
- Locating staff at same office site
- Delivering the same service jointly to agencies
- Combining delivery of one service with another
- Consulting with other agencies in a formal way

Federation has some well-known difficulties. One such is that it is difficult and often time-consuming to resolve conflict over the terms of a federation agreement. Few agreements can be written so clearly that all contingencies are spelled out and, of course, the unanticipated always occurs. Federations exist because of the desire for voluntary cooperation and should the thread of this cooperation be broken by conflict, a stalemate can occur and the enterprise is threatened. Voluntary cooperation involves a good deal of negotiation. There is nothing wrong with that, but sometimes there is no time for it and sometimes negotiation isn't successful. One of the strengths of centralized authority is that it only takes a single person who is in charge to make a (potentially quick) decision.

Case-Management Service-Delivery Systems

One strategy for solving integration and coordination problems in the complex system for service and benefit delivery is case management. *Case management* relies on settling the responsibility for organizing and delivering services and benefit packages on a single person—the case manager. This practitioner must assess client/consumer need, plan for the provision of services and benefits to meet those needs, and identify and acquire commitments from other organizations and service providers to deliver those services and benefits for a whole range of client/consumer needs (housing, medical care, employment, legal services, child day care, nutrition, personal counseling, and so on). Case management can go beyond just assembling "packages"; it can range from constant monitoring for quality to responsibility for seeing that clients/consumers get to the right places at the right times. It can also extend to actively advocating for clients'/consumers' rights on behalf of benefits and services that may be unjustly withheld. Case management is also a product of extensive frustration in the field with the high degree of specialization in the functions performed by different agencies. So specialized have these functions become that differences between services and eligibility rules virtually mystify the uninitiated. One of the case manager's tasks is to clarify for clients/consumers the service and benefit choices available and what is necessary to gain access to them.

Although there are many versions of how case management should be pursued, three styles illustrate the broad variability in case-management models.[9] The most simple approach proposes that the case manager act as a broker of services, one who has little direct contact with clients/consumers but simply identifies needs based on clients'/consumers' direct requests, locates organizations that offer relevant services and benefits, and refers clients/consumers to them. Responsibility for making direct contact rests with the clients'/consumers' own initiative. A second version of case management views the case manager as a therapist devoted to healing but one who actively pursues, monitors, and evaluates the provision of treatment, services, and benefits other than what the case manager can provide directly. That pursuit, monitoring, and evaluation occur in tandem with the therapist's/case manager's treatment/services. A third version, taking exception to the presumption of client/consumer deficit or pathology implied in the second version, seeks to organize and orchestrate resources focused on an assessment of client/consumer and client/consumer social network strengths and assets. This is done in an effort to support and augment these strengths in service of the clients'/consumers' greater functioning in an ordinary community.[10] Thus, the case manager's assessment of need is focused on strengths assessment rather than on diagnostic implications for treatment. Resource acquisition is done with a dual focus on person–environment interactions and with a strong commitment to client/consumer participation in decision making, resource acquisition, and quality monitoring. Deitchman describes these contrasts in the following way:[11]

> The client[/consumer] in the community needs a traveling companion, not a travel agent. The travel agent's only function is to make a client's reservation. The client [/ consumer] has to get ready, get to the airport and traverse foreign ground by himself. The traveling companion, on the other hand, celebrates the fact that his friend was able to get seats, talks about his fear of flying and then goes on the trip with him.

As Rapp and Chamberlain note, "The travel companion is an enabler engaged in a human relationship with the client but is not a therapist focused on the internal dynamics and psychiatric symptoms."[12] Indeed, there is some important research support from six studies over ten years for the success of the strengths-based case-management model. In two small experimental studies, one has shown statistically significant reductions in hospitalizations for the strengths-model case-management group, though one study did not.[13] A larger but post-hoc correlational study "suggests that clients in the strengths-model case management group had fewer hospitalizations or emergency room visits."[14] In other studies (both experimental and nonexperimental), other outcomes associated with strengths-based case management were community living skills and appropriate community behaviors,[15] greater overall physical and mental health,[16] greater tolerance of stress,[17] and reduced family burden,[18] among others.

As a design for service delivery and administration, the "strengths-based case management" model, Rapp says, requires certain organizational ("structural") features to be in place as *necessary conditions for implementation*.[19] Here are some examples; note their importance and particularity:

1. Team structure for service delivery: case planning, mutual support, passing on knowledge of resources, and so on.
2. BA-level workers can be case managers but "require access to specialists, particularly nurses . . . and experienced mental health professionals as team leaders."
3. Workloads for case managers shouldn't exceed twenty, nor average more than twelve to fifteen.
4. Case-management service should be of indeterminate length while expecting intensity to vary, of course.
5. Twenty-four-hour, seven-day-a-week access to crisis and emergency services, preferably involving the case manager.
6. "Case managers should have ultimate responsibility for client services, excepting medication, and retain authority even in referral situations."

Staffing with Indigenous Workers as a Service-Delivery Strategy

Indigenous Workers.   An *indigenous worker* is a nonprofessional who has had personal experience with the social problem of the clients being served.[20] As used here, the term *indigenous* refers to its common dictionary definition: originating in, growing, or living naturally in a particular region or environment. Thus, with respect to poverty, an indigenous worker is one who "lives naturally" in an environment of poverty. With respect to criminal deviance, an indigenous worker is a person who has been convicted of a crime and spent some time in prison. The classic example of the indigenous worker is the reforming alcoholic who is an active member of Alcoholics Anonymous (AA). The theory behind the indigenous worker strategy assumes that some social problems generate a particular culture or lifestyle or, according to Oscar Lewis, a "design for living" that has the social problem as a central reality to which life adjustments and responses must be made.[21] Those who have lived with a particular social problem have in fact become intimately acquainted not only with its reality but also with the cultural response to it. Such people know its customs, its language, and its common patterns. That knowledge, born out of experience, enables that person to establish communication more quickly and effectively with those who continue to live with a given social problem. Alcoholics readily speak of the unique subculture of the alcoholic experience—how it yields a common pattern of life and a common language for those life experiences and how difficult it is for an alcoholic to believe that anyone who has not experienced alcoholism can understand it.

There are other social problems that develop a strong subculture. The most obvious example is that of substance addiction, the habitual use of chemical substances. Addicts tend to form a discrete social group in their communities (though, as is the case with alcoholics and all other subcultures, loners exist among them); the life of individuals and the cultural group center on the central fact of demand, supply, and use of the chemical. Language, manners, and customs grow up around its use and are shared among group members. Knowledge of those cultural features of the addict's community gives the indigenous helper the critical edge in establishing communication and credibility more rapidly and more effectively. People with serious mental illness can become *prosumers*, integrating roles as consumers and professionals in fostering the community support of peers.[22] Perhaps less common—but certainly not less serious—is the use of indigenous workers to defuse encounters with staff of service-delivery systems that clients/consumers experience as humiliating, abusive, or traumatic. Keep in mind that social class, racial differences, prejudices, and biases can be the sources of experiences that are so humiliating and abusive that clients/consumers will do terrible things to themselves to avoid repetition of the experience: They will go hungry, refuse to seek medical care, or refrain from seeking redress when innocent and convicted of crimes that carry serious penalties.

Also understand that in some geographic areas where racial minorities comprise a very large proportion of the population, the actual encounter between such minorities and outsiders may be infrequent; after all, the literal meaning of ghetto is "an isolated section." Children of ghetto minorities may have their first encounter with people different from themselves only on visiting or being visited by a staff member of a social service agency. The encounter may be particularly revealing; having a black or Latino child feel the visitor's skin to see whether the white rubs off is not a scene that whites are particularly prepared to understand, much less handle well. The extensive use of indigenous workers can facilitate services and reduce serious misunderstandings, trauma, and abuse that can result from tense encounters between ethnic groups and naive whites. Use of the indigenous worker seeks to increase the probability that the staff member whom the client/consumer first encounters will be able to respond in ways that are culturally and socially sensitive and empathetic with the client's problem. Whereas the primary intent of using indigenous workers is to produce better service for consumers, there is good reason to believe that there also can be specific benefits for the indigenous worker as well. For example, the helper-therapy principle asserts that those vulnerable to a problem who set out to help others with the same problem are very likely to benefit simply by being involved in the helping process.

There is no clear understanding about why this is so; the principle is simply an empirical observation of outcomes. The helper-therapy principle may be just another version of the common wisdom that in helping another to learn, one learns as much in the process. The indigenous worker approach as a service-delivery strategy does have some basic problems and some limitations despite its appeal. Clearly, the indigenous worker idea is effective only with social problems that generate a subculture that is sufficiently unique so that it cannot be easily learned, understood, and incorporated by the ordinary nonindigenous helper. Also, it turns out that the career of a particular individual who performs in an indigenous worker role is fairly short. The tendency of the indigenous worker is gradually to take on the attitudes and values of the professional staff of the non-indigenous organization. That process goes by other names—socialization and cooptation, for example. It is certainly natural enough that a person should assimilate to the norms and outlook of those positioned to befriend, reward, and punish. It is not necessary to refer to a conscious motive on the part of organizations that employ indigenous workers to accomplish this; it is sufficient to cite socialization as a natural process in human groups.[23] Close observers of indigenous workers in Head Start and Community Action Programs (CAPs) report that it takes about eighteen months for the indigenous worker to be acculturated to the organization that pays the worker's wages. In other words, eighteen months may be about as long as one can expect an indigenous worker to retain a view of the social problem of concern that is sufficiently allied with client views so that it gives the indigenous worker a unique value perspective.

Referral Agencies in Delivering Social Service

Any system of agencies and organizations involved in delivering social welfare services and benefits can be a puzzle for clients/consumers and helpers attempting to solve problems. In any given metropolitan area, hundreds of agencies, programs, and organizations offer multiple services and benefits under widely varying conditions for diverse target populations. This is one reason why benefits and services are inaccessible to people who need them. Sometimes the organizations are so numerous and the nature of their services and entitlement rules so ill defined and difficult in terms of distinguishing one from the other that it requires direct experience to judge exactly where a certain client with a certain problem should be referred for services or benefits. Where this has been identified as a problem, one solution has been to create a special agency whose sole purpose is to ensure that clients/consumers get to the appropriate agency. Such a solution is the embodiment of an attempt to solve a problem of accessibility—a problem created by agency overlap, duplication of services, and the general disarray of the social welfare service-delivery system in the United States.

Referral agencies often assume a client/consumer advocacy role as well, viewing their responsibility as extending further than the simple supply of information to clients/consumers about the "best" source of help for their problem. Most referral agencies are also committed to advocating their clients'/consumers' needs to the agencies to which the clients are referred. The purpose of this advocacy is to ensure that once the application is made, the clients/consumers get the services and/or benefits to which they are entitled by right, policy, or law. In this sense, then, the referral agency acts as both a "front door" for all the community's agencies and as a "door widener" for clients/consumers to get what they need and what they are entitled to. Advocacy practices vary widely—following up with a phone call on each client to ensure that the client–agency contact was made, helping a client/consumer file an application for a "fair hearing," referring a client/consumer to legal counsel to get a special judgment as to whether the agency's actions or policy interpretations were correct. Some referral agencies broaden their functions to include what are commonly called "doorstep" functions; that is, the agency's reason for being is to serve all persons who "appear on their doorstep." They are free to serve as just a referral agency and, commonly, that is the most frequent service, but where services are not available or cannot be made available by some combination of expert choice of referral and client/consumer advocacy, the agencies' commitment is to serve the clients'/consumers' needs. It is in fact a radical professional commitment to undertake to serve all clients'/consumers' needs. One of the stated functions of doorstep agencies is that of constant monitoring and assessment of the adequacy and range of social services in the community, and of planning for additions or extensions when indicated by experience. Developed in Great Britain, and now worldwide, a whole program has been devoted to the creation of referral agencies and is directed toward the development of "Citizens Advice Bureaus" whose purpose is to provide referral services and, where necessary, client/consumer advocacy.[24]

Program Consumer/Beneficiary, Client-Controlled Organizations as a Service-Delivery Strategy

Organizations delivering social services or benefits organized and operated by the very people whom they serve has developed with some strength over the years. It has strong historical roots among groups driven by the "self-help" idea, for example, in the neighbor housing programs initiated in England in the mid-1800s when the idea seems to have first arisen of helping poor people in neighborhood groups arrange for funds to buy their own derelict houses and rehabilitating them with what we now call "sweat equity." Habitat for Humanity is a contemporary example. But such "mutual aid" societies for all kinds of purposes, both economic and sociocultural, have been developed by tribal societies (and later discovered by anthropologists) all over the world. In the contemporary world, they are often different than that; they are rather advocacy or activist political organizations among the poor or oppressed. Because they have no money or goods to share mutually with each other, their organizational focus is on ensuring that people actually receive what legislation or public policy has already established is due them as help in solving their difficulties. Examples are many: the National Welfare Rights group, Family Focus, and so on.

Racial, Ethnic, and Religious Agencies as a Service-Delivery Strategy

Instead of simply ensuring that there are staff members who either have a special cultural understanding or who speak a special language, a whole organization can be developed that is exclusively devoted to the special social welfare needs of specific groups. Various kinds of such service-delivery organizations currently exist: Some state income maintenance programs have established special units to serve Asian populations; at one point in the early 1970s, the Black Muslims were frequent sponsors of child care and emergency relief agencies for black inner-city populations; many metropolitan inner cities have had medical facilities that traditionally served only blacks. Probably the most common example of ethnic- and race-oriented service-delivery organizations are the black adoption agencies that responded to local black communities whose children were embedded in the public foster care systems. As Fanshel and Shinn, and others since have shown, the likelihood of these children leaving "temporary" foster care before they are self-supporting is distressingly small.[25]

At one time, it was believed that the black community did not have the foster parents or adoptive parents needed to serve these children. Those who pioneered black adoption agencies believed that the reason black people were not forthcoming to serve these children was the barrier to application posed by confrontation with an all-white staff and the formal nature of foster care or adoption application forms, as well as interviews required in a formal office setting instead of in the home or even in a familiar neighborhood. Also problematic were the extensive discussion of past psychological history and the high fees required. Adoption agencies to serve black consumers were created to construct a program that would give black applicants more reason to believe that their applications and life circumstances would be received with sympathy. Furthermore, it would avoid a confrontation with all-white personnel on unfamiliar grounds in unfamiliar neighborhoods. In fact, some of these agencies have been dramatically successful in increasing both the number of foster and adoption applications from black families and individuals and the number of permanent placements of black children. They demonstrate clearly that prior statements about the barriers presented by an all-white staff and the application process of the traditional child-placing agency were probably correct. It is worth noting that even though this service-delivery innovation seems to be an undeniable success, it still lacks widespread support and is still controversial. Nevertheless, in some places where black adoption programs have been operating for a few years, healthy black infants are being placed in adoption where they weren't before.[26] As important as these special ethnic agencies are in the solution of some severe social problems, this service-delivery strategy was not alone a sufficient answer. Availability of "adoption subsidies" was a crucial factor in the recruitment of black homes for black children."[27]

Black adoption agencies are a special contemporary example of the private voluntary program, which has been so prominent a part of the U.S. social welfare scene for so many years. It is easy to forget that before the 1930s, the major burden of the social welfare effort was carried by private voluntary agencies. Many of those voluntary agencies were ethnically and religiously oriented, oriented to alienated and often stigmatized subcultures that were similar in social status to today's U.S. black or immigrant Hispanic, Asian, and Caribbean population. Out of that social position grew ethnically and religiously oriented social welfare agencies intended to serve the needs of their cultural parent group. The black adoption agencies are an independent but parallel development, an interesting commentary on the hardiness of the ethnic self-help, mutual-aid phenomenon.

For the African American community, self-help institutions have been an urgent response to the oppression of a segregated postslavery society and the natural accompaniment to what was then called "race-work" (i.e., the social betterment of the black community). Among the themes were a fervent belief in self-reliance and the duty to help others in difficulties. Churches were a natural setting for this early effort. Inglehart and Becerra quote W. E. B. Du Bois, who stated that "charitable and rescue work among Negroes should first be found in the churches" and conclude that the African American churches were the primary caregiving institution for its community.[28] In later years the church would be joined by other social groups such as fraternities, lodges, and clubs, which established orphanages, homes for elderly people, and services to those who are homebound, among other things.

Under different and oppressive historical circumstances, Native American tribal peoples were subjected to a long series of paternalistic programs developed by the federal government and most often intended to weaken or undermine Native tribal culture. They were layed upon tribal peoples with little regard for Native culture and traditions—or their wishes for that matter. The Indian Child Welfare Act of 1978 finally moved public policy in a different direction when it placed the control of decisions about Native children in public care in the hands of the tribes with whom they had legal status. The tribal organizations the act created and financed are an important example of ethnic service delivery. Tribes had to move quickly and often from virtually no previous tribal welfare organization to develop a full-scale ability to make decisions about and provide care for their children. Tribes have had federal Title IV-E funds to develop this capacity and observers report that it has provided tribes with the means to increase benefits and services for their children. Many state officials believe that tribal children are spending less time in foster care and that the tribes are often taking care of their own children in their own communities under these ethnic agencies. Opinions among both tribal and state officials are divided on proposals to provide federal funding directly to tribal organizations.[29]

Ethnic self-help service-delivery organizations have emerged among many U.S. immigrant groups. Common among them are mutual-aid societies of various kinds that emerged in response to the common problems of new immigrants: illiteracy, unemployment, and isolation, with a lack of a safety net when disaster strikes. Many of these societies still exist—such as insurance or burial societies, patriotic societies, and lodges or clubs—providing a variety of welfare functions under their umbrella.[30] They are commonly known, among Irish and Italian immigrants, but less well known are the "mutualistas" of the Mexican immigrant community and the Chinese Consolidated Benevolent Societies that united the earlier clan and tong associations.[31]

In considering ethnic agencies, we have spoken of more or less formal organizations. However, it is important to be aware that nearly every emigrant group in the United States brought with it a natural "helping system" not comprised of formal organizations. These system must be used, supported, and nurtured whenever possible by existing public and private welfare organizations. Inglehart and Becerra describe natural helping systems among Mexican Americans, as well as among Chinese and Japanese immigrants. Delgado provides readers with interesting descriptions of contemporary natural helping systems in Puerto Rican communities which center around Puerto Rican food and botanical establishments.[32]

Religious agencies have a long history of providing benefits and services to poor and oppressed people, which any introductory social welfare text will acknowledge. Many of the larger sectarian social welfare organizations such as Catholic Social Services, Salvation Army, Jewish Family and Children's Services, and various Protestant welfare agencies deliver services at the local level through the support of public grants and purchase-of-service contracting (POSC) arrangements. Some religious congregations have become more active partners with the public sector in local service design and delivery.[33] Present efforts for expanding the role of religion in social programming received support during the Reagan administration and a major boost in passage of the Personal Responsibility and Work Opportunity Reconciliation

Act of 1996 (PRWORA) during the Clinton administration. In the PRWORA, Congress included a "Charitable Choice" provision to dissuade states from excluding faith-based organizations (FBOs) as contractors for their public welfare programs. The intent of Charitable Choice was to ensure a "level playing field" for religious organizations that it was claimed were being denied contracts unless they were willing to remove all traces of faith from their service programs. Since passage of PRWORA, so-called faith-based initiatives at the federal and state levels have emerged to provide technical assistance for potential religious service providers (such as grant writing information and skills) and to promote the use of public funds to support their role in providing community services.

Leading the way, in 2001 the White House Office of Faith-Based and Community Initiatives (OFBCI) was established by President George W. Bush through an executive order. A Compassion Capital Fund (CCF) was created as a key component of the president's faith-based and community initiative. The stated objectives of CCF are to

- Help faith-based and community organizations increase their effectiveness and enhance their ability to provide social services by building their organizational capacity.
- Work through intermediary organizations that serve as a bridge between the federal government and faith-based and community organizations. Intermediary organizations provide technical assistance and capacity-building subawards.
- Build the capacity of faith-based and community organizations working to combat gang activity and youth violence through the Communities Empowering Youth program.
- Award one-time capacity-building grants of $50,000 directly to faith-based and community organizations.[34]

By 2007, CCF had provided approximately $264 million to more than 4,500 organizations.[35]

Faith-based initiatives have been hotly debated, and positions taken on the faith-based movement have been passionate. At one extreme is the position that public social welfare services in a wide range of program areas should be turned over to faith-based providers. Those who hold to this position argue that the faith component attached to services has in the past made them more effective than today's services rendered by secular public employees.[36] Although there are proponents for this extreme view, most adherents of a faith-based initiative back away from the expectation that the religious sector could realistically replace all or most public social services. At the other end of the spectrum are some that are fearful that any further blurring of church and state is likely to erode support for a public commitment to social welfare.[37] A cautious middle ground is taken by those who believe there may be some good reasons why not all states have legislated rules and regulations deemed friendly to a wholesale expansion for partnership between public social welfare agencies and faith-based organizations. At issue are questions about separation of church and state, as well as administrative concerns about the capability of local congregations and other smaller faith-based providers to deliver social and human services by qualified personnel. The National Association of Social Workers (NASW) is a representative of this middle-ground approach.

In January 2002, NASW issued a position statement on "priorities for faith-based human services initiatives." The statement acknowledges that social service has its roots in charitable-voluntary agencies, and social workers are often involved in providing services in such venues. Also stated is the philosophy of NASW that maintaining a complementary relationship between public and private resources is desirable and necessary. The NASW position statement puts forth five fundamental principles of social service delivery that must be maintained in the public–private relationship. The principles address (1) accessibility to services, (2) accountability, (3) appropriate staffing, (4) separation of church and state, and (5) maintaining government responsibility. Particular to faith-based initiatives, the NASW priorities elaborate the position that any new publicly funded faith-based organization must provide services in an inclusive and nondiscriminatory manner, and existing nonprofit social service agencies must not be disadvantaged with respect to funding because they are not faith-based organizations. Also, safeguards must be implemented to ensure that services are appropriately coordinated, provided by qualified individuals, without requirements for religious observance, and without discriminatory practices in agency employment and in access to services.[38]

We agree with NASW and others who support the constitutional issue of separation of church and state when faith-based initiatives are implemented. It has the support of an authoritative view of the constitutional issues involved. As Kennedy and Bielefeld say: "The constitutional question is frequently not whether the government can provide services via third party surrogates (e.g., faith-based organizations) but HOW."[39] There tends to be an irresistible temptation in many cases to use human service programs as an opportunity to evangelize. The logistical issue of not requiring clients/consumers to attend religious services as an eligibility condition is not hard. The big problem is that some social treatments or interventions, particularly those concerning addictions, are based in part on the adoption of a new perspective and that often is religious. Consider, for example, the twelve-step programs in which "getting right with God" is one of the steps. It is a problem of significant proportion and we argue that the issue of separation of church and state should be preserved from challenges that propose to mix evangelism in any form in social programs.

Many of the religious programs being recruited by faith-based initiatives are run by churches that are very authoritarian. Where faith-based social programs are operated under the auspices of churches whose leadership is characteristically authoritarian—Roman Catholic certainly, but fundamentalist and charismatic Protestant just as well—a single member of the clergy (or very small elite group) is given great moral, administrative, and financial power. Where that is so, such congregations have little or no tradition or experience in calling church authority to account. The possibility for misuse of funds or abuse of operating policy requirements for use of tax funds is very great—human propensities for power, greed, and institutional self-serving being what history reveals them to be. To avoid that, accountability internal to the organization is essential. External monitoring and oversight have strict limits.[40]

In addition to ideological, professional, and practical issues concerning faith-based initiatives there has been the more sinister specter of political skullduggery. Initially, the CCF was an appropriation of $30 million with the goal of awarding grants to nonprofit entities (intermediary organizations) that would engage in technical assistance training for smaller community-based and faith-based organizations. However, according to insiders and watchdog observers, the Bush administration changed the purposes of the fund to include both technical assistance and funding for faith-based organization start-up and operational costs. David Kuo, former deputy director for the OFBCI, revealed a host of political influences and manipulations. One such example is the revelation that non-Christian grant applicants were sometimes excluded from faith-based funding even though White House officials insisted the money would be available to all.[41] Not only that, Bush administration and party officials were engaged in joint political outreach activity targeting African American ministers with promises of grants through the CCF. Furthermore, it was observed that White House OFBCI officials traveled to several areas of the country to engage in outreach for the CCF, but nearly all of the appearances occurred at party-sponsored events or at events with Republican candidates in close election races during the 2002 elections.[42] The pattern was repeated in 2004.

One leading scholar on religiously related social services, Bob Wineburg, points out that the Bush administration's faith-based initiative is really something different from the ongoing efforts to enhance the partnership between public funders and religious service providers. He refers to White House promotional activities as a "second faith-based initiative" with three intertwined motives: "*religious, social engineering*, and *votes*, namely black votes."[43] Wineburg observes that the architects on the *religious* side are mainly conservative and Evangelical Christians who promote government funds for churches and faith-based organizations that provide "relational social services"— services that "center on one's personal relationship to Jesus." Wineburg adds that the Catholics, Lutherans, and Salvationists who have been providing human services with public funding through the years "simply lost their souls and had become indistinguishable from the government."[44] The *social engineering* feature is being promoted by people who aren't necessarily true believers in faith-based social services, but rather they are opponents of a public sector social welfare system. "To them, government robs taxpayers of their liberty by prohibiting them from choosing whom to assist, when to do it, and how much to pay."[45] These social engineers believe that helping people in need should be done almost exclusively by the private voluntary sector. The third motive behind the second faith-based initiative is politics. "By creating an initiative that sends money directly to small black churches, there is the chance to increase the base of support among this traditionally Democratic block of voters."[46] The future directions of the so-called second faith-based initiative remain to be seen. We agree with Wineburg and other analysts that such motives and activities run counter to the development of healthy relationships between government and the private faith-based service providers.

Overall, faith-based initiatives are sometimes presented in concert with proposals to further devolve federal responsibilities for social welfare to state and local governments, and privatization of social welfare services. Although there is good reason to believe that government partnerships with existing and potential faith-based providers can offer positive advantages for the social welfare system, careful evaluation of the experiences to date appears warranted. In much of the promotion for faith-based initiatives is the largely untested hypothesis that faith-based services are more effective than services provided by personnel in secular organizations who are not expected to give the same proportion of care and moral inspiration.

A careful search of the literature for empirical studies comparing services from faith-based organizations (FBOs) with secular alternatives produces very little. One area of study relates to the popular trend of faith-based models to prepare prisoners in correctional facilities for release. Florida operates several correctional faith- and char-acter-based institutions (FCBIs) dedicated exclusively to the faith-based approach to rehabilitation and entirely funded and provided by voluntary organizations. Based on a process and impact evaluation of the Florida experience, researchers at the Urban Institute found that "staff, inmates, and volunteers overwhelmingly find value in the FCBI model and believe that it is achieving its goals of changing inmate behaviors, preparing inmates for successful reentry and ultimately reducing recidivism."[47] Another study of an FBO prison discharge program uses only client program satisfaction as an outcome measure, so effectiveness cannot be determined.[48] A study of an FBO Teen Challenge drug addiction program has no data from two-thirds of program participants so the findings can't be useful. At present the only other empirical and comparative studies find no clear support for the effectiveness of FBO programs. Kennedy and Bielefeld's quasi-experimental study of a small FBO job training/placement program in Indiana showed no significant differences in getting jobs and in wages received as between FBO and secular program trainees. The study had design and implementation problems (nonrandom assignment and a 30 percent dropout rate), so generalization is imprudent. But, surprisingly, the data show that the stronger the program was on a scale measuring faith-based commitment, the less likely were trainees to work full-time and have jobs with health benefits.[49] Another study in Indiana analyzed data on the characteristics of clients who seek and receive welfare reform services from FBOs. Findings indicated that clients who receive help from FBOs are more likely to be older, white, and married. Clients also report experiencing substantial economic strain, material hardship, and great need. Study results also suggest that FBOs are significantly more likely than secular organizations to have tightened service eligibility criteria.[50]

But the reader should notice that FBOs are important in other ways; in fact, the U.S. Department of Agriculture (USDA) data show that 60 percent of U.S. community food kitchens and pantries are run by FBOs and that they serve the lowest and most impoverished income groups in the country, those with few other resources. They are an important part of the U.S. safety net providing about 10 percent of the U.S. Federal Nutritional Safety Net (other programs are food stamps, commodities, and child nutritional programs).[51] Kennedy and Bielefeld also provide some useful conclusions about the special difficulties FBOs confront in implementing programs. One important consideration is how to allow government monitoring of grants without giving up the free exercise of religion clause in the Constitution which clearly protects religious organizations against "unwarranted intrusions." Another question is how to provide for and document the ability of the nonreligious client to opt out of religious exercises in the program. The knottiest problem is how to qualify "religious transformation," a common part of many FBO programs, as not transgressing the constitutional prohibition against the use of government funds for religious purposes.[52]

Privatization of Service Delivery

Privatization, as the term is used in social policy circles, has come to mean a number of things. At the extreme is the viewpoint that all of social policy programming should be left to the private sector—both with regard to funding and benefit/service delivery. The normative and more moderate viewpoint holds that current public social programs should be infused with as many private funding and service-delivery alternatives as are practical. We will focus on the funding issues of privatization later in Chapter 7. For now, we highlight privatization of service delivery.

Advocates of privatization argue that the introduction of market forces in the delivery of public services leads to healthy competition.[53] Through competition among service-delivery options, the argument is made that services can be provided with greater expertise and result in higher-quality services at lower costs. A how-to guide on privatization opportunities discusses the various types or methods that can be employed.[54] The following are most applicable to social service delivery systems. *Contracting* is the most widely used method of privatization for social programs.[55] Contracting involves the private sector taking responsibility for a new function or one formerly provided by government. The service-delivery agent (contractor) may be another public-sector organization, a private nonprofit, or a private for-profit business. *Franchise* involves giving exclusive right to a private firm for service provision within a certain geographic area. It can be thought of as "contracting with a twist."[56] An example would be a state government giving a private transportation company exclusive right to coordinate or provide nonemergency medical transportation to consumers of Medicaid in a three-county area. In the case of *vouchers* (as noted in Chapter 4), government pays for the service; however, individuals are given redeemable certificates to purchase a service on the open market. Some widely used vouchers are food stamps (now debit cards), housing vouchers, and vouchers for child day care. *Subsidies* (also discussed in Chapter 4) result in a government entity contributing financially or in-kind to a private organization to reduce the costs to clients/consumers. For example, developers of low-income housing are subsidized because they produce goods and services considered beneficial to the public interest.[57] *Service or "load" shedding* occurs when government stops providing a service and, if the service continues to be available, the private sector assumes responsibility. An example would be the downsizing or closing of a drug rehabilitation program, with a private nonprofit organization filling in the service gap. *Volunteers* may provide all or part of the service delivery for a government-funded benefit. Disaster relief carried out by the Red Cross and other private-sector organizations would be an example. *Self-help* privatization occurs when community groups and neighborhood organizations respond to a need not being provided (or partially provided) by the public sector—soup kitchens and food pantries, for example.

Scholars who have studied the growing trend toward privatization by contracting for social service delivery acknowledge examples of success, but also point out problems and issues. According to Becker, the bulk of privatization for service delivery in state and local governments has been to realize cost savings.[58] Any cost savings, he believes, have been mostly at the expense of employee health insurance and retirement programs—contributing to a severe erosion of these benefits. He concludes that "the inherent conflicts between just employment compensation, efficiency, effectiveness and opportunity costs are particularly problematic."[59] In their review of the literature, Nightingale and Pindus identify key points and conclude that there are success stories and examples of failure in all sectors. No one model (public, nonprofit, or private) is inherently better than another. The key factors to consider concerning service-delivery adequacy, equity, and effectiveness are whether there is clear accountability for results, clear criteria for performance, and clear public objectives. They note the following:

- Privatization is not inherently good or bad—the performance or effectiveness depends on implementation. There is no empirical evidence that the service provided by private contractors is inadequate. There is some evidence from research studies that the quality of services may be higher in private service-delivery systems than in public systems, but the findings may be biased in favor of the private sector.
- When public services are privatized, there is a reduction in the number of public employees, but there is not necessarily a reduction in total employment nor are workers always worse off.
- It is still too soon to know whether the most recent and highly publicized privatization efforts will be effective.[60]

Criteria for Evaluating Program Administration and Service Delivery

Introduction

The important question here is, what should we want in the way of a "good" service and benefit delivery system? We will offer several criteria specifically for evaluating service-delivery systems—features that characterize organizations good at accomplishing tasks with effectiveness and dispatch.[61] Thus, benefits and services should be, for example, (a) *integrated and continuous*, (b) *accessible to clients and beneficiaries*, and (c) *the organization delivering them should be accountable for its actions and decisions*. The traditional economic criteria used earlier in evaluating other program elements, *adequacy, equity*, and *efficiency*, are not useful here because they concern the actual benefit delivered, the end product. Our subject is the service-delivery system, only a means to that outcome, not the end product itself. By what standards should we judge these means?

Services and Benefits Should Be Integrated and Continuous

Social welfare organizations and systems often deliver more than a single program benefit or service. On that account, problems of integrating different program operations, benefits, and services are always an issue. For example, if system or program parts are not integrated, clients/consumers may be continually sent from one office to the next without understanding the reasons for being shuffled around; frustrating to say the least. A benefit-delivery system can be constructed to avoid that situation. For example, because people likely to qualify for the federal food stamp program are also likely to apply for benefits/services provided by state public welfare agencies, the food stamp program uses state-administered welfare agencies (e.g., the agency administering TANF) to determine eligibility and deliver benefits. This is an example of a service-delivery system integrating services by coadministration and colocation. It avoids determining eligibility twice and avoids the potential beneficiary having to go to more than one office to accomplish that task, saving some administrative costs in the process.

With deinstitutionalization and the closing of many state mental hospitals, patients with serious mental illness are being discharged into communities without medical care, vital medication, food, or housing. It is a serious problem in both integration and continuity of care. When a service- and benefit-delivery system continues to have such problems, the system is said to be fragmented. Certainly, that is generally the case in the United States, where individuals who are severely and chronically mentally ill among low-income groups without health insurance are being cared for in local jails and state and federal prisons. Linda Teplin of Northwestern University found that 9 percent of men and nearly 19 percent of women in local jails in her area were severely mentally ill; nationally, "more than 1 in 10 of all those in jails are known to suffer from schizophrenia, manic depression or major depression."[62] With the closing of the state mental hospital system jails have become the first line for the treatment of mentally ill people. And, without state mental hospitals, these individuals easily get into criminal difficulties and, thus, into state prisons, where they get what is nearly the only psychiatric treatment available for those unable to pay regular hospital and physician costs. That, despite the fact that it is "2–3 times more costly to provide treatment in prisons than in community clinics."[63]

Another leading example of service-delivery system discontinuity is the Social Security Disability Insurance (SSDI) program in which entitlement rules legislated by Congress require that a person declared disabled for work and, thus, entitled to SSDI monthly cash benefits is *not* entitled to Medicare benefits until one year later! There is an exception for individuals with disabilities on SSDI who have amyotrophic lateral sclerosis (ALS), which is commonly known as Lou Gehrig's disease. In the case of ALS, Medicare entitlement begins the first month the recipient receives SSDI cash benefits (approximately five months after an individual is deemed disabled). Other individuals who have disabilities and are receiving SSDI might be entitled to Medicaid, but that applies only if they meet a state or U.S. territory income limit for Medicaid—which may be greater than the SSDI benefit. Persons with disabilities might be entitled to Medicaid, but that applies only if they are very poor; if their SSDI benefit is more than (roughly) $550 for a single person, it is enough income to disqualify them for Medicaid. Thus, there is built into SSDI a systematic service and benefit discontinuity so that many who are assetless and financially distressed, who are very likely to need medical care, cannot receive it until two years after they are certified to be disabled.

Another important example of service system discontinuities and nonintegration are child welfare services in the United States, probably one of the most fragmented, disintegrated systems in all of the U.S. social services. Local juvenile courts make the decision to place children in state care and custody though they (commonly) don't administer child welfare services but rely on state or local welfare departments to do so. Thus, the decision to place children in care is divorced from the actual administration of care and both are divorced from the responsibility to provide funding for same. One could hardly devise a more fragmented, disintegrated, discontinuous system.

Services and Benefits Should Be Easily Accessible

Another criterion for good service-delivery organizations and systems is that they should be easily accessible to people who need them. Accessibility refers to the extent to which obstacles prevent ready use. Such obstacles might be geographic location, locations far away from where potential consumers actually live or work or far removed from public transportation. Another example can be identified in complicated application procedures requiring lots of reading or writing when the likely consumers may not be literate and having only English speakers for consumer groups when English is not their first language. If personnel cannot speak the language of potential clients, services and benefits are not fully accessible to them. That is an important issue in the United States, where there are always and in every generation significant immigrant and refugee subpopulations concentrated in particular areas. Today those would be Mexicans, Asians, Central Americans, Haitians, and, most recently, Russians, and Hindus and Muslims from the Indian subcontinent.

Cultural but not necessarily linguistic differences can also be an obstacle to access of needful clients to important benefits and/or services. Some Latinos, Asians, or Native Americans with serious medical or psychiatric conditions have sometimes been unable to take advantage of treatments prescribed by Anglo physicians and programs because Western medicine often has a very different style of healing. Native healers *(curanderos)* are commonplace among Latino cultures of all regions and certainly common to indigenous North American tribal groups.[64] Some medical programs have employed native healers as part of the treatment staff for relevant consumers.[65] With the blessing of native healers, use of Western procedures are likely to be more acceptable for these consumers.[66] It is a way of making services accessible.[67,68] Generally speaking, two strategies have been used to remove obstacles for use of or entry into programs and service-delivery systems: staffing with indigenous workers and constructing special referral agencies. See the subsections earlier in this chapter in which they are discussed at length.

Organizations Should Be Accountable
for Their Actions and Decisions

Accountability is the third ideal characteristic of a service-delivery system. The following example examines a service-delivery system, an agency concerned with child abuse as a social problem. Suppose a report was made to this agency of a case of suspected child abuse but the report remained uninvestigated for two months. Meanwhile, the child was beaten to death by one of the parents. The agency's accountability in this turn of events must be questioned. Be clear that what the agency is directly accountable for is the lack of response to the report.

The service-delivery agency can be said to have a system for accountability if the following conditions are met:

1. It is possible to identify which staff member decided not to respond to the abuse report.
2. It is possible for both the staff member and immediate superior to identify the specific organizational policy that justified that decision.
3. It is possible to identify the staff member's immediate superior for a quick supervisory review and opinion of the staff member's decision not to respond to the report (or lack of attention to it at all) with respect to its conformity to agency policy.
4. If there is substantive disagreement with the preceding opinions by outside third parties, there is a regular procedure (e.g., administrative hearing) by which such disagreements can be heard and resolved.

These are the minimum standards if accountability is to be a factor in the operation of a service-delivery system; more and better features might be involved. If organizations and service-delivery systems can respond to criticisms simply by denying that any overall policy is in operation, the organization cannot be held accountable. In other words, if *no* particular staff member can be held responsible, then, of course, no one can be held responsible. When failure to respond to a report of child abuse is associated (causally or not) with the subsequent death of a child, it is a travesty of justice to try to affix responsibility only to find that "no one was responsible." That is why accountability is such an important feature in the character of an organization; without it, irresponsibility and injustice go unmended.

Although many mechanisms are used to render service-delivery systems accountable as discussed earlier, two of the most prominent will be detailed: (1) administrative ("fair") hearings and procedures by which clients/consumers can appeal decisions that affect their benefits or services, and (2) constitutionally derived due process protections of clients'/consumers' procedural rights.

Administrative ("Fair") Hearings and Appeal Procedures.   Fair-hearing procedures are a common part of the service-delivery system of many social service programs. In fact, the Social Security Act requires a fair-hearing procedure for all programs established by the act (OASI, TANF, UI, DI, Medicare, and so on). A fair-hearing procedure is one in which a client or applicant is given the opportunity to appeal to an administrative tribunal or a judge who hears arguments of both sides. This tribunal reviews agency policy, practices, and enabling legislation and then renders a decision for or against the agency or the complainant. The administrative judge is duty-bound to hold the agency to decisions and actions that are consistent with agency policy, tradition, or legislative mandate. The judge can require the agency to reverse its prior actions or decisions and/or change its policies and procedures.

Fair-hearing systems most commonly use judges employed by the system that is in question. On that account, the U.S. fair-hearing system is not entirely independent of those who must submit to its scrutiny. On the other hand, the job performance of the administrative judges who operate the Social Security Administration (SSA) fair-hearing procedure are subject to review only by other administrative judges. However, during the early 1980s, judges were subject to unusual scrutiny by a new (Reagan-appointed) chief judge—clearly, the first historical record of blatant presidential political interference with the administrative apparatus of Social Security or the congressional power to set public policy for the agency.[69] The judges' association filed suit in federal district court asking for a desist order against such practice. The conclusion about presidential political interference was supported by the entire bipartisan committee, including prominent Republican congresspersons. State welfare departments administering income maintenance programs also have fair-hearing procedures, but note that in many state systems, the "judges" often are agency administrators with no supervisory responsibility for the decision being questioned and pressed into auxiliary service as administrative judges. Clearly, such judges cannot be completely free to make decisions that go against the interests of the organization that employs them. Every social practitioner should be able to counsel clients/consumers on use of the fair-hearing procedures in force in local social service and health agencies and income maintenance agencies. If they feel that policy decisions affect a client/consumer adversely and that a decision is inconsistent with past policy, is arbitrary or capricious, or is blatantly prejudicial or discriminatory, practitioners can and should help clients/consumers access fair-hearing procedures.

Practitioners should be prepared to help clients/consumers get fair hearings even if the policy interpretation that works to their disadvantage was made by the very agency for which the practitioner works—which is not uncommon. The first loyalty of a professional is to the client/consumer, and when there is a conflict of interest between client-consumer and organization, the professional obligation is to ensure that the client's/consumer's interest is served. That may mean that the client's/consumer's advocate may have to be someone other than the practitioner, and if that is the case, securing the services of another professional to advocate for the client/consumer on this one issue is one strategy.

Due Process Protections for Clients' Procedural Rights with Respect to Social Welfare Benefits and Services and Administrative Discretion.   Scholars and practitioners are in virtual agreement that policy rules are never entirely adequate as a guide to action or decision in concrete, practical, day-to-day situations. The human condition is too variable, so that even the best policy statements fall short of accommodating the complex and finely textured relationships between organizations and the people they serve. Absent a rule to guide action, staff members use the only recourse left to them—their own best judgment—which can be wrong in any given instance. Among writers and researchers on policy and organizational problems, such recourse is called *administrative discretion*. But, like strange and marvelous lights in the night sky, it needs careful watching. Administrative discretion can be a threat to the substantive rights of social service beneficiaries or service consumers. Administrative discretion can also be a threat to the procedural rights of citizens in claiming social welfare benefits or social services. *Procedural rights* are those elements in a decision-making process that are required for decisions to be made with the openness, fairness, and impartiality that natural justice demands. In the United States, federal and state constitutions provide for due process of law where interests in life, liberty, or property are at stake. Prior to the 1970s, social services or social welfare benefits were viewed as gratuities in which citizens had no property interests. These benefits were granted at the discretion—not the obligation—of the government. Reichs's concept of "new property" interest became ascendant, and the crucial case was *Goldberg v. Kelley*, decided in 1970.[70]

The key issue in that case was whether the constitutional due process requirements applied to welfare benefits. The U.S. Supreme Court held that they did indeed. Note that the Court did not find that citizens have a substantive right to welfare benefits, only that once a statute grants an interest or a right in a welfare benefit, then that interest must be protected by the constitutional due process requirements.[71] The Supreme Court recognizes that administrative discretion can indeed threaten the procedural rights that protect the possibility of just and equitable decisions. What does constitutional due process require of administrative decisions about eligibility for, continuance of, or changes in welfare benefits or services? Whereas it is true that the Social Security Act has always required programs to have a fair-hearing procedure as a way of redressing grievances, it was little used and the procedures were variable prior to the 1970s, when they became one of the principal battlegrounds for the welfare rights movement.

The following is Handler's appraisal of what is required of a fair-hearing procedure:[72]

- The right to timely and specific notice of the action taken by the agency and its basis. The norm is that the written notice must be in a form that the person can understand and allows reasonable time to prepare for the hearing.
- The right to appear at the hearing, to give evidence, and to argue a point of view. Sometimes allowing a recipient to present his or her story only in writing and not orally in public will not satisfy the due process standards. The Supreme Court has noted potential lack of writing ability by welfare recipients. The right to call witnesses exists generally but is not unlimited.
- The right to counsel. In recent years, the Supreme Court has retreated on this matter, though some precedent still stands.
- The right to confront and cross-examine witnesses.

- The right to an open or public proceeding. "Due process does not require an open hearing in certain kinds of administrative hearings (prison discipline cases and school cases)," according to Handler.
- The right to an impartial decision maker. The crucial issue is how much prior exposure to the case biases judgement. It appears that in some cases, the Supreme Court has allowed decision makers to have substantial involvement.
- The right to a decision based on the record and to written findings of fact and conclusions of law. It is very important to understand that in granting the application of due process requirements to "government largesse" (like welfare benefits and services), the Supreme Court conditioned the grant in important ways. The general principle is that due process requirements apply in any given specific instance only to the extent that there is a balance between the following three elements:
  - The seriousness of the grievance to the person receiving the welfare benefit
  - The need for any particular due process procedure in order to resolve the grievance fairly
  - The costs in time, money, and other resources to the administrative agency

This means that the balancing test described previously is the most explicit guide available to the general rules in determining what constitutes an acceptable attention to due process requirements.

Citizens and Consumers Should Be Participating in Organizational Decision Making

Citizen participation is the involvement of consumers and citizen representatives in policy decisions of a social service–delivery organization. Citizen participation is intended to increase the accountability of the organization to its consumers and the general public who pays the bills. Involvement of laypersons or consumers of agency services in policy decisions is believed to curb the career and professional self-interest of staff members. Such involvement exposes professionals to fresh viewpoints and, in the case of citizen participation by consumers, to a view of service from the receiving end. The point of consumer involvement is to constrain policy decisions toward the needs of clients rather than the needs of the community or the service-delivery staff. The problem with citizen participation as a strategy to increase organizational accountability is twofold. One, it doesn't happen very often; laypersons or service consumers are not given significant power over policy-making decisions. Two, if they are, they may not be very interested in taking that much responsibility. Nearly every author who writes about community participation notes the frequency with which citizen participation actually refers to token representation. Not only have observers of the scene in the United States—like Arnstein, Kramer, and Weissman—included this style of participation in their typologies of community participation, but also British policy analysts and observers note it with regularity.[73]

It should be clear that because power is the crucial factor, meaningful citizen participation cannot be said to occur unless it is actually exercised. The conditions for its exercise are as follows:[74]

1. Citizens must constitute a significant (perhaps one-third) voting block, not just a token portion, of the whole.
2. Citizens must have the right to initiate actions, not just respond to the agendas of executive managers.
3. Organizations must help citizen board members cope with formal procedures (like Robert's Rules of Order) and technical language they may find unfamiliar.

The War on Poverty of the late 1960s and early 1970s featured citizen participation as a central element in program strategy. The CAP (Community Action Program) agencies were a central administrative device by which program benefits and services were delivered to neighborhood target areas. CAP agency boards of directors were elected by the neighborhood areas they served. One of the five major Head Start program areas was parent participation in the policy-making and program evaluation efforts of Head Start, which itself was "governed" by an advisory board made up of the citizen consumers. It seems safe to say that the War on Poverty programs spent remarkable effort and energy orchestrating citizen and consumer participation. The net gain in citizen participation of any kind, let alone effective participation, was disappointing in most instances in both programs. One of the facts about which there is little debate is that volunteer participation in organizational decision making is a strongly class-biased trait. Citizen participation is essentially a middle-class phenomenon; middle-class people take to it naturally, apparently, whereas blue-collar people do not see it as either very important or potentially very productive (though they surely might not express it in exactly those words).[75,76] Neither Head Start nor CAPs serve middle-class populations, so it should not be surprising that participation efforts were unproductive. As Jones, Brown, and Bradshaw point out, it is not so much a matter of "apathy" as an essential pessimism about the likelihood of assuming an influential role.[77] Given documentation of the high probability that citizen participation was nothing more than tokenism in Head Start and CAP, it is a fair conclusion that blue-collar attitudes are in fact a correct assessment of the situation! Blue-collar people seem to have a grasp of this issue that neither professionals nor middle-class "joiners" seem to have. To balance the disappointing performance of the massive efforts by Head Start and CAP agencies to succeed in a full and serious citizen participation program, let us now turn to a description of a successful effort. Many believe that the Family Centre Project (also known as the Laurence Project) was the most significant antipoverty program ever undertaken in Australia. Perhaps it is best that its director David Donison speak for the project.[78]

> Radical, pioneering and iconoclastic in theory, and in practice full of human drama, the Family Centre project appeared to its staff to embody the very heart of the issues facing social work in the Australia of the mid-70s. The following description of the Project used by the Brotherhood of St. Laurence in its publicity material outlines the Project's essential elements. In 1972 the Brotherhood took the major decision to terminate its established Social Work Service and the Youth and Children's Services and to set up an innovative and experimental anti-poverty program designed to test new ways of assisting poor families. The overall objectives of the Family Centre Projects

were to demonstrate, with a small group of poor families who had been long-term clients[/consumers] of the Brotherhood, that changes in their economic and social conditions and opportunities were a pre-condition for change in their family and societal relationships, and that it was toward such changes that social work intervention would be directed. Through the first three years of the Project, the emphasis was on the redistribution of resources and power within the programme, with the implication that such changes are necessary in the wider community if power is to be effectively attacked. Among the features of the Project were:

(a) A universal income supplement scheme in which every family was entitled to a weekly subsidy to maintain its income at a set level;
(b) An emphasis on "development work" rather than "casework";
(c) A commitment to the "de-professionalisation" of the relationship between social workers and clients[/consumers];
(d) The introduction of programme in which the families ultimately took over the control and running of the Project;
(e) A growing emphasis on welfare rights, self-help and social action.

Another interesting and more recent example of citizen participation and empowerment as an accountability mechanism is the rise of citizen review panels for the purpose of monitoring, case by case, foster placement of children in long-term care. The function is to keep a constant public tab on children in public care to ensure that they do not somehow get lost from sight. These external reviews can occur either alongside the more ordinary case review systems that have been put in place in many states or can occur independently (in addition to them). Citizen review systems of this kind were stimulated by provisions of the 1980 Child Welfare Act.[79] Although their net effect on accountability awaits a future study, they have certainly stimulated considerable discussion and been effective in raising public consciousness of the problem of accountability with respect to foster care programs.

Organizations and Their Staff Must Be Able to Relate to Racial, Gender, and Ethnic Diversity

Organizations delivering social services cannot always resort to the creation of subunits serving ethnic or racial groups or hiring staff who are ethnically or racially similar to groups served by the organization. Absent that, direct service staff and administration have to be able to relate to ethnic diversity; Caucasians must learn to deliver services to whatever ethnic, gender, and racial diversity shows up on their front doorstep, and vice versa. Experience shows that it is wise to assume that professionals and other service-providing staff have been socialized into whatever were the cultural prejudices concerning ethnic groups and races, minorities of their families, and communities of origin. So, if their consciousness in this regard has not been raised, it is the responsibility of the program and its organizational host to do so. No program design, however well executed, can overcome staff attitudes where racism, sexism, and ethnic prejudice abound. Organizations need to seek consultation with their own staff members who have relevant ethnic and racial backgrounds or seek regular external consultation if no such staff exists. Service-delivery programs and their organizations should be evaluated on their attention to this issue. There is every reason to expect that racism, ethnic bias, and sexism on the part of service-providing staff management is present, that it has entirely insidious effects, and that it will not, somehow, go away by itself.

Summary

This chapter presented some leading and contemporary types of benefit and service-delivery organizations and discussed their strengths and weaknesses. Guidance for deriving program designs from program theory and program specifications from program designs were set forth. A set of evaluation criteria for the practitioner/policy analyst to use in judging the merit of specific real-life service-delivery organizations (or proposals for same) was offered, among which were the presence of a clear and credible program design, program specifications, service integration and continuity, program and organizational accountability, and the ability of the program and its host organization to relate to ethnic, gender, and racial diversity within its target populations.

EXERCISES

1. What is the difference between centralization and federation?

2. What practical difference would it make in which organizations you chose to work and in the day-to-day conditions under which you would work?

3. To what does due process refer? What does it have to do with human service or social welfare clients, programs, and policies?

4. How would you determine whether a fair hearing meets due process requirements of the law?

5. What are the major differences between administrative and professional discretion?

6. Describe a faith-based program and then write out a surefire method of discovering whether evangelization is present.

7. In applying for a job at a social welfare organization, you are told the agency surely has "a lot of citizen participation." What question(s) would you ask to determine whether that is really the case?

NOTES

1. For examples of logic models and how to develop them see W. K. Kellogg Foundation, *Logic Model Development Guide*, January 2004, www.wkkf.org/Pubs/Tools/Evaluation/Pub3669.pdf.

2. R. Savaya and M. Waysman, "The Logic Model: Incorporating Theory in the Development and Evaluation of Programs," *Administration in Social Work*, 29(2) (2005): 85–103; of course, the fact of successful program implementation will not guarantee proof that the program features "caused" the

outcome either. The only claim here is that it is a necessary condition for such an attribution, even though insufficient by itself.

3. C. A. Rapp, *The Strengths Model* (Oxford: Oxford University Press, 1998), p. 170.

4. Ibid., p. 175.

5. Ibid., p. 167.

6. Ibid.

7. Ibid.

8. T. Skocpol, M. Granz, and Z. Munson, "A Nation of Organizers: Institutional Origins of Civic Voluntarism in the United States," *American Political Science Review*, 94(3) (2000): 540–541; E. Brilliant and D. Young, "The Changing Identity of Federated Community Service Organizations," *Administration in Social Work*, 28(3–4) (2004): 23–46; D. J. Tucker, "Coordination and Citizen Participation," *Social Service Review*, 54(1) (1980): 17–18.

9. D. Moxley, *Case Management in the Human Services: Integrating Service and Support* (Thousand Oaks, CA: Sage, forthcoming).

10. C. A. Rapp and R. Chamberlain, "Case Management Services to the Chronically Mentally Ill," *Social Work*, 28 (1985): 16–22.

11. W. S. Deitchman, "How Many Case Managers Does It Take to Screw In a Light Bulb?" *Hospital and Community Psychiatry*, 31 (1980): 789.

12. Rapp and Chamberlain, "Case Management Services," p. 5.

13. M. Modrcin, C. Rapp, and J. Poertner, "The Evaluation of Case Management Services with the Chronically Mentally Ill," *Evaluation and Program Planning*, 11 (1988): 307–314; C. Macias, R. Kinney, O. W. Farley, R. Jackson, and B. Vos, "The Role of Case Management within a Community Support System: Partnership with Psychosocial Rehabilitation," *Community Mental Health Journal*, 30(4) (1994): 323–339.

14. C. S. Ryan, P. S. Sherman, and C. M. Judd, "Accounting for Case Management Effects in the Evaluation of Mental Health Services," *Journal of Consulting and Clinical Psychology*, 62(5) (1994): 965–974.

15. Modrcin et al., "The Evaluation of Case Management Services," pp. 307–314.

16. C. A. Rapp and R. Wintersteen, "The Strengths Model of Case Management: Results from Twelve Demonstrations," *Psychosocial Rehabilitation Journal*, 13(1) (1989): 23–32.

17. Modrcin et al., "The Evaluation of Case Management Services," pp. 307–314.

18. Macias et al., "The Role of Case Management," pp. 323–339.

19. Rapp, *The Strengths Model*, pp. 189–190.

20. M. Peterson Armour, "Alternative Routes to Professional Status," *Social Service Review*, 76(2): 229; D. Hardman, "Ten Characteristics of Empowerment Oriented Social Service Agencies," *Administration in Social Work*, 28(4) (2004); G. Brager, "The Indigenous Worker: A New Approach to the Social Work Technician," *Social Work*, 10(2) (1965): 33–40.

21. O. Lewis, "Culture of Poverty," *Science*, 188 (1975): 3–54.

22. C. Mowbray, D. P. Moxley, C. A. Jasper, and L. L. Howell (eds.), *Consumers as Providers in Psychiatric Rehabilitation* (Columbia, MD: International Association of Psychosocial Rehabilitation Services, 1997).

23. M. Ungar, S. Manuel, S. Mealey, G. Thomas, and C. Campbell, "A Study of Community Guides: Lessons for Professionals," *Social Work*, 49(4) (2004): 550–562; D. A. Hardcastle, "The Indigenous Nonprofessional in the Social Service Bureaucracy: A Critical Examination," *Social Work*, 16(2) (1971): 56–64.

24. Citizens Advice corporate Web site (2004–2007), http://citizensadvice.org.uk/; Citizens Advice Bureau of Bronx, New York, November 12, 2007, www.cabny.org/.

25. K. Santich, "For Foster Care Kids, Adoption Remains Elusive," *Tribune Business News*, McClatchy Publishing, November 3, 2007; D. Fanshel and E. Shinn, *Children in Foster Care: A Longitudinal Investigation* (New York: Columbia University Press, 1978).

26. In 2005 there were twenty-four African American adoption agencies in the United States. R. McRoy, R. M. Mica, M. Freundlich, and J. Kroll, "Making MEPA-IPEA Work: Tools for Professionals," *Child Welfare*, 86(2) (2007): 60; S. Duncan, North American Council on Adoptable Children (NACAC), "Black Adoption Myths and Realities," *Adoptalk*, Summer 2005; www.nacac.org/

adoptalk/blackadoptionmyths.html. Kansas City Black Adoption Program, J. Hampton, Director, personal communication, May 22, 1985.

27. M. Hansen and B. Hansen, "The Economics of the Adoption of Children from Foster Care," *Child Welfare*, 85(3) (2006): 559.

28. A. Inglehart and R. Becerra, *Social Services and the Ethnic Community* (Prospect Heights, IL: Waveland Press, 1995), p. 154.

29. E. F. Brown, G. E. Limb, C. A. Clifford, R. Munoz, and L. S. Whitaker, "Using Tribal/State IV-E Agreements to Help American Indian Tribes Access Foster Care and Adoption Funding," *Child Welfare*, 83(4) (2004): 293–296.

30. A. Gitterman and L. Schulman, *Mutual Aid Groups, Vulnerable and Resilient Populations* (New York: Columbia University Press, 2001), pp. 3–5.

31. Inglehart and Becerra, *Social Services*, pp. 159–160.

32. M. Delgado, *Social Services in Latino Communities* (New York: Haworth Press, 1998), pp. 51–71.

33. T. Tirrito and T. Cascio (eds.), *Religious Organizations in Community Services: A Social Work Perspective* (New York: Springer, 2003); B. Wineburg, *A Limited Partnership: The Politics of Religion, Welfare, and Social Service* (New York: Columbia University Press, 2001); R. Cnaan, *The Newer Deal: Social Work and Religion in Partnership* (New York: Columbia University Press, 1999).

34. U.S. Department of Health and Human Services, Administration for Children and Families, *Compassion Capital Fund Fact Sheet*, November 12, 2007, www.acf.dhhs.gov/programs/ccf/about_ccf/facts.html.

35. U.S. Department of Health and Human Services, (news release), October 19, 2007, www.hhs.gov/news/press/2007pres/10/pr20071019a.html; Links to faith-based initiatives can be found on federal and many state social welfare and human service Web sites. There is also a faith-based office in the White House (www.whitehouse.gov/government/fbci. For a national faith-based initiative advocacy organization with Web links, see the Web site for the Center for Public Justice (www.cpjustice.org/charitablechoice).

36. M. Olasky, *The Tragedy of American Compassion* (Washington, DC: Regnery Gateway, 1992); M. Olasky, *Renewing American Compassion* (New York: Free Press, 1996).

37. For an example of an organization opposed to faith-based initiatives, see the Web site for Americans United for Separation of Church and State at www.au.org.

38. National Association of Social Workers, *NASW Priories on Faith-Based Human Services Initiatives*, January 2002, www.socialworkers.org/advocacy/positions/faith.asp.

39. S. Kennedy and W. Bielefeld, *Charitable Choice at Work* (Washington, DC: Georgetown University Press, 2006), p. 169.

40. U.S. Government Accountability Office, "Faith-Based and Community Initiative— Improvements in Monitoring Grantees and Measuring Performance Could Enhance Accountability," *GAO Report* (GAO-06-616), June 2006, www.gao.gov/new.items/d06616.pdf.

41. National Association of Social Workers, Coalition Letter on the Faith-Based Initiative, September 23, 2002, www.socialworkers.org/advocacy/positions/faith2.asp.

42. D. Kou, *Tempting Faith: An Inside Story of Political Seduction* (New York: Free Press, 2006).

43. R. Wineburg, *The Underbelly of the Faith-Based Initiative*, Martin Marty Center, The Institute for the Advanced Study of Religion, University of Chicago Divinity School (*Sightings*, July 31, 2003), http://marty-center.uchicago.edu/sightings/archive_2003/0731.shml.

44. Ibid.

45. Ibid.

46. Ibid.

47. N. G. LaVigne, D. Brazzell, and K. Small, *Evaluation of Florida's Faith- and Character-Based Institutions*, Final Report (Washington, DC: Urban Institute, Justice Policy Center, October 2007), p. ix.

48. B. Wineburg, *Faith-Based Inefficiency* (Westport, CT: Praeger, 2007), p. 38.

49. Ibid.

50. Kennedy and Bielefeld, *Charitable Choice*, p. 169.

51. D. Reingold, M. Pirog, and D. Brady, "Empirical Evidence on Faith-Based Organizations in an Era of Welfare Reform," *Social Service Review*, 81(2) (2007): 245–283.

52. R. Brielfel et. al., *The Emergency Food Assistance System: Findings from Client Surveys in Food Assistance*, www.ers.usda.gov/publications/FANRR26/FANRR26-10/.

53. Kennedy and Bielefeld, *Charitable Choice*, pp. 157–159. E. S. Savas, *Privatization and Public–Private Partnerships* (Chatham, NJ: Chatham House, 1984).

54. W. D. Eggers, *Privatization Opportunities for States*, Policy Study #154, Reason Foundation, January 1993, www.reason.org/ps154.html.

55. Also referred to in the literature as purchase-of-service contracting (POSC).

56. U.S. Department of Health and Human Services, Administration for Children and Families, *A Guide to Developing Public–Private Partnerships in Child Support Enforcement*, www.acf.hhs.gov/programs/cse/rpt/pvt/contents.htm (accessed October 4, 2007).

57. Ibid.

58. F. W. Becker, *Problems in Privatization: Theory and Practice in State and Local Governments* (Lewiston, NY: Edwin Mellen Press, 2001), p. 184.

59. Ibid.

60. D. S. Nightingale and N. M. Pindus, *Privatization of Public Social Services*, prepared at the Urban Institute for U.S. Department of Labor, Office of the Assistant Secretary for Policy, October 15, 1997, p. 2, www.urban.org/url.cfm?ID=407023.

61. N. Gilbert and Paul Terrell, *Dimensions of Social Policy*, 4th ed. (Boston: Allyn & Bacon, 1998), pp. 150–151.

62. "Prisons Replace Hospitals for the Nation's Mentally Ill," *New York Times*, March 5, 1998, p. A1.

63. Ibid., p. A18.

64. D. Sharon, "Eduardo the Healer," *Natural History*, 52 (1980): 32–49.

65. W. McDermott, K. Deuschle, and C. Barnett, "Health Care Experiment at Many Farms," *Science*, 175 (1972): 23–30.

66. Ibid.

67. E. Ginzberg, "What Next in Health Policy," *Science*, 188 (1975): 1182–1186.

68. J. Goering and R. Coe, "Cultural Versus Situational Explanations for the Medical Behavior of the Poor," *Social Science Quarterly*, 51(2) (1970): 309–319.

69. D. Chambers, "The Reagan Administration's Welfare Retrenchment Policy: Terminating Social Security Benefits for the Disabled," *Policy Studies Review*, 5(2) (1985): 207–215.

70. J. Handler, *Protecting the Social Services Client* (New York: Academic Press, 1979), p. 31.

71. Ibid., p. 32.

72. Ibid., p. 28.

73. S. Damer and C. Hague, "Public Participation in Planning: A Review," *Town Planning Review*, 42(3) (1971): 224; D. Phillips, "Community Health Councils," in K. Jones (ed.), *The Yearbook of Social Policy in Britain, 1974* (London: Routledge and Kegan Paul, 1975), p. 106.

74. K. Jones, J. Brown, and J. Bradshaw, *Issues in Social Policy* (London: Routledge and Kegan Paul, 1979), pp. 106–108.

75. K. Newton, *Second City Politics* (London: Oxford University Press, 1976), p. 84.

76. For a dramatically convincing elaboration of this theme, see George Orwell, *The Road to Wigan Pier* (London: Golancz and Song, 1937), p. 37.

77. Jones et al., *Issues in Social Policy*, p. 106.

78. D. Donison, *Power to the Poor* (London: Blackwell, 1979), pp. 12–13. For a current description, see Tim Gilley, *Empowering Poor People* (Sidney: Brotherhood of St. Laurence, 1990).

79. L. B. Costin and C. A. Rapp, *Child Welfare Policies and Practice* (New York: McGraw-Hill, 1984), pp. 370–371.

7 How Do We Pay for Social Welfare Policies and Programs?

Analysis of Financing

Introduction

We begin this chapter by raising three basic questions and then give criteria for analyzing funding that will guide the analyst in sorting out the components of program funding. We summarize the major sources of funding and then examine these alternative funding arrangements as they apply to program examples. The chapter ends with discussion on devolution of social welfare programming, and the privatization revolution.

Beginning Questions and Criteria for Analysis of Financing

The following three basic questions outline the inquiry into understanding how social policy and program financing works, the positives and negatives of different approaches, and areas prime for modification and change. The criteria included are the same economic criteria we have used throughout the text—*adequacy, equity,* and *efficiency/effectiveness.*

1. Where does the funding come from?
   - Classification and categories of funding sources
   - Equitability in funding approaches

TABLE 7.1 Funding Sources for Social Welfare

Source	Policy and Program Basic Element
Private marketplace	1. Out-of-pocket payment for services/benefits
Private funding	1. Giving by individuals
	2. Bequests
	3. Service clubs
	4. Other charitable service-oriented giving
	5. Corporations
	6. Foundations
	7. Agency-based fund-raising
	8. Consolidated community fund-raising
Employee benefits	1. Health care insurance
	2. Retirement funds
	3. Other work-attached fringe benefits
Social insurance	1. Tax on employees and employers
	2. Tax on self-employed
	3. Tax on employers
Public/government funding	1. Federal taxes
	2. State and local taxes
	3. Fees and other revenue

2. What is the amount of funding?
   - Policy and program expenditures
   - Adequacy of funding measures

3. What approaches are used to fund programs?
   - Means of appropriation or reimbursement
   - Efficiency/effectiveness

Table 7.1 shows a classification of the funding sources available to finance social welfare programs. We will also use this schema of funding sources as the framework for description, analysis, and discussion of funding options.

Private Marketplace

In Chapter 1 we pointed out that the very notion of social policy suggests a collective, rather than individual, approach to social problems. However, there is a strong underlying philosophy in our society that individuals and families pay their own way when they have the means to do so. Examples like the following are familiar. When Margaret Smith could no longer maintain herself in her own home, her children arranged for long-term care at Resthaven Home. Ms. Smith has no resources other than her seventy-five-year-old house. She does receive a monthly Social Security benefit, but it is not enough to pay the full Resthaven monthly fee. Her family arranged for the sale of the house and has committed to pooling resources to pay for Ms. Smith's care without any outside funding assistance.

Rose and Joe Clark's fourteen-year-old son has suffered from emotional problems and their family doctor has made a referral to Hilltop Counseling Center. At this time only Rose Clark is working, but there is no provision in her basic health insurance to pay for counseling regarding emotional problems experienced by dependents. The Clarks have met with Hilltop administrators and have worked out a plan to pay for the needed counseling by making monthly payments for the counseling service. The family qualifies for a discount on cost of service, and a sliding-fee scale determines the scheduled amount the Clarks pay each month. Each of these examples represents an individual or family dealing with social problems via paying their own way in the private marketplace.

Private Funding

Private-sector financing of social welfare occurs in many ways; for example, charitable giving and bequests by individuals and families; support of religious congregations and other faith-based entities; agency-based and community-wide fund-raising initiatives; philanthropic giving by foundations and corporations; and contributing roles by fraternal organizations and other social associations or groups. Added together, the financial and in-kind contributions from the private sector represent important sources of funding for the nation's social welfare initiatives, particularly through the underwriting of nonprofit human service agencies. According to figures from the Giving USA Foundation, all giving totaled $295.02 billion in 2006.[1] Figure 7.1 shows the sources of contributions by percentage of total and the amounts given.

Giving by Individuals

Individuals are the most important source of contributions, as shown in Figure 7.1. Collectively, individuals gave $222.89 billion, or 75.6 percent of total contributions in 2006. However, not all contributions made by individuals to nonprofits are earmarked for programs we would call social welfare programs or social policy initiatives. In fact, only a little over 24 percent goes to support human services, health, and public/society benefits combined. The largest portion (32.8 percent) goes to religion.[2] An unknown proportion of contributions going to religion may end up supporting what we would consider "social welfare programs."

Sectarian social service agencies receive some support from their parent fundraising organizations. Jewish family and children's service programs receive assistance from United Jewish Communities (formerly United Jewish Appeal). Catholic social

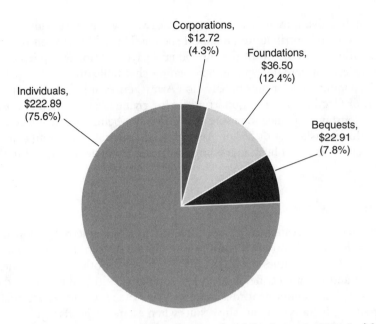

FIGURE 7.1   Sources of contributions for philanthropy in 2006 (in $ billions).

Source: Giving USA—2007, Giving USA Foundation.™

services are supported, in part, by Catholic Charities USA. Lutheran social services benefit from Lutheran World Relief. However, all three of these organizations' local social service programs depend heavily on other sources of funding—increasingly government funds for services purchased from them by public social agencies. Catholic Charities, for example, received 64 percent of its funding in 1996 from federal, state, and local governmental sources; only 5 percent of funding came from the Catholic Church.[3] At the congregational level, financial assistance is made available to faith-based programs and services. One large sectarian group, the Baptist Church, is a major proponent of separation of church and state and church leaders disapprove accepting governmental funds for their social programs. Local Baptist congregations help fund children's homes and other services.

What motivates people to give to nonprofit organizations? Three themes can be identified: a sense of personal responsibility to others; a person's relationships with others; and personal benefits such as receiving recognition, tax breaks, or pleasing an employer.[4] Not all giving involves a financial contribution or provision of in-kind resources. Countless individuals contribute to social welfare agencies as members of boards of directors and advisory committee members, volunteers who contribute professional and other services, delivering meals, providing clients/consumers with transportation, and a host of other support activities. Important also to fund-raisers for nonprofit organizations are reasons people do not give. Findings from a national study indicate that the major reasons people do not give are lack of money, lack of trust in a charity, and a charity's misuse of funds.[5]

Charitable giving by individuals is made easy. A working individual will find it very convenient to contribute to an appeal such as United Way when the employer agrees to withhold a portion of the individual's paycheck for that purpose. Simply checking the appropriate box will set up ongoing charitable giving arranged by some utilities. Dropping coins or bills in Salvation Army kettles at holiday seasons requires little effort or forethought. The opportunities for giving are so easy, in fact, that there is need for constant vigilance to ensure that one is not being misled and contributing to a cause that is dishonest or has unreasonable administrative costs attached. States' attorneys general are kept busy addressing scams and fraudulent activities in the name of charity.

Bequests

Closely related to the category of individual giving are bequests by individuals and families. As shown in Figure 7.1, contributions in the form of bequests amounted to 7.8 percent in 2006. A bequest involves leaving property or other resources designated in a last will and testament. Bequests enjoy popularity with individuals and families who have a strong commitment to a cause and also the ability to realize a tax advantage by giving. The tax saving usually results when estate tax is offset at the time of an individual's death. There are five basic forms of bequests: (1) unrestricted or general, (2) special bequests, (3) endowed bequests, (4) residual bequests, and (5) contingent bequests. Unrestricted bequests specify a certain dollar amount of property, usually cash, to be utilized for general purposes of the receiving organization. Special bequests are designated to support a specific program or project. Endowed bequests are established to provide a permanent fund for meeting the organization's general needs or a specific program or project—often established as a named fund. Residual bequests designate all or a portion of whatever remains after all debts, taxes, residue, and remainder of an estate. Finally, a contingent bequest takes effect only under certain conditions, for example, specified terms in the event that a spouse (or other) does not survive the person making the bequest.

Service Clubs

For many individuals, service clubs provide an outlet for volunteer involvement in charitable giving and community service. Service clubs come in a wide variety and have differing goals. Some are local in focus and others have a global mission. Many, if not the majority, have a selected area of service (and fund-raising) for which they have become recognized. Several examples of popular service clubs that are involved in fund-raising and service projects are Alpha Phi Omega, Kiwanis, Lions, Rotary, and Exchange.

Other Charitable Service-Oriented Organizations

There is also a diverse network of other organizations that play a role in charitable giving—far too many to list. Some have religious links, others are independent entities, and some are organizations that are quasi-public or public in nature. Examples of service organizations that have strong links to religious institutions or a historical religious beginning are the Shrine and Knights of Columbus. The Shrine of North America was founded by a group of men belonging to the Masonic Order. The Shrine operates a network of specialized Shriners Hospitals for Children (twenty in the United States and one each in Mexico and Canada) that treat children with orthopedic problems, burns, and spinal cord injuries, up to their eighteenth birthday, *free of charge*.[6] Funding for the Shriners Hospitals and care for patients is financed primarily through the Shriners Hospitals for Children Endowment Fund, which is maintained through gifts and bequests (by Shriners and non-Shriners alike). The Knights of Columbus is the largest lay organization of the Roman Catholic Church. Charitable giving in 2006 is reported at $143.8 million raised and distributed, and 68.2 million hours of volunteer service.[7] The categories of financial support are church support, community support (Special Olympics, programs for people with mental retardation or other mental and physical disabilities, disaster relief, and hospitals and related programs), and youth support (including World Youth Day, youth athletics, and scholarships and related programs).

Early in his career, entertainer Danny Thomas was inspired by St. Jude Thaddeus, the patron saint of hopeless causes. Upon achieving success, Thomas fulfilled a pledge to build a shrine to St. Jude. Through cooperation with the American Lebanese Syrian Associated Charities (ALSAC), a national fund-raising organization, Thomas established St. Jude Children's Research Hospital. The mission of St. Jude is to help find cures for children with catastrophic illnesses through research and treatment. Cost for patient care is covered by third-party insurance payments, and the ALSAC covers the expense for patients who do not have health care insurance.

Finally, there are service programs that are part of the public Corporation for National and Community Service funded by federal taxes through the National and Community Service Trust Act of 1993. The emphasis of these programs is on volunteerism. AmeriCorps is a network of three national service programs (AmeriCorps State and National, AmeriCorps Vista, and AmeriCorps National Civilian Community Corps). These programs engage individual volunteers in services to meet needs in education, public safety, health, and the environment. Senior Corps is a network of three national service programs that provide older Americans the opportunity to put their life experiences to work meeting community needs as mentors, tutors, and caregivers for at-risk and special needs populations. The programs of Senior Corps are Foster Grandparent Program, Senior Companion Program, and the Retired and Senior Volunteer Program (RSVP).

Corporations

Corporations account for a smaller overall percentage but nevertheless are an important source of contributions to charity. As shown in Figure 7.1, corporations' giving amounted to 4.3 percent of total contributions in 2006. Corporate giving involves a wide variety of business-sponsored philanthropic efforts, which Lauffer points out are "often described as the exercise of social responsibility that is good for business."[8] In addition to giving grants and gifts to selected nonprofit sector agencies, corporate leaders often become involved in community fund-raising efforts, and volunteer their services for nonprofit organizational improvement strategies such as planning, cost cutting, monitoring, and evaluating.

Foundations

Foundations are another major source of financial support from the private sector for social welfare programs. Foundations are required by law to spend 5 percent of their assets annually. As shown in Figure 7.1, contributions by foundations amounted to 12.4 percent of total contributions in 2006. According to the *Foundation Directory*, there are four different types of foundations: (1) independent, (2) company sponsored, (3) operating, and (4) community.[9] Independent foundations are grant-making organizations established to aid social, educational, religious, or other charitable activities. Financial support for independent foundations generally comes from a single source such as an individual, family, or group of individuals. These foundations tend to have broad discretionary giving practices; however, a large proportion of them limit their giving to a local area. Company-sponsored foundations are grant-making organizations with close ties to the corporation providing the funding. Giving practices of company-sponsored foundations tend to be in fields related to corporate activities or in communities where the corporation operates. Operating foundations use their resources to conduct research or provide a direct service. They are usually funded by a single source and make few, if any, grants. Community foundations are publicly sponsored organizations that make grants for social, educational, religious, or other charitable purposes in a specific community or region. Contributions come from many donors, including individuals, corporations, and other foundations. Community foundation grants are generally limited to charitable organizations in the local community of the foundation.

In addition to charitable organizations and foundations, other venues for private sector giving include agency-based and community fund-raising efforts. We examine them next.

Agency-Based Fund-Raising

Social agencies across the country engage in fund-raising events to finance their programs and services. In many cases an annual campaign is scheduled and individual solicitations are planned. Board members are generally expected to participate and contribute financially, at least symbolically. Other common methods for fund-raising are garage sales, golf tournaments, car washes, entertainment events, and raffles.

Community Fund-Raising

The history of federated community approaches to charitable fund-raising dates back to the late nineteenth century and the Charity Organization Societies (COSs). The COS movement was dedicated to developing improved ways to manage fund-raising for charity and promote scientific management principles in the delivery of services financed by fund-raising efforts. By the late 1920s Community Chests had replaced virtually all COSs, and more than 300 communities had established their own chests to centralize fund-raising and allocate funds to service agencies.[10] Today the dominant entity for community fund-raising is the United Way (UW). In some communities UW and Community Chest have been merged, with both organizational names used in promotional materials. A few communities continue to operate only a Community Chest, though the approach taken in fund-raising is similar to that described for UW.

The United Way movement consists of approximately 1,300 local community-based UW member organizations and a national leadership organization, United Way of America. Each local community UW is independent and governed and operated by local volunteers. Larger UWs typically also have trained staff involved as social planners, fund-raisers, accountants, and specialists in various practice areas. The mission of UW is "to improve people's lives by mobilizing the caring power of communities."[11] In addition to annual fund-raising campaigns, local UWs become involved in the identification of critical local issues and mobilization of resources through networking with community partners such as schools, government policy makers, businesses, organized labor, financial institutions, voluntary and neighborhood associations, community development corporations, and the faith community. The 2006–2007 UW annual campaigns totaled $4.07 billion, with additional resources leveraged beyond the campaigns (gifts for mobilization of special national projects, government grants to support critical community-based health and human services, sponsorship of special initiatives, bequests and planned gifts, and volunteer time).[12] When community-wide fund-raising campaigns take place, member agencies follow guidelines of agreement not to carry out their own fund-raising activities in competition with the community-wide effort.

Community UW agencies are experiencing changes that have challenged their hegemony over community charitable fund-raising in some places. According to Brilliant and Young, since the 1980s UWs are experiencing a declining role as fiscal intermediary (fund-raising and distribution) and economic regulator (overseer of how funds are spent). Their role as a community problem solver has been resurrected from earlier times—"focus on addressing community problems as a whole, rather than simply supporting or overseeing organizations that deliver services in the community."[13] Also, an emerging trend for UWs and competing federated charities is that of setting up and managing "charitable mutual funds." In this role they offer an attractive portfolio of charitable investments to assist potential donors in making decisions about where they want to invest their donations (e.g., youth services, services to elderly people, substance abuse treatment, etc.).

Adequacy, Equity, and Efficiency for Private Funding.   Private funding of social welfare in the United States is a useful ingredient in the overall mix for financing social welfare.[14] The various elements that make up private funding represent values critical to preserving the pluralist society in which we live. Important as private funding is, there is little evidence to support a view that there is the potential to finance the entire social welfare system through private funding, even with massive cutbacks in programs, benefits, and services.

Giving by individuals, corporations, and foundations is prone to sensitivities in the general state of the economy. In periods of economic growth, increases in wages and profits stimulate philanthropy. In times of disaster charitable giving can also be quite impressive—private donations following the tsunami in Southeast Asia, the earthquake in Pakistan, and Hurricane Katrina totaled about $7 billion.[15] There are also times when charitable giving tends to ebb. When the economy weakens and unemployment increases, benefits and services funded by private charity are needed the most. This dynamic alone raises serious doubt about any position suggesting that private charity can replace large cuts in benefits and services to individuals in need—a philosophy promoted during the Reagan administration. Finally, we raise the issue of adequacy when it comes to funding for the private voluntary sector. Although there are no specific benchmarks by which to measure adequacy in this area, examination of funding trends can be beneficial. A particularly helpful resource for information on private charitable giving from a national perspective can be found in the annual reports of the Giving USA Foundation. They provide a detailed analysis of giving trends from a historical perspective, including giving by individuals, corporations, and foundations. Another good source of information is the Foundation Center, which publishes *Foundation Giving Trends*. At the local level, the policy analyst will find useful information on the adequacy of private funding sources in community fund-raising campaign reports, audits of charitable giving organizations, and budgetary information from the private nonprofit service agencies that receive funding.

The public legislative and judicial arenas can have an influence on the adequacy of private funding. Tax laws and regulations in particular influence incentives to give. An example is the CARE Act debated in Congress in 2003. Advocates promote this kind of legislation as designed, in part, to stimulate charitable giving.[16] Critics fear that such measures support a new equation for charities: "More money, less oversight."[17] As noted previously, laws and regulations require foundations to divest a percentage of their holdings each year or suffer tax penalties. Individual charitable giving and bequests offer significant tax deductions to givers. But recently questions were raised in the powerful Senate Finance Committee by senators of both parties. At issue is the effectiveness of the 5 percent divestiture rule, given the huge increase in size of charitable foundations which has tripled in the last decade alone so that the assets of nonprofit foundations in 2007 totaled *2.5 trillion*. It seems to signal change not only toward increasing the amount foundations must spend each year but raising questions about whether many foundations were in business simply to perpetuate themselves.[18] One symptom of the problem is that even among foundation executives there is discussion of the urgent need to award very large grants simply to meet the 5 percent divestiture rule because of the amount of money they now have available. The basic problem discussed is finding enough organizations to award large grants to—organizations that have a large staff and are prepared to spend very large amounts of money over short periods of time. One hero of that scene is the Bill and Melinda Gates Foundation, which spends hundreds of millions of dollars on just such projects (i.e., AIDS and malaria programs in Africa).

Whereas the names of prominent "social entrepreneurs" like Bill Gates and Warren Buffet give a positive image to establishing and financing charities, some concerns may be noted. In a *Washington Post* article (October 8, 2007), Steuerle reported on some of the issues concerning collaborations between charities and businesses. He reported that such collaborations can be tricky—like the sale of a community hospital that was initially owned by a nonprofit, now owned by a money-losing for-profit and seeking to sell to another for-profit business. The deal depends on millions in local government subsidies. Other examples he gives are "credit cards bearing a charity's good name," and corporate logos associated with nonprofit and public events. The trend is that more and more adults are engaged in activities and with corporations that can be either charitable or profitable—a force he believes is unstoppable.

> As businesses and charities increasingly cooperate and compete to meet public and private demand, we will spend more of our time providing and receiving services once defined as primarily charitable.[19]

Steuerle concludes that the tax laws governing charitable giving and charitable status must be continually reexamined to help protect the charitable purpose of our contributions in this "polyglot of joint and competing ventures."

Even long-standing charity the Shrine has come under recent criticism.[20] An examination of Shrine records and interviews with former Shrine officials by the *New York Times* revealed serious mismanagement of money earmarked for hospitals. Among the findings concerning tax accounting procedures and oversight of spending, it was revealed that more than 57 percent of funds raised in Shriner activities in 2005 went to costs of the fraternity (including keeping temple liquor cabinets full and offering expense-paid trips to Shrine meetings and other events). These findings may be exceptional, but it is unlikely the Shrine is the only charitable organization for which such problems can be found.

Equity is not particularly an objective in private charitable funding. Individuals give to the causes in which they are interested or out of specific value commitments—their church or religious cause, the cause of their social club or organization, an appeal to feed hungry children, and so on. Corporations and foundations are free to select whichever special interest suits their fancy. Perhaps the closest example of attention to equity occurs in the case of community fund-raising. Even in the case of community fund-raising, however, there tends to be a bias toward supporting more traditional social programs over emergent grassroots initiatives that serve clients/consumers that are often considered *community deviants*—substance abusers, persons with HIV or AIDS, delinquent youth, and so on. One way to enhance issues of equity in community fund-raising and appropriations is for social workers and other human service personnel to become involved in advocacy efforts on behalf of individuals and families whose plight is not being addressed by either the public or private sector.

A lack of public oversight for private giving, coupled with legal loopholes, sometimes leads to abusive practices on the part of fund-raising organizations. The Internal Revenue Service (IRS) is the major federal agency concerned with charities' accounting practices. A relatively small proportion of IRS officials are deployed to audit charities and other tax-exempt organizations. The situation isn't much different at the state level. Especially revolting to individual givers is media attention to the salaries of executives and board members of some charities and foundations.[21] The high salaries may be perfectly legal, but the policy analyst can raise serious questions about the efficiency of charitable organizations when they spend large amounts of donated money on salaries and other overhead costs.

Private funding is a mix when it comes to efficiency and effectiveness. In some cases the act of giving and funding of human service programs is very clear and direct. In other cases the process may be convoluted and involve loss of resources due to administrative overhead, time delays, and other such problems. As noted previously, many of the private fund-raising organizations rely on volunteers, which can be quite efficient in terms of costs of raising money but inconsistent in effectiveness.

Employee Benefit Funding

Except for retirees, most people in our society who have health insurance rely on the fringe benefit package provided through their employer. There is wide variation in coverage and cost of the employment-related, thus "work-attached," health insurance benefits. It is an example of the insurance principle in financing social policy and programming. For social workers and other human service practitioners the concept of third-party insurance takes on importance in the funding of many private nonprofit agencies. The several parties are the social service agency, the client/consumer, and the third-party insurance carrier. The more comprehensive employment-related health insurance policies, for instance, provide services for employees and their dependents for mental health, substance abuse treatment, behavioral problems, and so on.

In addition to health insurance, employer-related insurance coverage often includes other policies such as long-term-care insurance, disability insurance, life insurance, and retirement pension plans.

We have become all too familiar with the vulnerability of employees to fraud and mismanagement of company retirement funds. The financial disaster at Enron Corporation and subsequent loss of retirement savings for former employees is one dramatic example. There are two major vehicles for employment-related retirement plans: defined contribution plans, such as monthly contributions to an employee's 401(k) fund; and defined-benefit plans, which are set up on the basis of an insurance annuity. The defined-benefit plans (pensions) are the subject of our discussion here.

Concerns about questionable policies and management practice of pension plans led Congress to enact the Employee Retirement Income Security Act (ERISA) in 1974. ERISA provisions include regulation of pension plans to ensure reasonable age and service requirements for retirement, reasonable vesting period, joint and survivor provisions, funding provisions, accounting and management standards, legal appeal procedures, and insurance provisions.

To protect pension plans, the federal government offers federal insurance for pension plans through the Pension Benefit Guaranty Corporation (PBGC). The insurance is a protection of financial assets much like the Federal Deposit Insurance Corporation (FDIC), which insures individual savings accounts. The cost of the PBGC insurance is funded primarily through pension plan premiums. When an insured pension plan is terminated, eligible beneficiaries are able to recover at least a portion of their retirement savings. However, only a little over half of all private pension plans are covered by the PBGC insurance. As of 2006, PBGC was protecting the pensions of nearly 44 million workers and retirees in about 30,330 private defined-benefit pension plans.[22] PBGC pays monthly retirement benefits, up to a maximum ($4,125 for single-employer plan in 2007) for about 612,000 retirees whose employer pension plans have terminated.[23]

Adequacy, Equity, and Efficiency for Employee Benefit Funding. Employee benefits have come under hard times for many people in the workforce. Funding for the social provisions of employer fringe benefits is strained in many cases. Few employees enjoy the advantages of high-quality health benefits (including such coverage as dental care, vision care, and psychiatric or counseling services). Costs for such benefits have been increasing at rates never before seen in history. The result is that funding for employee fringe benefits has eroded drastically. Added to that is the trend of many employers hiring primarily part-time employees in order to avoid paying costly fringe benefits. In the past, labor unions have been a counterbalance for protection of workers' benefits. In a few industries that is still the case today. In recent years union shops have lost much influence, particularly in states that have passed "right to work" laws that reduce union power and influence, and corporations can now bypass unions by moving jobs to low-wage countries like Mexico and China. On top of that, in 2006 only 12 percent of wage and salary workers were union members.[24]

Adequacy of funding for health care insurance has become particularly problematic. Escalating health care costs in the 1980s resulted in many companies turning to managed care options. In response to health care costs spiraling in the 2000s, some employers have dropped health benefits entirely. Many employers that have retained health benefits are selecting cheaper health insurance policy options with increased employee copayments, deductibles, and maximum out-of-pocket costs. Another approach is the use of Health Care Reimbursement Accounts (HCRAs) or Flexible Spending Accounts (FSAs), which offer a tax-exempt account funded by an employee or employer and used by the employee to pay health care expenses. Gaining in popularity is the use of Consumer-Driven Health Plans (CDHPs) that shift some of the responsibility for managing health costs to employees. These plans involve employer-funded "defined-contribution" untaxed expense accounts that employees manage to pay for health services and prescription drugs. CDHPs generally also involve at least the three following features: "(1) unspent money in the account accumulates for future years; (2) the account is accompanied by a high-deductible health insurance that pays for major expenses; and (3) the employee gets on-line support to track health care bills, maintain health, get information on provider quality, and get discounted prices."[25] "Opponents of CDHPs are concerned that these plans may take health benefits away from employees, give tax breaks to the rich, and leave the chronically ill behind in tradition[al] health insurance paying higher premiums."[26] Indeed! Readers should note that the United States, the richest country in the world, is also the only country in the Western industrial world that does not have a government-provided health care system. Nor can a case be made that the United States provides better health care for the average U.S. citizen.

Increased concerns relate to problems of funding adequacy for work-attached defined-benefit pension plans. Earlier in this chapter we discussed the role of the Pension Benefit Guaranty Corporation (PBGC) as an insurer of such pension plans in the private sector. Can the PBGC cover benefit costs for pension plans that fail, and can it protect workers' private pension plans? Underfunding of insured single-employer pension plans was projected at a record $400 billion in 2002. And, as a result of record pension underfunding and failure of a number of plan sponsors in mature industries, PBGC's financial position in that area showed a deficit level of $18.1 billion as of July 1, 2006.[27] It seems quite unlikely that PBGC can now protect workers' private corporate pensions.

Employers with defined-benefit pension plans are increasingly shifting to defined-contribution retirement plans—for example, 401(k) individual employee plans. Generally, it is a less costly and more efficient alternative for employers. It also enhances the principle of employee choice. Employees are typically given choices to consider regarding the investment funds for their 401(k) accounts. However, experience has revealed an equity issue for older workers near retirement age when an employer shifts to a defined-contribution plan. The effect in some cases has been a much lower retirement benefit for an individual retiring soon after the shift in plans takes place. Another issue, in general, confronts employees approaching retirement decisions. When the stock market is up, a retiring employee stands to realize a much bigger benefit than the employee who times his or her retirement during a market slump. Finally, there is the matter of an employee making poor choices about how to invest his or her 401(k) account and realizing too late in employment history to make up such losses.

The risks associated with 401(k) plans are compounded when employers practice deception or fraud in regard to the defined-contribution retirement plans described previously, which can be devastating for employees involved. A case in point occurred in 2001 involving the bankrupt Enron Corporation, a Houston-based energy and trading giant. Out of a sense of company loyalty (or subtle pressure), many Enron employees had invested their 401(k) equities in Enron stock. When Enron began to implode due to scandalous business practices, many current and former Enron employees scrambled to sell the Enron stock in their 401(k)s. However, they were forbidden to do so during a "lockdown" period required because Enron had hired a new company to administer its 401(k) plans. By the time the lockdown period was over, Enron stock was almost worthless.

Adequacy, equity, and efficiency of funding for employee benefits are influenced by the great variance in employee benefit plans. Earlier we cited that the government regulations of ERISA provide some safeguards for the adequacy and efficiency of funding for pensions. In addition, ERISA regulations address the equity issue by forbidding employers from having work-attached health care or retirement benefits that discriminate in favor of only one class of employee—management, for instance.

The bottom line, however, is that employers (public or private sector) are not required to fund employee benefits. It is beneficial to society when they do, but whether they provide the funding for benefits, and in what amount, is discretionary and can lead to inadequacy, inequity, and inefficiency in financing.

Social Insurance as a Publicly Mandated Funding Approach

Several of the nation's largest social programs are funded through social insurance: Social Security, Medicare, and Unemployment Insurance. Other examples are workers' compensation and employment-related insurance coverage for life, health, and disability. We begin our discussion with Social Security.

Social Security

Old Age, Survivors and Disability Insurance (OASDI) constitutes three different program elements of what we commonly call the Social Security program. The old age element (OASI) is insurance savings for retirement for those who work in employment covered under Social Security—approximately 95 percent of jobs are covered. Second, survivors of workers also are entitled to benefits. The third element is insurance for disability (DI). Social Security is financed through a payroll tax for all covered workers. This payroll tax (6.2 percent on earnings up to $102,000 in 2008) is matched by the worker's employer, making a total of 12.4 percent. Self-employed individuals pay the total 12.4 percent; however, they receive a personal income tax deduction for half of it. Funds from this tax are paid to the federal government and credited to two separate trust funds, the Old Age and Survivors Trust Fund and the Disability Trust Fund. Money from the trust funds is invested in special interest-bearing loans to the federal government, adding to the overall amount of funding available to pay beneficiaries as they retire, their survivors, or if they become disabled. Currently there are reserves in these combined trust funds to carry it through 2040. To avoid exhausting the trust funds, some modifications will need to be made (but notice that Social Security is in very good shape compared to private pension funds and, in fact, is not much different from many private funds offering guaranteed annuities). Those modifications will involve workers paying somewhat higher payroll taxes, of course.

The OASDI program elements utilize a formula set by Congress to determine adequacy of funding. You will recall in the discussion of benefit analysis in Chapter 4, beneficiaries realize a cost-of-living-allowance (COLA) at the beginning of each year based on changes in the consumer price index in order to keep benefit levels in pace with inflation. An additional feature is designed to help maintain adequacy of funding. Each year since 1971, the cap on the maximum salary level taxed has risen, based on a complicated formula that takes into account the existing cap level and changes in the national average wage. By way of comparison for a ten-year period, the OASDI tax cap on salary was $60,600 in 1994 and went up to $87,900 in 2004—a 45 percent increase! Funding increases have also been made from time to time by increasing the percentage of tax paid under OASDI.

In recent years, the social insurance principle has come on hard times in the Social Security system, largely because in past years Congress continued to expand benefit coverage, enacting larger benefits than were ever anticipated in earlier years when financing was being planned, and the ratio between the number of working contributors and the number of retiree beneficiaries has changed substantially. The prior contribution strategy on which Social Security is based is subject to a number of problems, one of which is insensitivity to demographic changes. Currently the OASI and DI trust funds hold surplus funds, but they will eventually be paid out in benefits— unless some changes are made. Clearly inferior are the drastic predictions of the "bankruptcy" of the Social Security system. Trustees for the Social Security system conduct analyses using alternative assumptions in estimates to project the future financial status of the trust funds for the short range (ten years) and long range (seventy-five years) and issue an annual report on their findings. Using a long-range set of assumptions in 2007, it was projected by the trustees that combined the OASI and DI trust funds would not reach exhaustion until 2041.[28] Planning continues in the exploration for alternatives, which will ensure adequate funding for the social insurance program elements of Social Security. Many alternative proposals include some measure of privatization (more on that later).

It is a great challenge to design a nationalized program of the magnitude of Social Security in a way to ensure perfect equity in either funding or provision of benefits. And it is a further challenge to maintain equity over the life of social insurance programs when they are set within the political process referred to earlier. Here are some examples of inequities that will help the policy analyst develop a sharp eye for applying the equity criteria for funding this and other social policies and programs.

Social Security taxes that fund OASDI can penalize dual-earner couples. Table 7.2 illustrates how a married couple with one wage earner compares with a dual-earner couple receiving the same annual wage-based income for the family of $150,000. Recall that each wage earner in 2008 paid 6.2 percent tax for OASDI up to a salary of $102,000. Even if Mr. Smith's salary were $1 million, his tax would still amount to $6,324. The Browns, on the other hand, would each continue paying the 6.2 percent tax until their salaries reached the $102,000 cap. Thus, the dual-earner household in this example will pay almost one-third more in OASDI tax as the single-earner household. But they will receive no more than 50 percent more benefits than if one spouse had never paid Social Security contributions at all (the maximum family

TABLE 7.2   Inequity for Dual-Wage Earners Paying Social Security (OASDI) Tax (2008)

Wages	Smiths	Browns
Husband	$150,000	$75,000
Wife	0	$75,000
Total	$150,000	$150,000
OASDI taxes	$6,324	$4,650 and $4,650
(Combined)	$6,324	$9,300

Source: Adapted from Jonathan Barry Forman, "Promoting Fairness in the Social Security Retirement Program," *The Tax Lawyer*, 45(4) (1992): 933–934. Reprinted by permission.

benefit is approximately 150 percent of the benefit of the spouse who has the better earning record). In an insurance scheme that was absolutely faithful to the insurance principle, the married couple's benefit on retirement would be based on the contributions of both the husband and wife, plus whatever interest and dividends accrued over the years during which the contributions were made. It must be said, however, that to date there is little average loss on this account because the average Social Security beneficiary has actually paid for less than what is received in benefits.

Another example of inequity for Social Security involving both the funding and benefit side of the equation can be observed by actuarial statistics. Ethnic minorities paying into the system generally have a lower life expectancy. The result is that as a group their contributions into the system do not result in as great a proportion of retirement benefits as holds true for whites. This is offset to some degree by the fact that a larger portion of ethnic minorities than whites become disabled or suffer chronic conditions and, as a result, more are able to benefit from the disability provisions of the program.

The feature that makes Social Security work to the advantage of those who are retiring now is that (1) there are income transfers at work and (2) profitability is not a factor (not least because there are no sales or marketing costs and administrative costs have always been much lower than in private insurance schemes). The Social Security system is, in fact, transferring income from those who are now working to those who are no longer working, persons who are retired or disabled, Medicare beneficiaries—and from high-wage earners to average-wage earners.[29]

Medicare

Medicare is a federal health insurance program for persons sixty-five or older, persons of any age with permanent kidney failure, and persons with certain disabilities. Medicare insurance is composed of four parts. Part A is hospital insurance (HI) Part B is a voluntary program of medical insurance, which covers physicians and other medical services. Part C, Medicare Advantage, is an alternative to Parts A and B which enrolls beneficiaries in a coordinated care plan or special fee-for-service plan. Part D is a voluntary prescription drug benefit program. In the case of Parts A, B, and D of Medicare, beneficiaries are responsible for deductible and coinsurance costs.

Medicare Part A is funded in the same way described earlier for Social Security. Workers pay an additional tax (1.45 percent on unlimited earnings in 2008) for HI. As in the case of Social Security, this is matched by a worker's employer, and total of 2.9 percent for the self-employed. These social insurance tax funds are also paid to the federal government and are credited to the Hospital Insurance Trust Fund. Currently, surplus funds exist in this trust fund but they may be exhausted even earlier than the Social Security trust funds. Projections by the Trustees for Medicare (health insurance) in 2007 estimated that under current program operations the health insurance trust fund would be exhausted by 2019.[30]

Persons who are sixty-five years old but do not have forty or more quarters of Medicare-covered employment may purchase the Part A premium. The cost in 2008 for purchase of the Part A premium amounted to $233 a month for persons who have thirty to thirty-nine quarters of coverage, and $423 if less than thirty quarters of coverage.

Part B of Medicare is funded for all Medicare beneficiaries through purchase of a premium. All persons eligible to receive Medicare Part A are entitled to enroll in Part B medical insurance. This part of the Medicare program is financed through a monthly premium paid by the enrolled person. The monthly premium is adjusted each year to cover 25 percent of program costs, and the remaining 75 percent is financed by the federal government through general funds. Beginning in 2007, single persons and married couples with higher annual incomes paid a higher percentage of the cost of Medicare Part B insurance based on reported income over a three-year period. These higher-income beneficiaries pay a monthly premium designed to equal 35 percent, 50 percent, or 80 percent of the total cost, depending on their income level by the end of the three-year transition period. Premium amounts change each year. Table 7.3 shows the premiums for 2008.

Part C (Medicare Advantage) is a policy directive that permits contracts between Medicare and a variety of different managed care and fee-for-service providers. Medicare beneficiaries may choose this program option over Parts A and B. Medicare Advantage plans include coordinated care plans, including health maintenance organizations (HMOs), preferred provider organizations (PPOs), and provider-sponsored organizations (PSOs); or private fee-for-service plans that reimburse service providers on a fee-for-service basis and are authorized to charge enrolled beneficiaries a set amount.

TABLE 7.3   Premiums for Medicare Part B—2008

You Pay	If Your Yearly Income Is	
	Single	**Married Couple**
$96.40	$82,000 or less	$164,000 or less
$122.20	$82,001–$102,000	$164,001–$204,000
$160.90	$102,001–$153,000	$204,001–$306,000
$199.70	$153,001–$205,000	$306,001–$410,000
$238.40	Above $205,000	Above $410,000

You Pay	If You Are Married but You File a Separate Tax Return from Your Spouse and Your Yearly Income Is
$96.40	Under $82,000 or less
$199.70	$82,001–$123,000
$238.40	Above $123,000

Source: U.S. Department of Health and Human Services, Medicare, Official U.S. Government Site for People with Medicare, Medicare premiums and coinsurance rates for 2008, November 9, 2007, http://questions.medicare.gov/cgi-bin/medicare.cfg/php/enduser/std_adp.php?pfaqid=1979.

In the case of Part D, which went into effect in 2006, beneficiaries must enroll in private insurance plans that are approved by Medicare. In 2007, a beneficiary paid a monthly premium that varied by plan, but estimated to average $22 a month.[31] In addition, the beneficiary was responsible for an annual deductible of $265. Medicare paid 75 percent of the costs from $2,400.00 to $5,451.25. If prescription drug costs for the year for a beneficiary exceeded $5,451.25, then Medicare paid approximately 75 percent of the additional cost. Individuals with low resource levels (assets for an individual less than $15,315, not including a home, or $20,535 for a married couple) may be eligible for assistance in paying premiums.[32]

Unemployment Insurance

The Unemployment Insurance (UI) program assists states and U.S. territories in providing a temporary source of income for workers when earnings are reduced or stopped because of temporary unemployment. It is a federal enabling program providing grant funding to states for administration of their unemployment compensation laws. The federal government sets broad guidelines for the unemployment insurance program, with states determining eligibility and benefit levels. Roughly 97 percent of all wage and salaried workers in the United States are in covered jobs. The program is financed through a tax on employers. Tax contributions are paid into a trust fund in the U.S. Treasury and credited to each state. The tax rate is determined by several factors including an employer experience rating based on employees who have qualified for unemployment benefits in the past and the fiscal health of a state's trust fund.

The future solvency of the UI program has not garnered as much concern as in the preceding case for OASI and Medicare. UI has changed only marginally through the years in terms of benefit expansion and benefit levels. However, the experience with UI has been that the trust funds for each state are very dependent on each state's economic circumstances. In good times (low unemployment) tax contributions lead to surplus funds, and conversely, high times of unemployment lead to exhaustion of trust fund monies. The federal government provides a very important safeguard in funding adequacy through an emergency fund, which is triggered by economic crises. The federal government also can step in with the Extended Benefit (EB) program when national unemployment reaches a certain level.

UI is designed to target people who lose their jobs through no fault of their own, as distinguished from people who are unemployed for other reasons. As a rule, UI does not provide benefits to unemployed workers who are new entrants or reentrants into the labor market, persons who have been discharged for misconduct, or those who quit their jobs voluntarily. In each case, however, their employer has paid unemployment insurance tax on their wages. Each state is responsible for financing its unemployment insurance plan, which consists of the Federal Unemployment Tax and an *experience rating* system. It is with the experience rating that variations in funding occur. An employer with an experience of high unemployment claims generally pays a higher tax rate until the employer can build up a reserve balance. In some states employers are allowed to reduce their experience rating by making additional contributions into the fund. There has been a gradual decline in unemployment insurance protection due to a decrease in manufacturing jobs and an increase in service sector jobs. *Compared to manufacturing industries, service industries have a disproportionately large number of part-time, intermittent, and temporary jobs that pay low wages. These jobs often provide insufficient earnings and employment to qualify workers for unemployment insurance.* Also, service workers are less likely to have the protections unions provide in assisting unemployed persons who become unemployed.[33]

Workers' Compensation

Workers' compensation is not a national social insurance program. Rather, it represents states' and U.S. territories' laws requiring employers to insure themselves against work-related accidents and illness. No state is required to have a workers' compensation program, and there are no federal minimum standards required of them. These laws ensure that employees who are injured or disabled on the job and their dependents are provided with fixed monetary awards in order to reduce the need for litigation. Benefits are also provided for dependents of workers who are killed as a result of a work-related accident or illness. Most states limit worker's ability to sue employers in the case of work injuries. The historic "trade-off" is that workers give up the right to sue for a disability benefit. Laws establish protection for employers by limiting the amount an injured employee can recover from an employer. Some laws also eliminate the liability of coworkers in most accidents. In addition to states' laws, there is a Federal Employment Compensation Act for federal employees, the Federal Employment Liability Act for employees of railroads engaged in interstate commerce, the Merchant Marine Act for seamen, the Longshore and Harbor Workers' Compensation Act for specified employees of private maritime employers, and the Black Lung Benefits Act for miners suffering from "black lung" (pneumoconiosis).

Workers' compensation laws in all states (except Texas) require compulsory insurance coverage, though many states do permit certain waivers. In most states employers may insure through private insurance carriers. State funds have been set up in approximately half the states, with the option for employers to purchase the insurance competitively through the state fund or from a private carrier. Employers in North Dakota, Wyoming, Puerto Rico, and the Virgin Islands must insure exclusively through a state fund. Several other states give the option of the state fund or self-insurance. Self-insurance by individual employers or a group of employers is allowed in a majority of states.

Adequacy, Equity, and Efficiency for Funding through Social Insurance.
Collectively, the nation's social insurance programs have established a safety net for countless individuals and families in our society when personal resources are inadequate to maintain basic standards for quality of living. As we have seen, however, there continue to be issues of adequacy, equity, and efficiency, all of which present serious challenges for policy makers. Particularly vexing is the issue of adequate future funding for OASDI and Medicare as these programs mature and societal demographics

change. Many Western industrial countries have comparable or better systems for retirement, more adequate provisions for injured workers, and surely much better systems for health care because they are universal and pay attention to health issues. Scandinavia, Germany, and Canada are examples. Proposals for infusing U.S. governmental programs with elements of privatization require careful study by the policy analyst. Readers should remember that none of the programs described so far actually require tax dollars for benefits even though participation is legally mandated. The social insurances only hold and distribute employer–employee contributions withheld from wages. From this point we will discuss social programs that require state and/or federal tax dollars to fund benefits.

Public/Government Funding

The U.S. social welfare system relies heavily on the public sector to fund the bulk of social policy and programming, particularly the large-scale public assistance programs. The funding methods are several, but primary among them is taxation at the various levels of government. Other public funding sources are fees and licenses, child support payments, fines, royalties, earned interest trust fund securities, and other miscellaneous revenue sources. Our focus in this chapter is on taxation as a funding source; we will want to briefly review where tax money comes from and its influence on different segments of the population, where it goes, and the methods used to appropriate funds for social programs or reimburse providers' benefits/services.

A listing of all social programs that receive funding raised by general taxation would be unwieldy to present, but the following are major examples of these programs and services:

- Temporary Assistance for Needy Families (TANF)
- Supplemental Security Income (SSI)
- Medicaid
- Children's Health Insurance
- Women, Infants and Children (WIC)
- Community Mental Health
- Social Services under the Social Services Block Grant (Title XX)
- Child Welfare
- Disability Services
- Aging Services

The collection of tax money is undertaken at all levels of government, and although folks grumble about paying taxes, it is probably the most widely accepted approach to raising funds for public use. However, there are some inherent social policy issues at the very heart of taxing practice. We address some of the key issues surrounding taxation before discussion of specific taxes used to finance social policy and programming. First, we look at the attributes of tax systems and taxation practice.

TABLE 7.4   Types of Tax Systems with Examples

Tax System	Tax Effects	Examples
Regressive	Takes a larger proportion of income from low-income people than from high-income people	Old Age, Survivors and Disability (OASDI) Social Security employment tax
Flat	Fixed tax rate, but takes a larger proportion of income from low-income people	Medicare Health Insurance (HI) employment tax State and local sales tax
Progressive	Takes a larger proportion of income from high-income people than from low-income people	Graduated federal income tax Most state income tax Federal estate tax Most state estate tax

"A tax is a tax is a tax," and everyone directly or indirectly pays. In that regard, we all carry part of the load. However, there are some major inequities in tax systems that affect the proportion of the burden carried by different individuals. In this regard, taxes are considered to be regressive, flat, or progressive. These three types of tax systems, along with examples, are identified in Table 7.4.

By definition, a regressive tax system taxes persons who have lower earnings at higher rates as in the example of Social Security employment tax. This can be confusing because the tax rate for Social Security tax is the same for all persons regardless of wage level. What makes it regressive is an earnings cap (discussed earlier) over which high-income wage earners pay no further Social Security wage tax. Another issue can be seen in regard to a flat tax system. Some say a flat tax is neutral (neither regressive nor progressive) as in the example of a sales tax. However, a flat sales tax has the effect of a regressive tax for poor people because a much greater proportion of their income is used to purchase the basic necessities—for example, groceries for home consumption, fuel to heat a home, and basic personal supplies. As such, this flat tax has the effect of being regressive since at any tax rate (say, 5 percent) it will require more of a poor person's resources needed for survival than in the case of a well-to-do person. Individual income tax systems are more progressive when the tax kicks in only for persons with incomes over the poverty level, and the rate of tax to be paid is graduated (increases) as income increases.

Other attributes add to the complexity and fairness of tax systems—tax credits, tax deductions, and tax shelters. Tax credits, as in the example of food purchases, child care, or earned income credit, serve as an offset in the amount of tax owed. Such credits can be very favorable to low-wage earners. Deductions are expenses, which defray the amount of income subject to income tax. Examples of tax deductions are health care expenses over a specified standard amount in the tax code and interest on mortgage payments for individuals and couples purchasing a home. Tax shelters come in the form of moving income into certain retirement accounts, pretax health expense accounts, educational saving accounts, and so on. Examples of the latter tend to favor middle-income and high-income persons and families.

Federal Government Taxes

The federal government levies taxes and charges fees in a number of areas. Federal taxes include individual income tax, corporation income tax, excise taxes, income tax of estates and trusts, and employment taxes (for Social Security and Medicare). Among the fees charged by the federal government, we note in particular the monthly charge for Medicare beneficiaries receiving medical care insurance. The federal individual income tax is the greatest producer for federal general revenue used to finance federally funded social welfare programs.

Most people who work for a wage are required to file an Internal Revenue Service (IRS) Form 1040 by April 15 of each year.[34] The IRS, a program division within the U.S. Treasury, collects the tax. This money is considered general revenue to pay for government expenditures appropriated by Congress in interaction with the administrative branch of the federal government. The federal individual income tax system raises over half the revenue collected by the federal government each year. It is an enormous amount of money—in the early years of the twenty-first century the amount has exceeded $1 trillion annually.[35]

Although the federal individual income tax system is progressive, and generally considered the most efficient way to raise revenue in this county, it is not without its problems. One of the problems relates to the federal alternative minimum tax (AMT).[36] The AMT was established in 1969 as a strategy aimed at millionaires, but relatively few paid the tax. The AMT is a complicated tax that imposes an additional tax on top of the basic income tax. The two income taxes have different deductions, exemptions, and tax rates, but unlike the basic income tax the AMT is not indexed for inflation. In 2006, 4.2 million Americans paid about $25 billion in AMT. In 2007, the number of taxpayers required to pay the AMT was expected to jump to 23 million with projections for 2012 at 38 million taxpayers.[37] Most of the additional taxpayers paying AMT make middle-class salaries, with 74 percent of those earning between $75,000 and $100,000 (and with two children) required to pay the AMT by 2010.[38] The unpopularity of this tax can be seen in the following:

> At first glance, the AMT may seem simple and fair. But for reasons nobody imagined when it was created, the AMT bulls-eye hangs not on folks with Cayman Islands bank accounts, but the upper-middle income families with lots of kids who happen to live in high-tax states. And it doesn't just raise their taxes. It plagues them with mind-numbing complexity.[39]

In December 2007 Congress acted to postpone for one year an expansion of the tax, but it will take further action to resolve this controversial issue.[40] Another problem is the "tax gap"—taxes owed but not reported or paid. Cheaters do it deliberately by underreporting income. And it is believed that most people who cheat are middle-income earners, while the largest tax loses involve illegal tax evasion from high-income levels.[41] A growing concern centers on tax evasion through offshore schemes in which individuals move funds into accounts "near" the United States, and hiding money overseas. In addition, there are complicated tax laws associated with the federal personal income tax system and honest mistakes are made that end up reducing the effectiveness of this tax.

State and Local Government Taxes

States and U.S. territories utilize three major types of taxes to raise revenues: (1) consumption or sales tax, (2) individual income tax, and (3) corporate income tax. Sales tax is the largest generator of state tax revenue and includes a general sales tax or selective sales taxes on products such as gasoline, utilities, insurance, tobacco products, and alcoholic beverages. Most states also utilize an individual income tax—though nine states do not have a broad-based personal income tax. Corporate income is usually apportioned among states according to how much sales, payroll, and property the corporation has in each state. Corporate income tax is complicated, and the tax burden is controversial. This tax tends to be largely borne by customers in the form of higher prices, by workers in the form of lower wages, and by property owners.[42] As a result, it can be difficult to conclude whether a state corporate tax is regressive or progressive (tax burden carried by corporate owners).

The largest generator of state tax revenue is sales tax. As we noted in Table 7.4, the state sales tax has a regressive effect since lower income people spend a greater proportion of their income tax paying for basic necessities, and hence pay a greater proportion of their income on the associated sales tax. States can choose to offset the effect of regressive sales taxes through various low-income tax relief approaches.[43] One popular approach is to exclude, reduce, or offset the tax as applied to food for home consumption. Another example is providing a refundable credit for low-income individuals, usually by offering the credit as part of the state individual income tax system. Yet another way to provide tax relief for the poor is through a credit for low-income working families with children. This approach is a supplement to the federal earned income credit, also done in conjunction with a state's individual income tax system. In some states sales tax relief is targeted to a special group or groups—senior citizen low-income renters, for example.

An advantage of state individual income tax, from a social policy perspective, is the progressive nature of a state tax in taking a larger proportion of income from the affluent than from the poor. Although some states tax very low-income individuals, personal exemptions, standard deductions, and low-income credits can fully exempt some taxpayers with low incomes. Another approach to shield the poor from the impact of taxes (particularly at times of tax increases) is to set an income below which low-income individuals and families are exempt from paying the tax.

Local governments utilize a variety of taxes, with consumption or sales tax and property tax as the major types. The greatest proportion of revenue for local governments is from taxes on property. Property taxes include taxation on homes, rental property, business property, farms, and ranches. Taxes on homes and rental property tend to be regressive because the ratio of home value to income and also of rental payments to income tends to decline as income rises. To the extent that business property owners do not pass on tax burdens to customers, they may be progressive. One way that states (and localities) use to provide low-income tax relief is through a tax relief approach called a *circuitbreaker*. A circuitbreaker involves a credit based on a household's residential property tax payments and its income—the greater a family's property tax and the lower its income, the higher the credit benefit. As in the use of low-income credits discussed earlier, the circuitbreaker may be a refundable income tax credit, or it may be administered separately from the income tax system. In most states where the circuitbreaker is applied, renters are also eligible—with percentage of rent treated as a property tax payment.

Adequacy, Equity, and Efficiency for Public/Government Funding through Taxation. "It is generally recognized that no tax plan can at once be perfectly fair, utterly simple, and economically neutral."[44] We have seen that regressive tax systems often provide the funding for social programming, particularly at the state and local levels. In that regard the taxes are harmful to the very people who receive the help. However, we also identified a number of ways that a tax system can provide tax relief for low-income individuals and families affected by regressive taxes. In the case of some tax systems, the policy analyst will note that a regressive tax may lead ultimately to positive income redistribution. As we noted earlier, Old Age, Survivors and Disability Insurance (OASDI-Social Security) is a case in point. OASDI payroll taxes are regressive in that earned income is taxed up to a maximum ($102,000 in 2008). However, on retirement, the Social Security program is structured to pay out benefits in greater proportion to low and moderate wage earners than to higher-wage employees. Given the extraordinary, unprecedented wealth and productivity of this country, the funding of the U.S. social welfare system is clearly inadequate. By almost any measure the U.S. welfare system provisions leave many of its poorest citizens with inadequate housing and health care and other deprivations. There is no doubt that many Western industrial countries do considerably better. The primary question readers should ask about "adequacy" is: why can't we do better?

Finally, there is the issue of complexity. Some taxes, sales taxes in particular, are generally simple for the taxpayer to understand and pay. Their collection does, however, require merchants to keep accurate records of accounting and the task of giving taxes collected over to governmental revenue agents. Then there is the problem for state and local governments that lose out on sales tax for individuals' purchases via the Internet and mail-order from out-of-state merchants. When tax relief is available for low-income individuals and families, it usually requires initiative on the part of the taxpayer to take advantage of the offer. And that implies an understanding of the tax break and in some cases an application for such relief. Tax codes for federal and state income tax systems are subject to continuous efforts at reform. Even though major efforts have been made to simplify the federal internal revenue tax code over the past twenty or so years, it still represents a high degree of complexity, and a large proportion of taxpayers rely on a service to fill out their annual tax forms for federal and state individual income taxes. As noted earlier, there is also the problem of taxpayers purposefully cheating the various tax systems.

Federal Government Appropriations and Reimbursements

It was not until 1913 that the federal individual income tax as we know it today came into being as an amendment to the Constitution of the United States. Prior to that time, the federal government had no power to collect such a national tax.[45]

Furthermore, the federal government was not really a player of any consequence in the nation's social welfare system, and for that matter, did not have revenues of a magnitude to assist states in their modest social welfare efforts. All of that changed during the twentieth century. As we reviewed earlier, the federal government is capable of raising huge sums of money through taxes, and also the federal role in returning revenues to the states (and directly to citizens) is substantial. The role of the federal government in making grants available to states from general federal revenues remained modest until the New Deal of President Franklin D. Roosevelt—beginning during the Depression years of the 1930s.

Several different arrangements are used in making federally collected general revenue money available for social policy and programs. In some cases, the federal government pays directly for social policy and program benefits and costs—SSI and food stamps are examples. In most cases, however, the federal government provides funding through various grants made to the states and U.S. territories. First, we will describe examples of direct federal payments, and then we will examine the federal grant-in-aid approach to states.

The Supplemental Security Income (SSI) program is administered by state governmental agencies. Funding for SSI comes from congressional appropriation of federal general revenue funds. States may, and most do, add their own funds to augment the SSI program; however, the basic program is one we consider an example of direct federal funding. Another such program is the Women, Infants and Children (WIC) program, administered by state and local governmental units. As in the case of SSI, WIC funding comes from federal general revenue. Additional programs, which receive direct federal funding, are the food and nutrition programs: food stamp program, school lunch and breakfast programs. Finally, we cite federal correctional programs, military human services, Veterans Administration programs, and the Indian Health Service as additional examples of direct federal government funding from general revenue. There are more that will be familiar to the practitioner/analyst.

Although the federal government uses a wide variety of granting approaches, we examine the two types of federal grants that are widely utilized for social programs involving a federal match of funds to state dollars for ongoing benefits and services. Table 7.5 identifies the two federal grant types (*categorical* and *block*) along with examples of social programs that are funded by each type of grant.

Categorical Grants.   The amount of state match for each of the larger public assistance categorical grants is determined by a formula, as noted in Table 7.5. The formula takes into account the social conditions of a state. As a result, each state's federal match can be somewhat different from the match in other states. However, for most social programs the major share of funding is the federal match (often over 70 percent). Medicaid provides a good example. The federal match for Medicaid services is a variable formula, which is adjusted annually. The federal matching rate is inversely related to a state's per capita income, with a range for the federal match from 50 to 83 percent. Federal matching for the U.S. territories is set at 50 percent with a maximum dollar amount limiting the funds each territory can receive. The federal match for program services continues for each dollar the state spends but with some limits built

TABLE 7.5   Federal Grants-in-Aid to States: Categorical and Block Grants

Categorical grant	1. Uses a formula to determine federal financial match of state dollars (typically based on):
	  • Population
	  • Per capita income
	  • Population at risk
	
	2. State plan designates a single state agency to receive the federal funding and administer the program or supervise local government administration
	
	3. Strict definition of program category, entitlement, and extensive federal rules and regulations on how the funds are to be spent
	
	4. Amount of federal funding based on reimbursement of entitled benefits or services provided
	
	Examples of social programs involving categorical grants:
	  • Medicaid
	  • State Children's Health Insurance Program (SCHIP)
	  • Women, Infants and Children (WIC)
	  • Child welfare foster care services
	  • Food stamps

Block grant	1. Sets criteria for funding new grants, or uses criteria from past state performance to determine amount of grant to state when block grant replaces categorical grant (typically based on):
	  • Program expenditures for a selected past base year
	  • Numbers of individuals/families who received benefits/services
	
	2. States given flexibility how funds will be parceled out to state agencies or local government administration
	
	3. States required to maintain effort (maintenance of effort, MOE) in comparison with standard of base year
	
	4. States given basic guidelines and flexibility on how the funds are to be spent
	
	5. Amount of federal funding based on funding cap for set time
	
	Examples of social programs involving block grants:
	  • Temporary Assistance for Needy Families (TANF)
	  • Social Services Block Grant (SSBG)—Title XX
	  • Alcohol, drug abuse, and mental health
	  • Maternal and child care
	  • Child care

into the reimbursement policy. For example, spending caps are placed on reimbursement for some hospital expenses, prescription drug charges, and payments to institutions for mental disease and other mental health facilities. In addition to funding for Medicaid services, the federal government provides a 50 percent match to states and territories for administrative costs (except for certain items that are matched at a higher rate).

An ongoing issue in the federal grant-in-aid process of financing state and local governments for social policy and programming, and other areas, is the question of federal control over funds granted. This issue concerns a "balance of power" between states and the federal government. The states form a union and agree to subordinate some of their powers to the federal government in order to further common goals. This relationship, referred to as *federalism*, shifts and changes over time.[46] Categorical grants represent the greatest federal control. These grants specify in detail how the federal funds are to be spent by states and require elaborate accountability to ensure that funds are spent by states in accordance with federal intent.[47] *Categorical grants* were initially used for the public assistance titles of the Social Security Act of 1935 to assist states in funding for aid to children and persons who are blind or disabled. Changes have occurred (and are ongoing) in the use of categorical grants, resulting in changes in federal/state relationships. As we noted earlier, in one case categorical grants for the public assistance titles for this population group were consolidated and federalized into the SSI program in 1974. In recent years, however, momentum is growing to replace categorical grants to states with block grants, a process often referred to as *devolution* of federal power and control for social programs.

Block Grants.   Block grants are fixed-sum federal grants to state and local governments for funding designated social programs. Block grants are authorized for a specified time period (i.e., five or ten years). As noted in Table 7.5, the federal government sets broad guidelines for states in how social programs are to be operated, giving states and, when applicable, local governments greater flexibility than in the case for categorical grants. However, as with categorical grants, most block grants require states to commit a revenue match.

In addition to federal grants-in-aid to states and U.S. territories, some social programs involve a reimbursement process to participants or benefit/service providers. The prime example is the Medicare program. The federal government appoints organizations engaged in the health insurance field (mainly insurance companies such as Blue Cross and Blue Shield) to act as contractors in administering Medicare. Contractors use federal guidelines to determine approved charges and make payments, directly or by way of reimbursement, to participants and suppliers of services.

Although the SSI program is not a social insurance program, Congress has made appropriations for funding increases sufficient to cover benefit COLA increases. By contrast, Temporary Assistance for Needy Families (TANF) represents a standstill budget of federal block grant funds to states and U.S. territories. Under the latter circumstances, states and territories will not have an incentive to increase cash income benefits for clients/consumers.

Adequacy, Equity, and Efficiency for Public/Government Funding through Appropriations and Reimbursements.   The net effect of federal tax collections, state demographics, differences in state economies, and the various federal appropriation and reimbursement approaches leads to an equity problem for states. At the macro level, analysts point to a "balance of payments" issue: that is, the amount of federal spending in each state in comparison to federal taxes and fee revenue dollars collected in each state. Although this balance of payments equity issue includes all federal expenditures (not just for social programs as we discussed earlier), appropriations for social programs and social insurance benefits are major inputs influencing the equation. In fiscal year 2005, the District of Columbia was the biggest gainer at $5.55 received for every dollar paid to the federal government. New Mexico followed as a top gainer state with $2.03 in return for every dollar paid in. New Jersey ranked lowest, receiving just 61 cents for every dollar paid in. Other states with a very negative balance were Connecticut, New Hampshire, and Nevada.[48] Although this equity issue may appear somewhat abstract, it is well worth watching by the policy analyst in terms of how the federal balance of payments can influence decisions of policy makers about social programs. Next, we examine how the federal funding approach to Medicare achieves its goal to increase equity among the states.

A primary goal in establishing Medicaid's statutory formula, whereby states with lower per capita incomes receive higher rates of federal reimbursement for program costs, was to narrow differences among states in their ability to fund Medicaid services. But it does not succeed very well because it moves twenty-one states further from the average, widening the average difference. Two factors constrain the formula. First, per capita income is not a comprehensive indicator of a state's total available resources and is a poor measure of the size of and cost to serve a state's people in poverty. Second, the statutory provision that guarantees no state will receive less than a 50 percent matching rate advantages many states that already have above-average resources to fund health care for their populations in poverty. If the U.S. Government Accountability Office (GAO) used an alternative to per capita income that more directly measures states' resources, number of people in poverty, and cost of providing services to this population—the formula would have reduced differences satisfactorily.[49]

Unfunded Policies

Not all social policies result in social programs per se. That doesn't mean there are no financial issues involved, but rather a different approach than we have discussed previously may be required to ferret out financing issues. The policy analyst will be concerned with how costs involving such policies are allocated, who pays, and what the costs are. Consider, for example, the social policy of "minimum wage." There is obviously a cost involved in minimum wage and, hence, a financing issue. However, unlike the cost of providing TANF clients/consumers with vocational training and/or child care, minimum wage is a cost to employers. Another example is the Family Medical Leave Act. This social policy requires covered employers to provide eligible employees with up to twelve workweeks per year of job-protected leave to care for the employee's newborn child (or adopted or foster care child); to care for the employee's spouse, child, or parent who has a serious health condition; or because of the employee's own serious health condition. There are costs to employers and coworkers who donate work hours, but no funding is required to operate a social program. Additional examples in the category of "other" are the Child Care Credit and Earned Income Tax Credit (EITC). In the case of both these social policy provisions the costs are borne primarily by the governmental units (federal and state) in lost tax revenue and most likely by additional costs to consumers for the products made by employees who use Family Medical Leave.

Finally, there is the issue of unfunded mandates. Legislators have been prone to pass legislation that compels both public and private organizations to implement policies at their own expense, or the costs are to be incurred by consumers or others. We have presented some examples throughout this text. Unfunded mandates can be legislated at all levels of government. As states have been required to take on a greater role in funding social programs, sensitivities to unfunded federal mandates have heightened. In 1995, Congress passed the Unfunded Mandate Reform Act, which helped diminish new unfunded mandates on state and local governments. However, as Congress adds rules and regulations to reauthorization of block grants (including new set-asides and cost ceilings), some have the effect of unfunded mandates to states.

Devolution

American social welfare programs have *evolved* as a collaborative effort of federal, state, and local government. As discussed earlier in this chapter, these government entities participate in funding, regulating, and providing benefits and services. A key time period in the evolution of American social welfare occurred during the Great Depression of the 1930s. The federal government, under President Roosevelt's "New Deal" administration, took a bold new leadership role for planning, funding, and setting guidelines to regulate public social welfare programs. Prior to that time, public assistance had been the sole domain of state and local governments (along with the private sector). In addition to the social insurance programs that were established in 1935, a central feature defining American federalism (federal–state relationship) was the use of federal categorical grants of money to states to fund their public assistance programs.

For the first time in U.S. history the 1935 Social Security Act established categorical grants for public assistance programs for children and persons who are elderly or blind to be operated by the states and territories. It provided federal funding for them as well as federal statutes and regulations governing how they should be run. State and local governments had to match federal dollars at some levels so that a funding stream was established and based, in part, on the number of recipients that were served. Whereas categorical grants tend to be open-ended, in some cases Congress has set a cap on the amount of federal funding that is available for a particular social program. Through the years additional social welfare measures supported by federal funding for medical care, disability services, aging services, and so on have been added to the mix and financial incentives have been offered to states for program expansion. The *evolution* of an emerging American *welfare state* appears to have peaked during the economic growth periods of the 1960s and 1970s, and thereafter came under increasing attack from conservative politicians and others who argued that the country had gone too far in creating a dependence on the federal government for social welfare. Ronald Reagan, elected president in 1980, became a champion for the movement to reduce federal spending and responsibility for public social welfare by devolving costs onto states. During the past quarter-century the allocation of specific responsibilities among governmental levels for social welfare programs has shifted in significant ways toward the states, and the trend suggests the *devolution*[50] of the welfare state.[51]

A principal ingredient of devolution (along with privatization and charitable choice) has been a shift in the approach to federal funding for public assistance programs. The shift is away from categorical grants to block grants for state-operated programs. Recall that categorical grants create an ongoing federal funding stream that increases as eligible recipients increase. On the other hand, block grants are fixed-sum federal grants (with time-limited authorization) to state and local governments for funding designated social programs. *Proponents* view block grants as a way to eliminate some of the inconsistencies among programs serving similar populations and as a way to empower states and provide them with far more flexibility.[52] Other arguments that have been advanced in favor of block grants are that they encourage state and local governments to experiment, hence, become more effective in providing benefits and services; they are less complex in terms of federal rules and regulations; and they serve to control federal spending. *Opponents* are concerned that the block grant mechanism will provide an indirect means of reducing federal spending for key social programs.[53]

Finegold, Wherry, and Schardin trace the history of block grants back to the 1960s, when President Johnson and a Democratic Congress enacted the Partnership for Health program and the Safe Streets Act program. Three subsequent surges in the use of block grants were each associated with Republican control. In 1971, President Nixon proposed consolidating 129 different programs into six block grants, but a Democratic Congress rejected Nixon's original consolidation proposal. However, by the end of President Ford's administration Congress had created new major block grants—including the Community Development Block Grant (CDBG) and the Comprehensive Employment and Training Act (CETA) program. During President Reagan's administration seventy-seven catagorical grants were consolidated into nine block grants. Then in 1996, the Republican-controlled Congress approved the block grant for Temporary Assistance for Needy Families (TANF), included in the Personal Responsibility and Work Opportunity Reconciliation Act of 1996 (PRWORA).[54]

PRWORA is regarded as a landmark in the devolution movement. The act was signed into law by President Clinton, following his veto of other block grant proposals and earlier versions of the "welfare reform" bill. A major feature of PRWORA was elimination of the categorical grant for Aid to Families with Dependent Children (AFDC) and replacement with the TANF block grant. PRWORA also promoted privatization by setting flexible provisions for states to contract out major administrative functions and purchase of services for TANF and several other social programs. In addition, the act supported "charitable choice," encouraging states to contract with faith-based service providers for purchase of services.

According to Finegold et al., the lessons researchers have learned from the experience of block grant development over the past forty years can be summarized as follows:

- Funding gradually declines—initial funding for block grants has not been consistently higher or lower than funding for the programs they replaced, but the "real value" of block grant funding tends to diminish over time.

- Creeping categorization reduces flexibility—over time Congress erodes the flexibility of block grants by adding restrictions, requiring that a share of funds be set aside for particular purposes, or creating new categorical programs with the same or related objectives.
- Administrative efficiency and cost savings are most evident when state administrative capacities already existed at the time of block grant implementation.[55]

A particularly serious issue regarding adequacy and equity involves the more recent (1900s and 2000s) conversions to block grants. Over the years, judicial decisions gave sharper focus to the concept of *entitlement* to public assistance. The public assistance programs (e.g., AFDC, Medicaid, Food Stamp) created individual rights to benefits. "Litigation over these rights to benefits has resulted in court orders to provide benefits to whole categories of individuals denied assistance."[56] Recent block grants, TANF in particular, do not create these same rights. In fact, language in PRWORA makes clear that "no individual entitlement" to TANF assistance is granted for any state program funded under Section 103.

Policy analysts and policy advocates predicted future widespread shifting to block grants in the years following passage of PRWORA. Congress has debated extending devolution through the block grant approach to other major social welfare programs, particularly the Food Stamp Program, Medicaid, and child welfare. In addition to TANF, a number of other social welfare programs are funded through block grants (i.e., the child care program and the State Children's Health Insurance Program (SCHIP) block grant funded from inception). Although the block grant approach continues to be a popular idea to devolve the federal role in social welfare funding, the extent to which it has led to devolution has been more limited than many had predicted. "Not only were efforts to block-grant the full range of programs unsuccessful, where block-granting did occur, it was not the halfway house" to full divestiture of federal accountability and financing responsibility that some had envisioned.[57] And, the largest public assistance fiscal burden to federal and state government, Medicaid, remains a categorical grant funded program.

The Privatization Revolution

The privatization[58] revolution in social welfare is occurring at all levels of government, but it is particularly apparent at the state level. William D. Eggers, an advocate for privatization, notes that state fiscal crises combined with the growing revolt against new taxes is forcing state policy makers to search for ways to cut costs in delivering state services. "Governors and state legislatures are seeking innovative approaches to fundamentally restructure, downsize, and 'rightsize' state government in order to avoid continuing budget problems."[59] In one form or another, privatization has been applied in virtually all areas of social welfare programming. For social programs, *contracting* is the most prevalent of the several techniques for privatization attributed to Eggers in Chapter 6. Governmental programs contract out with private-sector contractors for program administrative/management functions or purchase of service.

Privatization Applications and Issues

The discussion that follows is a brief review of the application and issues created by privatization in four selected social program areas: (1) TANF case management, (2) child support enforcement, (3) the food stamp program, and (4) child welfare.

Privatization and TANF Case Management.   Case management can include TANF eligibility, intake and diversion activities, benefit determination, the development of the individual responsibility plan, assessment of the need for services, case monitoring and tracking, and sanctions for noncompliance with TANF requirements.[60] Following passage of PRWORA in 1996, the emphasis in public welfare changed from providing cash assistance to preparing welfare consumers for work, and placing them in jobs. States were given much more autonomy through their block grants than they had received previously under AFDC categorical grants. Of particular significance, unlike AFDC, TANF *no longer prohibited states from using personnel from private organizations* to perform eligibility determination for cash assistance. Many states and localities have taken advantage of this flexibility by changing not only the services they offer, but also the type of organization that delivers these TANF services. According to a GAO survey in 2001, about 13 percent of all federal and state maintenance-of-effort dollars for TANF administration and services were spent on contracts with the private sector.[61] The percentage has surely increased since that report was made.

In 2003, Mathematica Policy Research reported the results of its research on privatized TANF case management covering six states and a tribal agency. It used a case study research approach in what is likely the most in-depth study of privatization since TANF was inaugurated. The study sites followed one of two models of privatization: (1) sites that privatized all TANF case management and processing functions, including eligibility determination; and (2) other sites that privatized only employment-related case management functions. The various contractors included national for-profits (MAXIMUS and Affiliated Computer Services); affiliates of national nonprofits (examples—Catholic Charities Diocese, Lutheran Social Services, and Salvation Army); and local and regional nonprofits (including faith-based and secular organizations). This study provides a rich documentation on how privatization is working out in the various study sites. McConnell, Burwick, Perez-Johnson, and Winston list seven key lessons that emerged from their case studies:

- Agencies must prepare to address the challenges of privatization.
- The procurement process must be fair and transparent.
- Contract design affects the level of competition.
- Performance measures should be targeted, yet comprehensive enough to avoid unintended consequences.
- It is possible to design contracts that include performance incentives but limit risk to contractors.
- Public agencies must dedicate resources to monitor the work of contractors effectively.
- Public and private agencies must find ways to coordinate services.

McConnell and colleagues conclude:

> These lessons offer important guidance to public agencies facing the challenges of privatization. However, many significant questions remain for future research to address, including whether TANF recipients receive more effective services from private organizations than from public agencies, whether some types of private organizations provide better services than others, and given the new responsibilities it places on public agencies, whether privatization saves taxpayers money. Answers to these questions will allow public agencies to make informed decisions about the future direction of welfare privatization.[62]

It is clear that TANF, the most recognized welfare program, is undergoing significant changes as a result of the privatization revolution. How that will affect service delivery and program funding are significant issues to follow in future policy analysis.

Privatization and Child Support Enforcement (CSE).   CSE, a relative newcomer to the social programs under the Social Security Act, was established in 1975 through Title IV-D of the act. It includes the following service components:

- Locating noncustodial parents
- Establishing paternity
- Establishing support orders
- Collecting support payments
- Providing services for noncustodial parents

All states and territories operate a CSE program. Several Indian tribes also have a CSE program. State CSE programs are financed by a categorical grant system with three major funding streams. The largest funding stream is a federal reimbursement of 66 percent for allowable child support activities; another is a 90 percent match for laboratory costs in determining paternity; and the third is child support collections, split between the state and federal government. In addition, an incentive system provides additional funds for good performance.[63]

State CSE programs rely on state-of-the art technology to carry out many of their service functions, and this has proven attractive to private data management and processing concerns. PRWORA strengthened CSE programs by providing additional tools to enhance the collection of child support. One important example is the federal requirement that state governments establish automated registries of child support orders and a directory of new employees for quickly tracking and locating parents owing support. In addition, states are turning to private firms because of difficulties in servicing growing caseloads with available staff and budgetary constraints. The federal government has prepared a planning guide that is useful for states considering privatization and could be perceived as an encouragement to do so.[64]

States most commonly contract with the private sector for the collection of past-due support, especially those considered hard-to-collect. Under the terms of most collection contracts, states pay contractors only if collections are made, and payments to contractors are often a fixed percentage of collections. Privatizing collections has enabled states to collect support they would have been unable to collect without hiring additional staff. In fiscal years 1994 and 1995, contractors in nine states collected nearly $60 million and were paid about $6 million.[65]

A report by the GAO found that by 1995, a total of twenty states had privatized one or more child support services statewide and eighteen states had privatized services at the local office level. The study also identified twenty-one contracts for full-service child support operations, forty other contracts for collections and related location services, eight contracts for location only, and nine contracts for payment processing services. Most of these services were contracted out to four major contractors.[66] The extent of contracting is considerably expanded if one considers the hundreds of contracts with private-sector providers for services not covered by the GAO study.

Observed results for privatized CSE services in comparison to preprivatized services are sketchy. In 1997, a GAO study concluded that state and local governments have experienced mixed results in their efforts to reduce costs and improve services through privatization.[67] A small-scale GAO study the next year concluded that fully privatized offices performed at least as well as or better than public CSE programs in locating noncustodial parents, establishing paternity and support orders, and collecting support owed.

> The relative cost-effectiveness [68] of the privatized versus public offices, however, differed among the comparisons we made. Specifically, Virginia's and Arizona's privatized offices were more cost-effective—60 percent and 18 percent, respectively—than their public counterparts. However, in Tennessee, one public office was 52 percent more cost-effective than the privatized office we reviewed, while the remaining privatized office in Tennessee was about as cost-effective as its public counterpart.[69]

Privatization and the Food Stamp Program (FSP).   The FSP helps low-income people buy the food they need for good health. Benefits are provided to eligible consumers on an electronic card that is used like an ATM card and accepted at most grocery stores. Early versions of a federal food stamp program date back to 1939. The modern FSP began with pilot programs in the 1960s. The Food Stamp Act (1964 and 1977) authorizes federal funding through the U.S. Department of Agriculture and administered by state and local governmental offices, with administrative costs shared between the federal and state governments. U.S. territories and Indian tribes are also involved in administering the program. Privatized functions within the FSP have existed for many years in the areas such as developing computer software, operating electronic benefit transfer systems, and training. However, the Food Stamp Act *requires that state civil servants make all the decisions about eligibility* for clients/consumers to receive benefits.

Texas and Florida have each requested waivers to privatize substantial parts of the eligibility determination process. In 1997, the Texas waiver was denied. In 2004, Texas proposed to close more than half its local offices, largely replacing them with kiosks and call centers that would determine eligibility based on materials received over the telephone and Internet.[70] In 2002, Florida received permission to use private contractors for eligibility determination in six counties, with the Senate Appropriations Committee directing that no additional waivers be granted until efforts of privatizing food stamp eligibility determination in Florida be evaluated.[71] In opposition to organized labor and Democratic leaders, Indiana's governor signed a deal to privatize administration of the state's food stamp program to a consortium led by IBM.[72] When the U.S. House of Representatives Committee on Agriculture convened in July 2007 to consider the 2007 farm bill, an amendment was submitted to allow states greater flexibility to contract out administrative operations to private entities. The amendment was defeated, jeopardizing existing state practices and disallowing states' incremental efforts to privatize the eligibility process.[73]

Privatization and Child Welfare.   Although there is ongoing debate regarding privatization of social services in general, in child welfare state and local governments have paid private, voluntary agencies to provide child welfare services since the early 1800s.[74] The extent to which privatization occurs today in child welfare is reflected in a report by the U.S. Department of Health and Human Services (DHHS). Based on a survey of local child welfare agencies, it is reported that 58 percent of all family preservation services, 42 percent of all residential treatment, and 52 percent of case management services for adoption are being contracted out.[75] Assessments of privatization in this field have turned up some very mixed results.

An extensive review of the literature on privatization efforts in child welfare, published by the University of Kentucky, focused on quantitative studies comparing newly privatized services with public services with respect to outcomes for children.[76] Only five empirical studies of such comparisons were found, accompanied by many technical problems that made conclusions hazardous to generalize. However, some privatized programs had better outcomes for children, some had worse, and one showed no differences at all. The research problems were many beginning with the fact that there is no single model of privatization, so program efforts differed considerably and midstream program changes sometimes made conclusions difficult. The study observes that the expected cost savings from privatization were not borne out by experience.[77] In McDonald and Berry's study of a major child welfare reform effort in Kansas, they found a significant improvement in adoption placement and one year later when the privatization managed care system was put in place those gains continued.[78]

Privatization in child welfare appears to have worked best when the public contracting agency is well prepared and capable of entering into contracting relationships using sound management principles. Up-front planning, use of pilot projects, and phased implementation have characterized child welfare privatization initiatives in most jurisdictions. Thus, most have been able to avoid some of the serious problems that occurred in Kansas and other places involving widespread privitization. However, privatizing to solve a public agency's systemic issues or simply for ideological reasons appears only to compound problems. And underfunding services will not likely achieve high standards for adequacy, equity, or efficiency/effectiveness no matter whether services are provided by direct public agency delivery or purchase of service contractors. Conclusions reached in an extensive assessment of six jurisdictions with privatized child welfare services are as follows:

> There has been some success in matching good candidates (private agencies) with the programs being designated by public agencies, and creative thinking has been clearly brought to many of the processes. On the other hand, many other aspects of these efforts proved inadequate. The financial methodologies frequently were unworkable, if not disastrous. Monitoring and evaluation posed significant difficulties, both for private agencies that were expected to comprehensively monitor and report on program achievement, and for public agencies that were attempting to undertake new quality assurance roles. Finally, outcomes and performance measures proved to be a major hurdle for most of the programs.[79]

Other Privatization Concerns

Some other concerns can be raised about privatization. Policy issues arise regarding the appropriate use of proprietary (for-profit) organizations for social programming, performance-based contracting, and privatization of the social insurance programs.

Proprietary Contractors. The use of large for-profit corporations as contractors in contracting out some or all of a public program's administration raises some serious concerns. One example, among many, of a large for-profit contractor involves the federal government's contract with MAXIMUS, Inc., to provide administrative oversight for implementation of the Ticket to Work program. MAXIMUS has been a major player in contracted projects for state government, particularly in the areas of work resources, child support enforcement, child welfare, and children's services. Another example involves federal contracts with large firms like Booze Allen-Hamilton to provide technical assistance to Head Start programs. These contracts replace a system of multiyear grant awards to experienced technical assistance and training organizations, many of which are private nonprofit organizations with years of experience and expertise in early child education and human services. The track records of the new contractors are not primarily in fields directly related to Head Start. Other examples of large-scale private for-profit corporations that have bid for a piece of the action in managing privatized welfare programs include such companies as IBM, Lockheed Information Management Services, Anderson Consulting, and Unisys. Common concerns have been recognized in the use of corporate contractors, including the established precedent for corporations to bail out of projects they ultimately find to be unprofitable, monopolistic pricing once they gain a large share of the market, cost-cutting measures such as closing offices and eliminating jobs of public employees, and efforts to control salaries through lobbying against public sector unions.[80] It is questionable whether maximizing corporate profits will prove compatible with the interests of those in need.[81]

The entrance of proprietary contractors in social welfare is seen by Sanger as changing the environment profoundly. She believes they are welcomed for the cost savings and efficiencies they promise, but their substantial and growing presence is a cause for trepidation. She notes that in the 1990s the revenues of for-profits tripled, growing to nearly 40 percent of those of nonprofits.[82] The for-profit contracts are concentrated in the welfare-to-work area. For aggressive firms one for-profit CEO projects a $12 to $15 billion market for welfare service contracts.[83] Her qualitative study of four of the largest for-profit service providers concludes that the retreat of government providers may create several profound problems in the future. First, the rapid increase in nonprofit programs has created a "brain-drain" in the public services as important numbers of the most competent public services staff are drawn to the nonprofits by substantially better salaries and freedom of operation.[84] Sanger believes this creates a deep hole in the capacity of the public sector to offer future services should the for-profits ever begin to retreat under the pressure of reduced profits. Second, there may be plenty of reason to think they might, as welfare caseloads consist of more and more clients with severe barriers to employment.[85] Third, the issue of accountability for nonprofits continues to be a matter of concern: "the incentives of performance-based contracts may also induce . . . providers to reduce needed but more costly services, quicker rather than better and more lasting (job) placements (beyond the bonus period) and preferences for clients who are easier to place rather than those with multiple barriers (and thus in need of more costly interventions)."[86] Privatization critics Kahn and Minnich are even more skeptical. They believe that the profit-making culture of corporations is in sharp contrast to the public good culture. Using these corporations for social programming threatens not only the social welfare system, but even more seriously, "democratic commitments to the public good."[87] It is hard to tell whether these are overreaching concerns, but the influence of this sector on the achievement of adequacy, equity, and efficiency in funding bears careful watching.

Performance-Based Contracting.   Another feature of privatization we note here is the use of performance-based contracting rewards. With performance-based contracts, contractors are offered an incentive of greater revenues for achieving program objectives at or above certain levels and in some cases penalized when performance is below set levels. Focusing on performance changes the relationship between the government agency and the contracting agency because the reputations of both are at stake for achievement of specified results. For both parties, there is motivation for success in achieving predetermined social program objectives.

Performance-based contracting is not without some problems. Behn and Kant list a number of them. Performance contracting:

- May inhibit experimentation
- May encourage innovation in cost cutting but not in service delivery
- May stifle overachievement
- May not provide for start-up costs
- May inhibit symbiotic relationships
- May reward promises, not performance
- Must rely on outputs, not outcomes
- Uses measures that can distort behavior

- May encourage creaming (selecting clients/consumers most likely to succeed)
- May undermine equity and fairness.[88]

Another problem is the difficulty in always being able to specify some numerical criterion by which good and bad performance can be distinguished. The potential conflict over how the enduring profit motive in performance-based contracts creates incentives to shave services in ways that, although not mentioned in the contract, may degrade them. Clearly, successful performance-based contracting requires partners from both government funding agencies and contract providers who are sophisticated in pricing, administrative controls, and close monitoring.[89]

Privatization involving performance-based contracting has gone *hand in hand* with the principle of managed care in areas where applicable—particularly health-related (including mental health) and other services where discrete units of service can be specified. As discussed earlier in this chapter, managed care is a common methodology in health insurance plans. The basic features of managed care are aimed at cost containment to control inefficiencies in the consumption, allocation, or production of services that contribute to higher than necessary costs. Managed care methodologies applied to social services include the following. Reimbursement for services is based on a case rate rather than on a fee for service. Using a *case rate*, a flat fee is paid for a client's/consumer's treatment or service based on his or her diagnosis or presenting problem. A specified period of time is set for units of treatment or service. The service provider accepts financial risk, though that may be offset somewhat when the provider is given flexibility in how it meets the client's/consumer's need. *Capitation* is a term used to indicate a specified amount paid periodically to the provider for a group of specified services, regardless of quantity rendered. With capitation, a reimbursement system involves paying providers a fixed amount to service a client/consumer over a given period. Providers are not reimbursed for services that exceed the allotted amount. A *community rating* feature may be applied when there are variations for average costs of providing services to all clients/consumers in a geographical area or by class—on the basis of such factors as age, at-risk need, permanency of presenting problem, and so on. Managed care methodologies can create major problems when cost data are not available at the outset and on a real-time basis. Managed care has been criticized generally because of a tendency in the use of cost containment to withhold needed services or provide incomplete services because of time limits specified in rates set for reimbursement. An interesting application of managed care coupled with performance-based contracting for permanency planning is to reward service providers for their promptness in moving children out of temporary foster care to a permanent placement.

In contrast to our privatized way of doing things (i.e., private health insurance—private employer-based insurance—and various transmogrifications of managed care) a single-payer health care system offers greater promise for adequacy, equity, and efficiency. *Single payer* refers to a federal system of health care in which the federal government assumes payments for health care. It's not perfect, but it appears to be more adequate and much more equitable. We seem to be going toward a medical system where there are two tracks: one for the wealthy who can pay for expensive insurance and the other who use emergency rooms because few hospitals will risk turning away uninsured persons. By any account other than from the insurance industry and big pharmaceutical companies, our current system is overly costly, certainly has not reduced medical costs, and has clearly not resulted in any improvement in comparison with other industrialized nations on longevity, infant death rates, maternity care, and so forth. Among industrialized nations the United States ranks at or near the bottom. And the profits of hospital corporations and Big Pharma (large pharmaceutical and biotech companies) have been on an upward swing over the years with nothing to show except a big chunk of working-class and lower-income folks going uninsured, big CEO salaries, and increased stock prices among health care providers and Big Pharma. The U.S. health care system is the most expensive in the world. However, a study of cross-national surveys of adults' health experiences in Australia, Canada, Germany, New Zealand, Great Britain, and the United States revealed that the U.S. health care system ranks lower than several other countries in patients' perspectives in several different variables of performance. The United States ranked 1 (first) out of 6 on effectiveness, and 3 on timeliness, but it ranked 6 (last) on patient safety, patient-centeredness efficiency, and equity.[90]

Privatizing Social Insurance Programs.   Medicare is already heavily privatized. It was designed that way in the beginning. As discussed earlier in this chapter, private insurance carriers play a role in processing Medicare claims, and private sector hospitals and health care providers are reimbursed by the government for their care and services. Medicare Part C, Medicare Advantage, involves contracts between Medicare and a variety of different managed care and fee-for-service entities. Many beneficiaries who have chosen this program over Parts A and B have received satisfactory services. However, as reported in the *New York Times*, unscrupulous methods used by private insurance companies to persuade Medicare consumers to sign up for the private plans are causing great concern. And, the fastest-growing type of Medicare Advantage plan generally does not coordinate care, nor save money for Medicare. The chief actuary for Medicare indicated that the additional payments to Medicare Advantage plans (above and beyond the costs of traditional Medicare) are causing higher premiums for all beneficiaries and speeding depletion of the Health Insurance trust fund.[91]

Medicare Part D involves an extensive system of private insurance companies offering beneficiaries prescription drug plans approved by the government. This new feature of the Medicare program has resulted in lowering drug expenses for those who need large quantities of prescription drugs, a catastrophic cost feature, and economic benefits for persons who are low income or disabled. However, there are no restraints on drug companies over costly products and excess profits, or provisions to allow government negotiation on prescription drug costs. Proponents of this privatized system argue that market competition among providers is resulting in lower Part D premiums and will do so in the future.[92] Opponents cite statistics showing that consumer costs are rising because Congress has specifically forbidden Medicare to negotiate the prices of the huge amount of prescription drugs directly with pharmaceutical manufacturers. Pharmaceutical manufacturers spent large amounts of time and effort to secure this congressional provision.[93] This will be an important area for the practical public policy analyst to follow in regard to the success of a government program with major elements of privatized administration and benefits.

The proposals for Social Security (OASI) reform are many. At a time when there was a federal government budget surplus, a number of proposals were put forth that would apply part of the surplus to Social Security measures, including such a proposal from the Clinton administration. A common theme in the majority of proposals is to change from the current pay-as-you-go (PAYGO) system to one with investment-based personal retirement accounts. Some proposals promote a change from the current system to a pure investment-based system, whereas others include a mixture of PAYGO and investment-based accounts. The idea of privatizing Social Security through stock market investments lost some momentum following the downward cycle of the market after 2000; however, President Bush unsuccessfully pushed for Social Security privatization as a major feature of his domestic policy at a time of a record budget deficit in 2005/2006. It is worth noting that Chile, a modern thriving economy, privatized its social security system in the 1970s. That change was not a success: The cost of running the system has been very high due to fees, commissions, and especially marketing costs, exceeding 10 percent of contributions in the past few years. This has significantly reduced the participants' net rate of return.[94] Any and all serious proposals to change Social Security from its current system should be carefully examined in terms of a comparison on criteria for analysis we have selected for this text—*adequacy, equity,* and *efficiency.* Analysis should include assessments of the direct impact of revenues collected for Social Security, benefits received (or to be received) by individuals and families, and the income-transfer distributional effects.[95] Can workers really effectively manage their own investments if they are to use their OASI contribution accounts for investing in the stock market? As millions of citizens found out, coping with the big swings in both stocks and bonds and mutual funds is a tricky and complicated proposition. Even sophisticated investors are not immune to big mistakes. Although they may have enough money to recoup a loss in retirement income, most workers will not and one mistake can reduce retirement income to a vanishingly small amount. The oldest investment wisdom says that you don't bet the farm, and OASI is the city fella's or gal's equivalent.

Much of what we have discussed in this section is in the formative stages of development. It can be a challenging area for policy analysis, often requiring specialized methodology beyond what can be expected for application by the practical policy analyst. However, readers of this text are most likely to be on the front lines where the impact of policy developments can most keenly be observed. The practical policy analyst can make an invaluable contribution in documenting the effects on clients/consumers and making this information known to advocacy groups and other change agents working toward just treatment for those affected by privatized social policies and programs.

Summary

This chapter presented a detailed overview of the methods utilized to finance social welfare policies and programs. Both private and public funding sources were described within the framework of three guiding questions:

1. Where does the funding come from?
2. What is the amount of funding?
3. What approaches are used to fund programs?

Criteria were applied to assist the practical public policy analyst in evaluating the equity, adequacy, and efficiency of funding through the public sector, employee benefits, social insurance, and taxation and public/government funding through appropriations and reimbursements to social welfare programs. The chapter closed with discussion concerning privatization and problems that have been observed with the privatization movement in social welfare. We observed that although private funding is very important in programming the U.S. welfare system, it does not, in itself, meet the requirements for adequacy. Equity is not a particular objective of private funding, and it does not lead to an equitable society. A strong case can be made that private funding does lead to efficiency and effectiveness, but that usually happens when there is a collaborative relationship with the public sector. Employee benefits have played an important function in creating needed social safeguards for working individuals and their families. However, a trend reveals that these safeguards are disappearing for the middle class and nonexistent for the working poor. Whereas some employed individuals have adequate health care and retirement benefits, many do not. Adequacy, equity, and efficiency are all problematic when analysis is applied to these benefits. The social insurance programs offer the greatest hope for adequacy, equity, and efficiency. As we have seen, however, they are increasingly in jeopardy when it comes to adequate funding for the future. Some hold that privatization will answer any funding needs for the future, but results so far indicate troubled waters when it comes to providing an adequate safety net for all U.S. Citizens.

EXERCISES

1. Select a nonprofit human service agency in your community. What are the funding sources for that agency? Does the agency conduct fund-raising drives and, if so, what are they?

2. Identify two or more foundations in your community or state that fund human service programs. What guidelines do they use to fund human services?

3. What are the differences between defined-benefit and defined-contribution retirement savings plans?

4. What is the sales tax rate in your state and in your community? Are groceries taxed? Are there any tax breaks for low-income individuals and families?

5. How does funding of social insurance programs differ from grant-funded programs?

6. What are the major differences between federal categorical grants and block grants?

7. Has your state (or U.S. territory) experienced an economic slowdown? What is being done to preserve budgets for human service programs?

8. Identify a privatized social service in your community. What systems of accountability are in place to monitor the services?

NOTES

1. *Giving USA—2007* (New York: Giving USA Foundation), p.1.

2. Giving USA Foundation, 2007, www.givingusa.org/gusa/resources.cfm.

3. P. Flynn and O. Benali, *Catholic Charities USA 1996 Annual Survey* (Alexandria, VA: Catholic Charities USA, 1997).

4. R. L. Edwards and E. A. S. Benefield, *Building a Strong Foundation: Fundraising for Nonprofits* (Washington, DC: NASW Press, 1997), p. 8.

5. V. A. Hodgkinson, M. S. Weitzman, S. M. Noga, and H. A. Gorski, *Giving and Volunteering in the United States: Findings From a National Survey* (Washington, DC: Independent Sector, 1992).

6. The Shriners of North America, 2007, www.shrinershq.org/Shrine/.

7. Knights of Columbus, *Knights Set New Record for Charitable Giving*, June 8, 2007, www.kofc.org/un/newsrelases/detail.cfm?id=403832. The number of members of the Knights of Columbus probably includes individuals who are policy holders of their life insurance offering.

8. A. Lauffer, *Grants, Etc.* (Thousand Oaks, CA: Sage, 1997), p. 130.

9. M. M. Feczko (ed.), *The Foundation Directory—1996 Edition* (New York: Foundation Center, 1996).

10. Lauffer, *Grants, Etc.*, p. 155.

11. United Way of America, *About United Way*, 2007, http://national.unitedway.org/about.

12. Ibid.

13. E. Brilliant and D. R. Young, "The Changing Identity of Federated Community Service Organizations," *Administration in Social Work*, 28(3–4) (2004): 28.

14. It is estimated that private spending for social welfare in 1992 equaled about two-thirds of public spending for social welfare. R. Hoefer and I. Colby, "Social Welfare Expenditures: Private," in R. L. Edwards (ed.), *Encyclopedia of Social Work*, 19th ed., 1997 supplement (Washington, DC: NASW Press, 1997), p. 274.

15. J. Diamant, "Of the Private Donations, Half Went to the Red Cross," *Charity Navigator*, August 29, 2006, www.charitynavigator.org/index.cfm?bay=content.view&cpid=486.

16. Council for Advancement and Support of Education, The Charity Aid, Recovery and Empowerment ("CARE") Act of 2003, 2003, http://case.org/govtrelations/taxpolicy/givingsummary.cfm.

17. S. Strom, "New Equation for Charities: More Money, Less Oversight," *New York Times*, November 17, 2003, p. E1.

18. Stephanie Strom, "How Long Should Gifts Just Grow," *New York Times*, November 12, 2007, p. A1.

19. C. E. Steuerle, *Blurring the Line Between Charities and Businesses*, Urban Institute, October 9, 2007, p. 2, www.urban.org/url.cfm?ID=901119.

20. S. Strom, "In Shriner Spending, a Blurry Line of Giving," *New York Times*, March 19, 2007, www.nytimes.com/2007/03/19/us/19shrine.html?_r=1&th=&oref=slogin&emc=th&.

21. B. Stamler, "The Gray Area for Nonprofits, Where Legal Is Questionable," *New York Times*, November 17, 2003, p. E1.

22. Pension Benefit Guaranty Corporation, *2006 Annual Report, 2007*, www.pbgc.gov/docs/2006_annual_report.pdf.

23. Pension Benefit Guaranty Corporation, *Communications and Public Affairs Department, Fact Sheet, 2007*, www.pbgc.gov/media/key-resources-for-the-press/content/page13540.html.

24. U.S. Department of Labor, Bureau of Labor Statistics, "Union Members in 2006," *News*, January 25, 2007.

25. HealthyBenefits.com, *Why Is There Movement Toward Consumer Driven Health Care?* 2003, www.healthybenefits.com/MOVE.HTM.

26. Ibid.

27. Pension Benefit Guaranty Corporation, *2006 Annual Report*.

28. The Board of Trustees, Federal Old-Age and Survivors Insurance and Disability Insurance Trust Funds, *The 2007 Annual Report of the Board of Trustees of the Federal Old-Age and Survivors Insurance and Disability Trust Funds* (Washington, DC: U.S. Government Printing Office, 2007).

29. H. Aaron, *Economic Effects of Social Security* (Washington, DC: Brookings Institution, 1982), pp. 12–16, 67–73.

30. *2007 Annual Report of the Boards of Trustees of the Federal Hospital Insurance and Federal Supplementary Medical Trust Funds*, p. 31, www.cms.hhs.gov/reporttrustfunds/downloads/tr2007.pdf.

31. U.S. Department of Health and Human Services, *Projected Medicare Part D Costs Drop By 30 Percent Monday* (press release), January 8, 2006, www.hhs.gov/news/press/2007pres/20070108.html.

32. Centers for Medicare and Medicaid Services, *U.S. Department of Health and Human Services Medicare Eligibility Tool*, January 22, 2007, www.medicare.gov/MedicareEligibility/home. asp?dest=NAV|Home|GeneralEnrollment|PremiumCostInfo#TabTop.

33. M. Nichols and I. Shapiro, *Unemployment Insurance Protection in 1994* (Washington, DC: Center on Budget and Policy Priorities, 1995).

34. Filing the 1040 in 2007 was not required for single persons earning less than $8,750 or for married couples filing jointly earning less than $17,500. U.S. Department of the Treasury, Internal Revenue Service, 1040EZ, Instructions 2007, www.irs.gov/pub/irs-pdf/i1040ez.pdf.

35. U.S. Department of the Treasury, Internal Revenue Service, Table 1—*Summary of Internal Revenue Collections, by Type of Tax, Fiscal Years 2001 and 2002*, 2003, www.irs.gov/index.html.

36. For a discussion on how the AMT is computed see L. E. Burman, "The Alternative Minimum Tax—Assault on the Middle Class," *Milken Institute Review*, Fourth Quarter, 2007, www.urban.org/UploadedPDF/1001113_Burman_AMT.pdf.

37. C. Edwards, "The Alternative Minimum Tax: Repeal Not Reform," *Tax & Budget Bulletin*, Cato Institute, No. 45, May 2007.

38. Ibid.

39. Burman, "The Alternative Minimum Tax," pp. 12–13.

40. D. Herszenhorn, "Congress Averts Higher Tax Bill for Middle Class," *New York Times*, December 20, 2007, www.nytimes.com/2007/12/20/washington/20cong.html.

41. NOLO, *Fraud and Tax Crimes*, www.nolo.com/lawcenter/ency/article.cfm/objectID/95D63E1.

42. C. McLure, "The State Corporation Income Tax: Lambs in Wolves' Clothing," in H. Aaron and M. Boskin (eds.), *The Economics of Taxation* (Washington, DC: Brookings Institution, 1980), pp. 327–346.

43. N. Johnson, *Which States Tax the Sale of Food for Home Consumption in 2003?*, Center on Budget and Policy Priorities, January 13, 2003, www.cbpp.org/1-13-03sfp.htm.

44. D. Rankin (ed.), "Taxes: Who Should Pay and Why?" *National Issues Forum* (Dayton, OH: Domestic Policy Association, 1985), p. 5.

45. During the Civil War a tax was levied on the incomes of Union citizens.

46. C. Tubbesing, "The State-Federal Tug of War," *State Legislatures*, 25(7) (1999): 52–57.

47. For some categorical grant programs states may receive a waiver from the rigid national requirements when it can be demonstrated that a particular state approach can be cost-effective and not harmful (or an improvement) to serving client/consumers.

48. J. S. Moody, "Federal Tax Burdens and Expenditures by State: Which States Gain Most from Federal Fiscal Operations?" *Special Report* (Washington, DC: Tax Foundation, July 2003, No. 124).

49. U.S. Government Accountability Office, "Medicaid Formula: Differences in Funding Ability Among States Often Are Widened," *GAO Report* (GAO-03-0620), August 11, 2003, www.gao/gov/atextd03620.txt.

50. In the literature the term *devolution* is also referred to as "new federalism," in recognition of the changing relationship between the federal government and the states regarding social policy/programming.

51. R. P. Nathan and T. L. Gais, "Is Devolution Working? Federal and State Roles in Welfare," *The Brookings Review*, 19(3) (2001): 25–29, www.brookings.edu/press/review/summer2001/nathan.htm.

52. I. V. Sawhill, "Block Grants: Past, Present, and Local Perspectives," a Brookings Public Forum, Panel One: Federal, State, and Local Perspectives, Brookings Institution, October 15, 2003, www.brookings.edu/events/2003/1015welfare.aspx?p=1.

53. K. Finegold, L. Wherry, and S. Schardin, "Block Grants: Historical Overview and Lessons Learned," *New Federalism—Issues and Options for States* (Washington, DC: Urban Institute, April 2004) (Series A, No.A-63).

54. Finegold et al., "Block Grants."

55. Finegold et al., "Block Grants."

56. Finegold et al., "Block Grants," p. 2; attributed to R. S. Melnick, *Between the Lines: Interpreting Welfare Rights* (Washington, DC: Brookings Institution, 1994).

57. P. Winston and R. M. Castaneda, *Assessing Federalism: ANF and the Recent Evolution of American Social Policy Federalism*, Urban Institute, May 2007, www.urban.org/publications/411473.html.

58. Evelyn Bandoh makes a distinction between the terms *privatization* and *outsourcing*, with *privatization* referring to the transfer of entire program infrastructure from government to another service provider. She defines *outsourcing* as involving the government competitively contracting with vendors to provide specific services. We prefer to use *privatization* as it is more broadly defined in the literature. We also prefer to use the term *contracting* over *outsourcing*, though we can agree that the two terms can usually be used interchangeably. Evelyn Bandoh, "Outsourcing the Delivery of Human Services," Welfare Information Network, *Issues Notes*, 7(12). (October 2003), www.financeproject. org/Publications/outsourcinghumanservicesIN.htm.

59. W. D. Eggers, *Privatization Opportunities for States*, Policy Study #154, Reason Foundation, January 1993, www.reason.org/ps154.html.

60. P. Winston, A. Burwick, S. McConnell, and R. Roper, *Privatization of Welfare Services: A Review of the Literature*, Mathematica Policy Research, May 2002, www.mathematica-mpr.com/publications/ PDFs/privatization.pdf.

61. U.S. Government Accountability Office, "Welfare Reform: Federal Oversight of State and Local Contracting Can be Strengthened," *GAO Report* (GAO-02-661), June 2002, www.gao.gov/new. items/d02661.pdf.

62. S. McConnell, A. Burwick, I. Perez-Johnson, and P. Winston, *Privatization in Practice: Case Studies of Contracting for TANF Case Management*, Mathematica Policy Research, Final Report, March 2003, www.mathematica-mpr.com/publications/PDFs/privatize.pdf.

63. U.S. Congress, Committee on Ways and Means, *2004 Green Book* (Washington, DC: U.S. Government Printing Office, March 2004), pp. 8-60–8-61.

64. U.S. Department of Health and Human Services, Administration for Children and Families, *A Guide to Developing Public-Private Partnerships in Child Support Enforcement*, www.acf.hhs.gov/ programs/cse/rpt/pvt/contents.htm (accessed October 4, 2007).

65. U.S. Government Accountability Office, "Child Support Enforcement: States' Experience with Private Agencies' Collection of Support Payments," *GAO Report* (GAO/HEHS-97-11), October 1996, p. 2, www.gao.gov/archive/1997/he97011.pdf.

66. U.S. Government Accountability Office, "Child Support Enforcement: States and Localities Move to Privatized Services," *GAO Report* (GAO/HEHS-96-43 FS), November 1995, p. 2, www.gao. gov/archive/1996/he96043f.pdf.

67. U.S. Government Accountability Office, "Child Support Enforcement Privatization: Challenges in Ensuring Accountability for Program Results," *GAO Report* (GAO/T-HEHS-98-22), November 4, 1997, p. 3, www.gao.gov/archive/1998/he98022t.pdf.

68. Cost effectiveness was defined as the ratio of each office's administrative costs to collections, expressed as the cost to collect $1.

69. U.S. Government Accountability Office, "Child Support Enforcement: Early Results on Comparability of Privatized and Public Offices," *GAO Report* (GAO/HEHS-97-4), December 1996, p. 2, www.gao.gov/archive/1997/he97004.pdf.

70. D. A. Super, *Policy Considerations Relating to Privatization in the Food Stamp Program*, Center on Budget and Policy Priorities, October 28, 2004, www.cbpp.org/10-28-04fa.pdf.

71. McConnell et al., *Privatization in Practice*, p. 4.

72. K. Dilanian, "Labor Moves to Bar Welfare Privatization," *USA Today*, October 26, 2007.

73. U.S. House of Representatives, "Ag Committee Republicans Vote to Protect States' Rights," *News from the Agriculture Committee Republicans*, July 20, 2007, http://agriculture.house.gov/republicans/press/110/pr070720.html.

74. M. G. Rosenthal, "Public or Private Children's Services?" *Social Service Review*, 74 (2000): 283.

75. Kansas Action for Children, *Privatization of Child Welfare Services in Kansas: A Child Advocacy Perspective* (Topeka, KS: Author, 1998).

76. Freundlich and Gerstenzang, *Assessment of the Privatization*. Other earlier descriptive studies, sometimes quite local and detailed, are available; for example: Kansas Action for Children, *Privatization of Child Welfare Services in Kansas: A Child Advocacy Perspective* (Topeka, KS: 1998); L. Snell, *Child Welfare Reform and the Role of Privatization*, Policy Study #271, Reason Public Policy Institute, October 2000, www.rppi.org/ps271.html.

77. D. Van Slyke, "The Mythology of Privatization in Contracting for Social Services," *Public Administration Review*, 63(3) (2003): p. 296.

78. T. P. McDonald and M. Berry, "Adoption Trends in Kansas: Managing Outcomes or Managing Care?" *Children and Youth Services Review*, 22(2) (2000): 161–274.

79. M. Freundlich and S. Gerstenzang, *An Assessment of the Privatization of Child Welfare Services: Challenges and Success*, (Washington, DC: CLWA Press, 2003), pp. 293–294.

80. H. J. Karger and D. Stoesz, *American Social Welfare Policy: A Pluralist Approach* (Boston: Allyn & Bacon, 2002), p. 168.

81. N. Bernstein, "Giant Companies Entering Race to Run State Welfare Programs," *New York Times*, September 15, 1996, p. 1.

82. M. B. Sanger, *The Welfare Marketplace: Privatization and Welfare Reform* (Washington, DC: Brookings Institution, 2003), p. 73.

83. Ibid., p. 96.

84. Ibid., pp. 101–104.

85. Ibid., p. 98.

86. Ibid., p. 104.

87. S. Kahn and E. Minnich, *The Fox in the Henhouse: How Privatization Threatens Democracy* (San Francisco: Berrett-Koehler, 2005).

88. K. R. Wedel, "Designing and Implementing Performance Contracting," in R. L. Edwards and J. A. Yankee (eds.), *Skills for Effective Services Management* (Silver Spring, MD: NASW Press, 1991), pp. 335–351.

89. R. Behn and P. Kant, "Strategies for Avoiding the Pitfalls of Performance Contracting," *Public Productivity and Management Review*, 22(4) (June 1999): 474–478.

90. The Commonwealth Fund, *New Cross-National Comparisons of Health Systems: U.S. Ranks Lowest in Patient Surveys, Has Greatest Inequity for Lower-Income Patients*, April 4, 2006, www.commonwealthfund.org/newsroom/newsroom_show.htm.

91. R. Pear, "Methods Used by Insurers Are Questioned," *New York Times*, May 7, 2007, www.nytimes.com/2007/05/07/washington/07medicare.html?pagewanted=print.

92. M. B. McClellan, T. P. Miller, R. B. Helms, et. al., *Medicare Part D and Prescription Drug Prices*, Policy Fact Sheet, American Enterprise Institute for Public Policy Research, January 5, 2007, www.aei.org/publications/pubID.25420.filter.all/pub_detail.asp.

93. Medicare Rights Center, *Truth Is the Best Medicine. Get the Facts on Prescription Drug Costs*, National Legislative Association on Prescription Drug Prices, January 19, 2007, www.medicarerights.org/truthrx_myth2.html.

94. S. Edwards and A. E. Edwards, "Social Security Privatization Reform and Labor Market in Chile," *Economic Development and Cultural Change*, 50 (2002): pp. 465–489.

95. P. A. Diamond (ed.), *Issues in Privatizing Social Security* (Cambridge, MA: MIT Press, 1999); M. Feldstein and J. B. Liebman (eds.), *The Distributional Aspects of Social Security and Social Security Reform* (Chicago: University of Chicago Press, 2002).

8 Analysis of Interactions among Policy Elements

Introduction

Policy elements, like entitlement rules and financing methods, are not singular and isolated; they are almost always interactive. So far, we've looked at policy elements one at a time and now we need to consider how they interact in live situations. They interact in sometimes surprising and unforeseen ways: intended or by accident; complex or simple; to the advantage of some or to the serious disadvantage of others. A convenient way to speak of these interactions is to use the following simple classification of five interaction types:

1. *Coentitlement:* The use of one form of benefit automatically entitles a beneficiary to another.
2. *Disentitlement:* The use of one benefit automatically makes a beneficiary ineligible for another.
3. *Contrary Effects:* The operation of one policy or program feature cancels out the effect of another feature.
4. *Duplication:* An intended or unintended receipt of the same benefit form arises from more than one source for the same purpose.
5. *Government-Level Interaction:* Benefits or services administered or financed at one level of government affect those at another level of government (e.g., federal and state levels).

These classifications are neither mutually exclusive nor exhaustive, but they are believed to account for the main types. A discussion of each, along with a clarifying example, follows.

Coentitlement

In most child welfare programs that offer foster home care services, a child is also eligible to use the sponsoring agencies' resources for medical care or therapy. As a rule, foster care services come as a package even though there might be a separate price, a separate billing, and even a separate staff who administer them. Some social agencies that offer congregate meals for elderly persons (nutritious main meals free or at low cost) also offer transportation services that are free or subsidized. Both are examples of *coentitlement* as an intentional policy. Simultaneous availability of two types of benefits is advantageous in that the benefit is more accessible or used more consistently by more people, or it increases the effectiveness of one benefit because of the simultaneous use of the other. Some coentitled benefit packages are very extensive. (Though it is now less extensive, the TANF program is a good example of that.) Whereas full elaboration cannot be given because, as you may recall, TANF is state administered and state designed and, therefore, varies widely state by state, here is a partial list of the benefit types for which TANF children and their caretakers are most often eligible.

1. The cash benefit based on the number and age of children.
2. Medical care (under Medicaid) is paid in full on presentation of a medical card. Coverage includes prescription drugs, appliances, and immunizations.
3. Child care.
4. Food stamps are benefits for which TANF families are automatically entitled in most states (because the income and asset rules for TANF are so much more stringent than for food stamps).
5. WIC benefits (Women, Infants and Children nutrition program), which supply extra food stamps for food believed especially appropriate for children under age three and for pregnant women. The intention is to ensure proper nutrition for families at the poverty level.
6. Vocational training. Note that all mothers of children over age five must either enroll or register for employment with the state employment service.
7. Supportive services through the Social Services Block Grant (Title XX) provided by vendor payments to personal counselors for fragile families, special education, or health services.
8. Family planning services: advice, medical care, birth-control appliances, or birth-control drugs by prescription. Abortion is included in many states.

Excepting the cash benefit, these benefits are given sometimes by administrative rules and regulations and sometimes at the administrative or professional discretion of the operating agency. Although coentitlement is automatic from a policy perspective, clients/consumers are not always informed of such coentitlement; to obtain the benefit or service, they sometimes must ask for it. One way practitioners can serve their clients/consumers is to have current and accurate information about these kinds of coentitlements. Other examples of coentitlement abound simply because most social problems require a number of services simultaneously. Most child abuse programs maintain temporary shelter care facilities, and most shelters for battered women maintain counseling and medical services. Traditionally, workers' compensation has not just a single goal but a whole set: income replacement, medical care, workplace safety, and rehabilitation. It must, therefore, have a diverse set of coentitlements: cash benefits, medical payments, rehabilitation counseling, prosthetics (e.g., artificial limbs and braces). A set of multiple goals will almost always imply the presence of coentitlements. Attention should also be called to instances in which entitlement to multiple benefits is unintentional. That type of interaction will be referred to here as a "duplication" discussed later.

Disentitlement

When legislators, program designers, or administrators wish to avoid the added expense of one person receiving duplicate benefits for the same social problem, they will install an entitlement rule that specifically rules out receipt of one benefit while simultaneously receiving another. A disentitlement policy that probably affects more people than any other is the one Congress installed in the DI program. Any person receiving Social Security Disability benefits must report whether he or she also receives workers' compensation; if so, then the dollar amount of the workers' compensation benefit must be deducted from the disability benefit. Many workers totally disabled in a work-related accident are also covered under DI. Although it may seem unfair to disentitle a worker from a part of the DI benefits on the basis that the injury was work related and the person receives workers' compensation, a reasonable case can be made for it under the present circumstances of both systems. First, workers do not pay for the full cost of Social Security Disability benefits, and they pay nothing at all for workers' compensation insurance. Second, the Social Security system is in good shape now but may be under some strain after 2042 due to demographic changes of more retirees with less workforce. (With a good economic recovery, Social Security trust funds might be *well off* by that year!) Third, Social Security DI benefits are not extravagant but they are generally more adequate than workers' compensation *and* they continue beyond the eight- to ten-year limitation on workers' compensation. Those facts suggest that there is a case for prohibiting two such simultaneous payments.

A different disentitlement is embedded in most workers' compensation legislation. As mentioned, benefits are restricted to eight or ten years. The intent of workers' compensation laws is to compensate workers for workplace injuries, thus placing the cost burden for that injury on industry, which is expected to pass it on to the consumer by incorporating the cost into the price of products or services. But, if workers' compensation benefits cease in eight to ten years and the worker continues to be disabled, he or she will almost certainly apply for and receive Social Security Disability benefits. Consequently, the Social Security system is certain to be saddled with a cost the industry and its consumers should pay—an effect that no doubt contradicts the basic historical rationale behind workers' compensation legislation.

Another classic instance of interaction among policy elements, in this case, between an entitlement rule and a program goal, is called the *relatives-responsibility* rule. It requires parents and children to exhaust their own resources on behalf of each other before any one could be eligible for public assistance benefits. This historical example (no longer in effect but still discussed as a possible solution to some problems) was nearly universal in the United States up to the mid-1950s. Relatives-responsibility policies, whatever merit they may have had, led to all kinds of mischief, chief among which was that they often disentitled those the program was most directly intended to benefit. Requirements were so strict in many places that unless both parents and their adult children could pass a means test for public assistance, no family member was eligible. Some elderly parents simply went without, knowing that an application for assistance would be denied because their children were marginally able to give them money, but then their children and their grandchildren would be seriously deprived.

The relationship between parents and adult children can become painfully complicated when one is newly dependent on the other for regular financial support. These and other reasons complicate a relatives-responsibility policy. Much of the problem with relatives-responsibility policies vis-à-vis eligibility stems from the rise of the nuclear rather than the extended family as the paramount economic and social unit in modern Western industrial society. The relatives-responsibility policy arose in the context of multigenerational households that had few elderly members. Such a norm made functional sense in the context of a more rural and agrarian economy.

Contrary Effects

Contrary effects produce both a negative and positive condition in which the effectiveness of at least one benefit characteristic is canceled out or seriously diminished. Recall that the ideal social welfare service-delivery system is characterized by integration, continuity, accessibility, and accountability. This section will consider two kinds of contrary effects. One is concerned with the unforeseen problem that an improvement in one of these ideal characteristics is likely to decrease performance in another ideal characteristic. Think about what happens when an administrator increases organizational integration. As discussed in Chapter 6, the common way to do that is to centralize authority over various program operations, for example, placing a single person in charge of many separate services to young mothers (health, family planning, nutrition) so that all clients are told about all services, and services are scheduled with attention to the need for simultaneous benefits. With one person "running the show," problems would be more easily resolved. Yet, however appealing such integration might be, it can create other problems; from the preceding example, integration redistributes (centralizes) authority by adding another layer of administration, which can mean a reduction in organizational accountability to consumers. That is, when (not if) the organization makes a mistake, there is one more layer of decision making through which the aggrieved consumer must pass before ultimately reaching a decision maker who might be the only person who can right the wrong. Note that the problem is made serious only if an organization fails to take accountability seriously. The point is that an organizational change like centralization always creates other problems, but those problems are serious or disabling only if the organization is unaware of the paradoxical nature of the enterprise it is tinkering with.

Is it possible for the opposite problem to occur—*for an increase in accountability to decrease accessibility?* Yes. Imagine the reaction of organizational employees to increased public criticism or a recent scandal. The most human reaction, most would agree, is to move more slowly, move with greater certainty, and reduce the occasion for taking risks in decision making and in the conduct of ordinary organizational affairs. That certainly slows the work of the organization and on that account decreases accessibility of benefits and services to those who need them.

A second contrary effect is an increase in the tendency toward organizational "paper trails," that is, copying all decisions made and referring constantly to written policy so that in the event of a demand to account for actions and decisions, the "evidence" of history and policy consistency is ready at hand. Does that mean that public criticism of organizations is unjustified? Not at all. Increased organizational attention to policy clarity and consistency generally has a positive effect for clients/consumers. Do paper trails always signify bad outcomes? Again, no. Paper trails can protect an ethical professional who is legitimately opposing organizational leaders on behalf of needful clients/consumers.

At one time the view of Congress was that the entitlement rule restricting payments to licensed nursing homes was designed to ensure high-quality medical care for the aged; but in some unknown number of instances, it was producing poor care in miserable institutional or nursing home surroundings even though some relatives would have provided home care if they could have afforded to give up working so they could stay home and care for their elderly loved ones. The Medicaid waiver program has expanded greatly. States had to show that each person who uses it would have occupied a nursing-home bed were it not for care received by relatives at home. The rub was that some states used the program so much that they ran into another policy feature that prohibited its expansion, a contrary effect. States were allotted Medicaid waiver money on the basis of a proportion of existing nursing-home beds. Some states used it to the maximum, but because they have (wisely) discouraged the provision of new nursing-home beds, the further use of the waiver program became impossible. This "contrary effect" was removed when Congress (sensibly) removed the limits on states' use of Medicaid funds for services that kept elderly individuals at home, conditional only on states showing that such services were less costly than the nursing-home alternative.[1]

Other examples of the interaction of eligibility rules and goals come easily to mind. Deinstitutionalization of persons with mental illness is just such an example. When mental institutions were first experimenting with it, there was often an open-door policy so that the facilities of the hospital were always available. It served many patients well. But many believed that other patients became so comfortable with the sheltering arms of the hospital that it created an institutional dependence resulting in surprisingly high hospital admission rates alongside dramatic reductions in total hospital censuses. It was a type of (unexpected) contrary effect. And, of course, another contrary effect was that it took away the motivation of a community to provide general hospital care for its own mentally ill citizens.

One of the recent controversies about the Social Security system centered on the need to resolve an instance of a contrary effect. In this case it concerned the payment of a minimum benefit for the Old Age and Survivors Insurance (OASI) program. The original Social Security Act conceived of the minimum benefit as a temporary measure to provide benefits to retirees, but through no fault of their own, they had not yet worked long enough to build up an adequate benefit.[2] Currently, the majority of those receiving minimum benefits are not the workers for whom it was intended but for those who have *always* worked for very low wages, albeit over their entire lifetime. The original framers of the Social Security Act intended to cover those working full time in the primary workforce. This minimum benefit has placed Social Security in the position of making up for the low-wage features of the U.S. labor markets. The reason it became a problem is that the Social Security trust fund is now a bit pressed to meet its regular obligations—continuing the minimum benefit coverage creates even more obligations not paid for by contributions. This adds a fiscal threat to the trust fund and that is the contrary effect we are illustrating here: one policy (good thing in itself) creating substantial problems for another policy element—the trust funds financing method. The contrary effect was resolved in some measure by Congress in 1983 when it prohibited further *new* minimum benefit approvals.

Duplication

The next interactive effect we will consider is duplication, specifically the *unintended* duplicate receipt of social welfare benefits or services as described in the earlier discussion on coentitlement. Coentitlement is in fact a form of duplication, but it is distinguished by the fact that it is intentional. At one time a widely publicized instance of duplication was what the popular press has called *double dipping*, the simultaneous receipt of Social Security retirement benefits *and* federal civil service or armed service retirement benefits. That particular duplication was clearly unintended by Congress in the construction of any of the three federal retirement systems. Few, if any, anticipated early retirements from the civil or armed services such that a person could work for the next ten years and, thus, become entitled to Social Security retirement benefits. The result, of course, is a windfall for armed forces and civil service retirees and one with which the financing methods were not prepared to cope. In the mid-1980s Congress folded most federal retirement benefit systems into the Social Security system, as a general policy solution to the problem.

Notice that the most immediate reason why unintended duplication occurred in the preceding example is that the entitlement rules overlap in ways that were not anticipated. Such duplication occurs not only among programs that deliver material benefits, but also actually are more frequent among programs that deliver social services. One of the most striking studies of social services delivery in the 1960s was reported as what was generally known as the "St. Paul Study." Among its many findings was that 10 percent of the midwestern metropolitan area study population received 95 percent of the social services. Of relevance here are the conclusions about the extensive duplication of services, even within this relatively small proportion of the population. Not only were the services strongly concentrated, they were unintentionally double-dosed. That situation was not unique to the 1960s. A brief glance at the usual organization of services in most metropolitan areas today would produce striking examples.

How many "counselors" does a child have who is adjudicated by almost any local juvenile court? Here is a catalog of bad examples of services that are duplicative, uncoordinated, unnecessarily expensive, and possibly destructive for the child involved. First, there is the juvenile officer who nearly without exception is officially charged with advising and supervising the child. Then there is very likely to be the school counselor who also has official responsibility for counseling activities, albeit in relation to the child's life at school. Note, however, the few school counselors who would tell you that they only counsel about school problems. It is entirely likely that the same child will have a counselor at a local mental health clinic, and if the child's family receives welfare benefits (TANF perhaps), there will be a social worker from the welfare department who has counseling duties. Nor is this necessarily the end of the list. Think of the family minister and the group leader of the local Boy Scouts or Girl Scouts who may (rightly enough) feel called on to serve this child in a counseling function.

Summary

Chapter 8 presented several important types of intended and unintended interactions between policies of closely related but separately administered policies and programs. The practical analyst should be alert to the presence of the consequences of at least four types of policy interactions:

1. Coentitlement
2. Disentitlement
3. Contrary effects
4. Unintentional duplication

Interactions between operating characteristics of social policy and programs can only be evaluated against their contribution or their detraction from the ability of the program or policy to contribute to the solution of the social problem of concern. In contrast to other operating characteristics, note that there is no inherently negative policy interaction; interactions are "good" or "bad" only insofar as they prevent some other operating characteristic from reaching its own ideal state.

NOTES

1. H. Reester, R. Missmar, and A. Tumlinson, *Recent Growth in Medicaid Home and Community-Based Service Waivers*, Kaiser Commission on Medicaid and the Uninsured, Henry J. Kaiser Family Foundation, April 2004, www.avalerehealth.net/research/docs/medicaid_hcbs.pdf.
2. E. Burns, *The American Social Security System* (Boston: Houghton Mifflin, 1949), p. 95.

PART THREE

Analysis of Social Policies and Social Programs Using Basic Concepts and Evaluation Criteria: An Example

Introduction

This final section of the book demonstrates how the concepts discussed in Parts One and Two can be used in analyzing social policies and social programs. Note that they can also be used to design a new social policy or program. That will not be done here because, for most social workers or human service practitioners, the main problem is to understand the imperfect, day-to-day world of existing policies and programs. Included in the example will be some suggestions for policy or program (or legislative) changes that are implied by the analysis. Adventurous practical analysts may want to try their hand at designing a social policy or new program. The most utopian impulse sometimes generates the best new programs. To demonstrate that this method has widespread usefulness, the example in this chapter will deal with the social problem of child abuse and programs and policies that are familiar to social work and human service practitioners.

We will begin with a serious study of the social problem viewpoints important in shaping the enabling legislation and program designs.

9 An Example of Social Policy and Social Program Analysis

Selected Features of Federal Child Welfare Legislation since 1970 Concerned with Child Abuse

The Social Problem Context

The first step in a social policy analysis is to analyze the underlying social problem, here the physical abuse of children. We will use various sources: government documents, reports of research, professional journals, and discussions of the policy implications of the legislation found in the journals and sometimes the quality media that have a reputation for reliability (e.g., *New York Times*). Documentary sources such as legislative hearings and Senate and House Committee reports will give us a view of what Congress had in mind about the social problem of child abuse—definitions, causal explanations, and the like. Major legislation might include the Child Abuse Prevention and Treatment Act (CAPTA) of 1974 (P.L. 93-247), as amended in 1988, 1996, and 2001; Promoting Safe and Stable Families Amendments of 2001; the Keeping Children and Families Safe Act of 2003 (P.L. 108-36), and, finally, the Indian Child Welfare Act (ICWA) of 1978 (P.L. 95-608). Summaries and reviews of the legislation, the legislative history, as well as committee reports and hearings that preceded it can be found most easily at various Web sites, but one of the best is www.thomas.loc.gov. Commentaries on the legislation can be found on "think tank" Web sites such as the following:

- Center on Budget and Policy Priorities (www.cbpp.org)
- Center for Law and Social Policy (www.clasp.org)
- Children's Defense Fund (www.childrensdefense.org)
- Child Welfare Information Gateway (www.childwelfare.gov)

- National Indian Child Welfare Association (www.nicwa.org)
- Congressional Research Reports for the People (www.opencrs.cdt.org)

A second source for information and analysis of social problem issues are the human service, social work, and academic journals. They will contain data on the problem as well as causal explanations, but note that they will have their own ideological perspective. A computer search of relevant databases such as LexisNexis, JSTOR, Criminal Justice Abstracts, Public Documents Masterfile, GenderWatch, PolicyFile, Academic OneFile, Proquest Research Library, Medline, PsycINFO, and Social Work Abstracts is helpful because it often gives you electronic access to citations and the complete text of an article. Of course, you can always do an old-fashioned review of annual journal indexes that will locate relevant titles of articles and research reports. Examples of journals of particular use for our immediate purposes are *American Journal of Orthopsychiatry, Child Abuse and Neglect; Child Welfare; Children and Youth Services Review; Child Maltreatment; Social Service Review; Social Work; Social Work Research and Abstracts; Journal of Social Service Research; Journal of Social Policy;* and *Policy Studies Review.* Readers should never overlook British, Canadian, and Australian professional journals because they often contain useful and important research and intervention program reports.

It is useful to check reliable, reputable national newspapers and periodicals on a topic because careful investigative journalism can be a good source of social problem data and policy history and status: for example, the *Washington Post;* the *New York Times;* the *Wall Street Journal,* some British newspapers, notably the *London Times* and the *Manchester Guardian,* and periodicals such as the *New York Review of Books,* and *Atlantic.* Don't assume that the British and European press have inadequate coverage of U.S. issues. Some of the best policy and program commentary and empirical research have been done not by universities but by prestigious research institutes, prominent examples of which are the Brookings Institution, the Urban Institute, the Center for the Study of Democratic Institutions (Princeton University), and the Institute for Research on Poverty at the University of Wisconsin. The institutes just listed are ideologically liberal. Conservative examples are the American Enterprise Institute and the Rand Institute. Readers and students should be aware of the temptation to read only abstracts or summaries of research findings because that can lead to serious trouble. Abstracts and summaries of research findings often give only the most positive perspective on the findings and seldom will alert the reader to serious shortcomings. Each study must be carefully examined for features that make its conclusions suspect, questionable, or downright wrong (e.g., bad sampling, poor measurements, or invalid statistical conclusions). An advance look at their research can be found in their publications, whose titles can be obtained by a search of your university or college library online catalog for holdings or on the Internet Web pages of each institute. A major benefit from such reports is that they often contain excellent bibliographies.

Definition of the Social Problem

The first step in the social problem analysis is to sort out how the social problem is defined, find descriptions of major subtypes, and locate estimates of its magnitude.

Most social problems present definitional problems and child abuse is no exception.[1] Because it won't do to try to understand all of them, it is useful to simplify. We'll do that here by restricting our social problem focus to *physical* child abuse, the type of child abuse that is arguably the least ambiguous although the least frequent. And it will reduce the complexity when we begin to think of explanations and interventions. We need a definition to begin our analysis, so let's use the definition of physical abuse summarized from definitions in state legislation by the U.S. Children's Bureau: "'any non-accidental physical injury to the child' and can include striking, kicking, burning or biting the child or any action that results in a physical impairment of the child."[2] Qualitative distinctions among types of physical abuse are ordinarily a matter of severity ranging from moderate to severe to fatal.

Having established a definition, the social problem analysis must now turn to the issue of incidence—how much physical child abuse is there? It is a vexing question as so much depends on the definitions used. The chief source of national information on abused and neglected children is the National Child Abuse and Neglect Data System (NCANDS), maintained by the U.S. Department of Health and Human Services. Based on data collected from the states through NCANDS, approximately 3.3 million allegations of child abuse and neglect were made to child protection service agencies in 2005, with about 62 percent reaching the report stage and either were investigated or received an alternative response.[3] A total of 28.5 percent of the investigations that reached the report stage were determined to involve at least one child as a victim of child abuse and neglect, with 1,460 resulting in fatalities in 2005.[4] We must be careful to distinguish between incidence based on reports and that based on substantiations because 66 percent of reports are neither substantiated nor "indicated" abuse.[5] There are a few more recent estimates of incidence for states and/or for smaller subgroups of maltreated children. A study of substantiated child maltreatment among infants in Virginia published in 2005 reports an incidence of 6.5 per thousand, whereas a seven-year study of physical abuse among Alaskan infants less than a year old (published in 2004) reported an incidence of 4.6 per thousand live births; there is also a national Canadian study that reports 5.4 per thousand rate of substantiated cases of physical child abuse.[6] On the basis of these studies, physical child abuse is clearly an important social problem. Most experts believe that these figures should be interpreted as minimal estimates because they are based on official reports, which cannot take account of large-scale *unreported* child abuse (e.g., middle- and upper-income households are unlikely to be reported for child abuse). The NCANDS figures are likely to be the best available as they improve on most earlier data based only on police reports, whereas the NCANDS data were taken from hospitals, schools, and other major agencies as well. Still, as Pecora and colleagues observe, abusing parents can purposely avoid medical care and can obfuscate by switching physicians, and certainly medical recognition of physical child abuse is not a perfect art. Even with good practitioners, medical personnel can be reluctant to label middle- and upper-income parents as abusers of their children.[7]

The preceding data on national incidence obscure wide variability between states: Washington, Arizona, Colorado, Mississippi, Virginia, Pennsylvania, New Jersey, and Vermont had substantiated rates of child maltreatment from 0.0 to 6.0 per

1,000 children under age eighteen, whereas in Alaska, Florida, District of Columbia, and Massachusetts, these rates were greater than 20 per 1,000.[8] Such variability is not only about cultural ideas of "right" child rearing: Rodwell noted more than a decade ago that what specific behaviors constitute child abuse or neglect also depend on the willingness of a locality to provide services, and its tolerance for subcultural variation.[9]

The Ideological Perspective

#12 The next step in the social problem analysis is to identify the underlying ideology. It is important because it will help the reader understand differences in problem definitions and causation. Recall that ideology is a statement about what is preferred and how things "should" or "ought" to be—in this case, with respect to physical child abuse. It should be distinguished from statements asserting what actually "is." There are many sources for social problem ideology: major recent legislation of relevance (and documents like committee hearings and reports that constitute part of the legislative history), professional journals, publications of child advocacy organizations, and so on. Media statements by important political players and professional "experts" can be of special importance and in that context can be quite explicit about ideology. But political figures and professionals working in child protection organizations usually have self-interests at stake, so their statements aren't always clear and forthcoming about ideological perspectives, perhaps out of concern that offending some audience or constituency may be costly. And legislative acts are often intentionally vague. Capturing the ideology of a social problem often requires a good bit of inference. Following are examples of such inferences. Readers should keep in mind that our concern here is with *public policy*, beliefs embedded therein, not just private beliefs. Be forewarned that sometimes downright conflicting ideological positions can be inferred from legislative provisions, reports, and documents; there is no guarantee that legislation will be all neat and tidy, as the following analysis will show.

A good source for the understanding and identifying contemporary ideology about physical child abuse is the Adoption Assistance and Child Welfare Act of 1980 (P.L. 96-272), and its many amendments through 2003. It is not enough to say that in the act, the ideology is that parents should not physically harm their children. Though that certainly is the case, more detailed statements can be made. For example, because we can legitimately infer from the fact that this act continued funding for child abuse reporting systems, it affirms an ideological position that the state has a right to invade the privacy of the family in order to (as Garbarino says) "know what's going on" for children there.[10] Note that it is not an unqualified state right because there is strong indication of a counterideology in the provisions of P.L. 96-272 prohibiting the removal of children without judicial determination. It limits state invasions of the privacy of families, so it is clearly an ideological position affirming citizen rights over administrative (but not judicial) power.[11]

Because it requires services precisely to prevent placements outside families where possible, this act expresses a clear ideological preference for children remaining with kin wherever possible. That same ideological persuasion can also be inferred because the act requires a least restrictive environment (LRE) feature of foster care placement, where "least restrictive" is defined as placement with own kin as first priority, extended family next, and nonrelative care last and least preferred.[12] Where blood kin are not available for children, permanent, adoptive families—fictional kin—*should* have a priority over long-term foster care with nonrelatives as is implied in the act's provisions for subsidized adoption for some children. Permanency and kinship are the cultural/ideological preferences here.

It is also worth noticing that there are other ideological commitments expressed in the legislative history of the act. For example, the legislative history will clearly tell us that the provisions for subsidized adoption were passed over the objections of those whose ideology was that people should not be "paid for being parents." Note the act requires that subsidies be given only after "reasonable search for adoptive placements which do not require a subsidy."[13]

With respect to the ideology, the Adoption and Safe Families Act of 1997 (P.L. 105-89) is substantively similar to the 1980 act; that is, although children should be protected from abuse, physical or otherwise, retention of kinship ties should be given very high priority. Barring that, permanent families for children should be the priority: Its provisions strengthen subsidies for adoption, give fiscal incentives to states for increasing adoptions of children in foster care, provide for the study of expanding and making permanent foster care with kin ("kinship-care") and attempt to promote state policies that avoid children remaining in foster care over long periods of time (foster care "drift").[14]

The Indian Child Welfare Act (ICWA) of 1978 contains a clear departure from the ideological position discussed earlier concerning the right of the state to invade family privacy on behalf of children. *ICWA requires a higher standard of proof for removal of Native American children from their parents than for removal of non–Native American children—that is, "proof beyond a reasonable doubt."* The historical background of this provision is the forcible administrative removal of thousands of Native American children from their families and tribal communities for placement in government and private boarding schools (up through the early 1900s), on the theory that Native American children needed to learn farming, white customs and the English language. In the 1970s, it became clear that thousands of Native American children were still being placed in state-funded foster care with little probability of their return home to their families.[15] Worse, nearly 53 percent of Native American children were placed by their states in non–Native American homes.[16] The ideology of the ICWA can be inferred here in a straightforward way: Great caution should be exercised in removing Native American children from their parents and tribal community, and when they are, any kind of temporary or permanent placement should be within a Native American family or tribal community. Barth and others draw similar conclusions.[17] Another example of identifying the ideology underlying a social problem is found in Christopher G. Petr, *Social Work with Children and Their Families.*[18] Petr's "value based framework for practice" has a great deal in common with the ideology implied in the legislation just discussed. Among the eight basic elements of Petr's framework is "family centered practice," which speaks of Petr's ideological commitment to the priority of the family and kin we found implied in the provisions of the Adoption Assistance and Child Welfare Act of 1980 (strong emphasis on family reunifications, placement prevention, and so on). But Petr does carry it a good deal further, for in his hands, it means that families alone should *control* intervention choices, outcomes, needs, and the sharing of information. There is not much in the act that implies that.[19] Petr's framework element least restrictive environment shares the act's definition of LRE: Any placement away from parents should give priority to kin first.[20] Readers will find other elements of Petr's framework familiar, for example, "respect for diversity and difference."[21] However, Petr's element of "achieving outcomes" is, in one sense, contrary to the outcome-focused provisions of the 1997 version of the act (Adoption and Safe Families) because it turns out to be an argument *against* ultimate-outcome measures. Although Petr favors measuring the effects of practice, it is with short-term, intermediate process measures, quite different than establishing the worth of interventions by measures of *how it all turns out* for people in trouble. That would seem to put Petr with one but not both feet in the same ideological camp with the 1997 act.[22] He has respectable reasons and well-reasoned arguments for his position, of course.

There are ideological perspectives on child abuse contrary to those stated earlier. Here is Duncan Lindsey, editor-in-chief of *Children and Youth Services Review*, speaking of "Child Abuse: The Red-Herring of Child Welfare":

> For in response to . . . the horrors of child abuse, public child welfare has been transformed from a system serving a broad range of disadvantaged children into one designed primarily to protect children from battering and sexual assault . . . (so that most) children who come to the attention of . . . agencies . . . (as) the victims of neglect or inadequate care are (now) virtually excluded from receiving assistance.[23]

Lindsey's point is that the incidence of battering and sexual assault is small relative to other social problems that affect children. His opinion is supported in part by the data.[24] He concludes that intervention programs are not generally effective (true with exceptions). Lindsey then draws an (ideological) conclusion that, on these accounts, *basic child protection should be administered by the police* in order that the child welfare system can be freed to address the total well-being of a much larger number of children.[25]

Causal Analysis

The next step in analyzing the social problem of physical child abuse, child battering, is to identify causal explanations used to understand this problem. There are many; Tzeng, Jackson, and Karlson list twenty-four for physical child abuse alone.[26] Many experts think of these theories as in three types: (1) explanations focused on factors within individuals, (2) explanations focused on factors in the surrounding sociocultural and economic environment, (3) explanations focused on ecological factors occupying the interactional space between both of the preceding types of factors.[27] The reader should be clear that *no general theory of physical child abuse has been unequivocally confirmed and shown to be superior to competing theories.* The research reviewed here is often significantly compromised by small clinical samples and comparison groups with selection bias and differential attrition, among other problems.[28] Despite the recent, admirable growth in research on child abuse, it is quite clear that we are only beginning to understand a few of the basic issues.

The *individual focused theories* on child battering are concerned with the attributes of parents in the main—think here of the paradigmatic example, the 1960's studies of Henry Kempe, from whose research came the term "Battered Child Syndrome."[29] They range from focus on the characteristics of their personalities, their psychological states, their ability to bond with their infants to a focus on the presence of severe mental disorders of parents. Most of these studies show confirming evidence, interesting, perhaps potentially important, but so weak as to be altogether unpersuasive when it comes to use in practice. Here are some examples. Many studies find that abusing parents do indeed have unrealistic expectations for their children compared to nonabusers, though not all such parents abuse their children.[30] Some studies are useful in correcting long-cherished but wrong generalizations, that is, that child batterers are psychotic or severely mentally ill. Actually, only a small proportion of battering adults have ever had such conditions, at least as defined in standard psychiatric classification schemes such as the American Psychiatric Association's *DSM-IV-TR*.[31] On the question of the relationship of race/ethnicity to child abuse, the research, as of now, is equivocal—some studies affirm the relationship, others don't. It is clear that the differences between races and ethnic groups are small in any case.[32] Of course, substance abuse is a major factor in all types of maltreatment.[33] Finally, there is now considerable doubt about whether the idea that those who have been abused as children will then abuse their own children is generally true. Actually, research has always shown clearly that *most* parents who have had such experiences don't, in fact, abuse their own children, and, more interesting, there is some support for the idea that when they don't, they seem to have had an emotionally supportive parent, partners, or friends.[34] Most people do.

Among other things, *sociocultural-type* theories focus on economic factors such as poverty, where the research consistently shows strong relationships to child battering. But notice that most poor people don't abuse or batter their children, so poverty by itself is not causal.[35] Some researchers think they have found a complicated link between the two: Low-status employment emphasizing subordination to authority translates into authoritarian styles in child rearing. Unemployment and job loss create crises (constants for families in poverty) that are themselves associated with increased parental irritability, arbitrary discipline, and physical punishment. A good many studies support their association with physical abuse.[36] And, of course, this explanatory type is concerned with cultural sanctions toward corporal punishment of children. Clearly, the U.S. population is more accepting of physical punishment for children than Canada or England and some Asian countries.[37] But although corporal punishment is somewhat politically incorrect among middle-class America these days, the respected Diana Baumrind's review of the research challenges commonly accepted beliefs; for example, she concludes that nonabusive corporal punishment is: "not harmful when administered deliberately for disciplinary purposes and legitimately belongs in the disciplinary repertoire of parents."[38] She also reminds us of some findings that could be important in designing interventions: that the importance of singular maternal attachments is not supported by cross-cultural research; that personal "warmth" is good for children in other ways but is *not* associated with secure attachment of children to mothers and may not even be necessary to same; that unconditional approval is *not* associated with preschool competence.[39]

Ecological explanations turn on complex interactions between persons, parental pairs, families, social networks, cultural influences, and environmental factors, all taken together. Here are some interesting interactional findings. Yes, some abused parents from poverty backgrounds do abuse their children but those who do are *also* in unstable, intimate relationships during the first four years of their child's life.[40] Violence between intimate partners is likely to be associated with violence to young children.[41] Abusive families display fewer social interactions, especially positive ones, with their children, larger families are susceptible to low levels of positive and high levels of negative interactions, and all are heightened by crowded housing conditions.[42]

Sociobiological theory takes an evolutionary perspective on social behaviors and understands them as survival strategies for species, ultimately genetic, to continue the species gene pool. Sociobiology theory (following Tzeng et al.) predicts that parents' adopted children are more likely to be abused than genetic children, children with disabilities are more likely to be abused than children without disabilities, and stepfathers will direct more energy toward their own than toward their stepchildren.[43] Research studies find some but not strong support for these propositions.[44]

Learning theory considers observational learning, operant conditioning, and social context as crucial to explaining human behavior. As applied to child abuse and aggressive behavior, its principles have some obvious applications: People literally learn how to be aggressive, learning when and where aggression is appropriate to social norms, and learning the consequences of aggression. Indeed, studies show that children who observe their parents being aggressive or violent in the course of family interactions will probably include aggression in their own kit bags, for example.[45] Tzeng and colleagues believe that learning theory can be used to "re-educate parents about parenting and . . . taught new better stress coping skills and communications processes."[46] Other research suggests that they may be correct.

Gainers and Losers

The obvious losers from this social problem are abused children, but, of course, society itself is a loser when its stock of human capital is degraded, abused, or disabled. There are few gainers who somehow profit from the abuse of a child. But there is no social problem without a sizable set of winners, and, clearly, one of the most obvious winners here is the abuse perpetrator: Abuse reaffirms their power in the family and is a clear message to those who would dispute it—including spouses as well as other children. Indeed, in the United States there is considerable support for the rights of parents to be completely free of interference from official government in physically punishing their children. Were there a social consensus on corporal punishment or on the idea that injuring children is always a socially shameful act, could it be that physical child abuse would disappear? A primate biologist who has studied the abuse of young in primate groups in the wild has reviewed the human child abuse research and concluded that abuse among humans is a result of "an unsocialized child and an inconsistent parent living in a social system where there is ambiguity about child rearing practices and discipline."[47]

The Judicial Context

Judicial decisions have framed child abuse policy on all sides. Constitutional questions concerning the right to be free from harm (Eighth Amendment) and the right not to be deprived of either property or liberty without due process (Fourteenth Amendment) are often potentially applicable to child protection where removal of children from biological parents is involved. Here are several examples of important court decisions establishing or extending social policy about abused children. Investigations of complaints of child abuse must inevitably compromise the privacy of a family. But where workers harass parents by threats of prosecution or initiate court actions with little evidence, the judiciary has created a potential for civil liability and damages against them.[48] Stein says, in general, social workers *don't* have to give "Miranda warnings" prior to interviews during child protection investigations if they are being conducted in the family home or the worker's office.[49] And, in at least one federal jurisdiction, in 1989, when social workers were being sued for failing to monitor a foster home placement of two girls who were sexually assaulted, a federal circuit court granted social workers nearly absolute immunity, Stein says, "for all actions taken from the time dependency begins until dependency ends."[50] Administrators and practitioners need to take notice of the U.S. Supreme Court ruling on the rights of fathers in proceedings terminating parental rights: It cannot be assumed that fathers are unfit parents just because mothers have been so adjudged, says the Court. "These and other Supreme Court decisions make clear that the rights of unmarried fathers who have lived with and cared for their children and have legally established paternity cannot be terminated without notice to the father and a determination of his fitness as a parent."[51] Readers may wish to keep current with other legal issues found in such volumes as MacMurray and Carson's *Legal Issues in Violence Towards Children*.[52]

The Historical Context

The first statute concerned with child abuse and neglect was a timid 1735 law passed in Massachusetts when, under British common law, children were thought of as non-persons with no standing or rights. They were, literally, an adult possession. In the middle and late 1800s, organized "child saving" appeared. From its very beginning, this social movement understood children from a strongly "scientific," rationalistic view—natural beings who were to be understood from the perspective of whatever positivistic science (as opposed to theological ideas) had to say about them.[53] Children were the evolutionary future and, thus, to be "saved," not in the theological sense, but in the Darwinistic sense! And, unthinkable a century earlier, it was not necessarily or only a matter for private organizations because child savers thought it was quite all right for the government to interfere in private affairs for the public good, for the sake of children. These days, the best known child-saving agency from those turn-of-the-century times may be the Children's Aid Societies because of their sponsorship of "orphan trains," which sent eastern seaboard "street-corner" children (mostly full orphans) west for adoption by farm families. That was heady child saving indeed to think of these children sent to the healthy air of the virtuous West, where bad things didn't happen in the popular imagination of that age. In fact, the Children's Aid Societies were preceded in time by private organizations devoted solely to protecting children and animals from abuse: the Societies for the Prevention of Cruelty to Children and Animals (SPCCA). The first of these was the New York SPCCA, founded in 1874, and it and others on the eastern seaboard brought the abuse of children in this newly urban and industrialized country to the consciousness of the American public.[54] There were nearly two hundred such societies in the United States and Europe by 1910. The New York SPCCA program was devoted primarily to child protection in a law enforcement mode; in fact, many SPCCA field staff were sworn officers with certain police powers. Their child protection was pursued through coercive means: warnings, moral persuasion, surveillance, and imprisonment at hard labor on occasion. Its preferred mode of intervention was to remove children from families and place them more or less permanently in institutions.[55] Costin believes that "the intent was to bring salvation to children by a permanent break from parents and substitute mass culture for an immigrant culture."[56] Costin quotes from a report of the New York SPCCA: "ignorant people must be compelled to do what is right by the strong arm of the law."[57]

The Massachusetts SPCCA branch developed along quite different lines. Cognizant of the problems of immigrants and different standards of child rearing and family life, the Massachusetts SPCCA thought that child abuse was partly a problem of cultural assimilation.[58] By 1907, it abandoned policing to focus on remedial action and services to strengthen family life, child protection being only one part of their responsibility. SPCCAs the country over moved toward the Massachusetts SPCCA program idea rather than that of the New York Society. Early in its history, its practices focused on substitute and noninstitutional *family care* for abused children, provided citizenship classes in settlement houses, child care and the provision of kindergartens for immigrant children, and "friendly visiting," of course.[59] In the Progressive Era, after the turn of the century, the social problem of child abuse faded into the background. Costin believes that was due, in part, to the political focus of the Progressives on the external causes of social ills, on improving the quality of life not just for those considered "unfortunate" but through more or less "universalistic" programs that were directed at *all* the nation's children. Accordingly, the Progressives sponsored and passed legislation on maternal and child health for which almost all families were eligible.[60] In the social work profession, child abuse assumed a low profile as the profession became increasingly preoccupied with personal and counseling services.[61] That was followed by the economic disasters of the Great Depression in the 1930s when the professional perspectives were swept up in the situational disasters—unemployment, hunger, and housing—that were its consequences.[62]

The social problem of the physical abuse of children finally reappeared as a public issue in the 1960s with the discovery by radiologists of characteristic patterns in

X-rays of the broken bones of battered children.[63] Following from that, Henry Kempe popularized the idea of the "Battered Child Syndrome." Child abuse became a child-saving issue on the same basis that exploitative child labor and orphaned children had nearly a hundred years earlier: children, innocent victims, essentially helpless in terrible circumstances, were being exploited and injured at the hands of aggressive adults. Indeed, it took on the character of a social movement, just as had child labor a century earlier. When the Child Abuse Prevention and Treatment Act was passed in the 1970s, the country had long accepted the idea of public, rather than private, initiatives to intervene in social problems and the child-saving movement had surely helped prepare that ground. The policy initiatives were characteristic of the features that, in some ways, the child-saving movement had pioneered: not only federal leadership but also a preference for program designs influenced by the most recent research findings, strong roles for "experts" and professionals offering "treatment" interventions focused on families and individuals with much program implementation in the hands of the private sector. Notice, however, that the focus of the federal legislation is on individual children, clearly a legacy from the child-saving movement. There is a certain contradiction here because, as will be seen later, much of the research on child abuse implies that children are being abused because of unemployment, crowded housing, and cultural ambiguity about child rearing and corporal punishment in particular, not the ignorance and/or the neuroticisms of individual parents. History goes some way toward explaining that contradiction as a legacy from the child-saving movement. It is also a historical fact that the United States is a reluctant welfare state, unwilling as always to make public provision for secure employment, adequate housing stock, and accessible medical care for its citizens, even if there is good reason to think that a universal provision along those lines might go some way toward preventing an important proportion of child abuse. When the 1974 Child Abuse Prevention and Treatment Act was passed, its sponsor was shocked that there was not a single federal agency that had any legal responsibility for the problem.

The Social Program and Policy System

Introduction

Up to this point, the work of our policy analysis has been at a broad level, necessary so the reader can discover those vital things that explain how the program came to be and how its shape will have been influenced by history, ideology, and politics of the moment. Now our work turns to describing the details of how a specific program is supposed to work. Notice that there are always two general kinds of things for the policy analyst to do: (1) describe the program and (2) judge its worthwhileness.

Readers should be warned against their own ambition—don't try to analyze a whole piece of legislation, certainly not a whole social policy system or even large agencies. In fact, the readers' first attempt should be "bite-size," a small program or subprogram with homogeneous goals and objectives that can fit on a single page. That will probably be an administrative subunit in a social agency: for example, a food kitchen for homeless people, one small program unit serving, say, therapeutic foster care, or a case management unit for individuals who are chronically mentally ill.

Goals and Objectives

The first task is to describe goals and objectives. The program used throughout this chapter to demonstrate our policy and program analysis method is a child abuse prevention program roughly modeled on the work of Wolfe and colleagues, but that we shall call the Adolescent Relationships Program (ARP).[64] The basic program idea is to focus prevention on high-school-age students who have a high probability of becoming both teen parents and being violent toward their own children and those of intimates. Research shows that these are teenagers who (a) live in violent neighborhoods and (b) have either regularly witnessed family violence or experienced it themselves. Studies indicate these adolescents are very likely to engage in serious dating violence (both sexual and physical aggression) plus considerable difficulty in ending such relationships.[65] Studies also show that the developmental process for violence in teen dating seems to parallel that of violent families; that such violence appears at around fifteen to sixteen years of age, when, in a year or so, attachment relationships of longer duration will begin.[66] It is relevant to child battering because *research findings show clearly that abuse of adult intimates and child battering are very likely to occur together.*[67] In short, the program theory is that from their families and neighborhood, children learn that violence is normative, acceptable behavior and a useful way to resolve conflicts with others—reinforced, of course, by media and cultural models. The program theory assumes that coercive violence strategies are gender specific and that peer and family apply socialization pressures to adopt them. The program goal is to reduce child battering by both male and female adolescents. Specific objectives of this program are for adolescents to

1. Learn awareness of how their tendencies toward abusive behavior began (e.g., understanding power and control in relationships, victim/batterer gender socialization, sex-role stereotypes)
2. Learn that violent attitudes and behaviors are not normative, rather the reverse (e.g., peer, media, and family role models)
3. Learn specific skills for building nonviolent relationships and specific behavioral responses to abuse (or the tendency to abuse) in their own relationships (e.g., choosing partners, defining powerful relationships through equality, empathy, and emotional expressiveness)[68]

These are what are called *intermediate objectives;* that is, if these are achieved, it is logical to expect that the probability for child battering is significantly reduced. ARP is a program that could be funded under many of the broad and very loose legislative mandates for child abuse prevention in the United States. Let's assume it is funded by a state Children's Trust Fund. We'll take some liberties here—the program is actually Canadian. The design leads from the fact that, from a policy perspective, the success of most "after-the-fact" intervention programs for child batterers is either not impressive or not enduring.[69] ARP is a preventive, "before-the-fact" program with all the obvious advantages. The ongoing research on the program we are about to study is encouraging.[70]

Our next task is to make a judgment as to the merit of the goals and objectives: How good are they? We judge that they turn out to be good ones for the most part. First, they are clearly concerned with outcomes that can stand justified on their own merit, not just "means" to some distant end. Second, they are defined with sufficient clarity so that they can (potentially) be measured. Third, the terms of the objectives fit closely with the theoretical concepts of physical child abuse. The theory on which the program is based is consistent with one of the causal explanations found in the social problem analysis. But *performance standards* cannot be found anywhere in the program description, and that is a lack. Not stating them might be acceptable if the program is a *prototype* (never before implemented). It is important because if no specific expectations are set out for program success then it could be considered a success if only a single (or two or four) participant achieved the objectives. Doubtless, neither the program designers, the staff, nor those who supply program funds would be satisfied with that. When a program goes "public," performance standards ought to be public since that has the virtue of "keeping everybody honest." The temptation to adjust expectations to fit performance (and say "good job") is very strong when investment in program achievement is high. And it almost always is.

It is useful in any discussion of goals and objectives to notice the extent to which they concern social control issues. In this instance, that is very much the case: This program wants to change behaviors that are socially deviant to those that are normative. Clearly, this program is deeply committed to social control of the first order. Of this, more will be said later in the section titled "Administration and Service Delivery."

Eligibility Rules

Program participation is limited to the following:

- Age between fourteen and sixteen years.
- Enrollment in a particular high school.
- Those from a family known to the local protective services office because violence has occurred. The participant might not have been abused but must have witnessed family or neighborhood violence over a significant period of time.

For our present purposes, let us proceed as if these were the complete set of eligibility rules. Our first question is: What type of eligibility rules are these? The rule maker is clearly the program administration—thus, we have *administrative rules* here. No administrator can add or ignore these eligibility rules so there is no *administrative discretion* here about these eligibility rules. Other types of eligibility principles (rules) are eliminated by the fact that there is no money or reference to legislation or judicial decision.

Now, are these "good" eligibility rules? First, *do these rules fit the social problem analysis* to which this program intends to contribute at least a partial solution? The answer is yes, indeed they do, because these rules target those who research shows are at some documented risk of child battering. But it is also clear that they limit the program to a small sector of the target group. That is acceptable as long as that is all the program claims to do.

Another criterion on which we should judge eligibility rules concerns whether program participation *stigmatizes*. To be stigmatizing, program participation has to be known to the public, and the observing public must know that participation is associated with social deviancy. It seems hard to imagine that attending these program activities in the ordinary public high school could go unnoticed by other students. Aren't students immensely curious, not to mention observant, about what their peers are doing and why? It might be possible to obscure participation, but it would take some clever planning indeed. Public knowledge about participation seems likely to create stigmatization since the program itself is about a serious social deviancy (family violence). At any rate, it is a matter to which program staff should be alert: Left unattended, it could be the cause of program nonparticipation, high dropout rates, and so on, and conclusions might be truncated by "creaming effects."

Other criteria for eligibility rules are *off-targeting* and *over-* or *underutilization*. The former is not an issue here because these eligibility rules closely target potential participants. *Underutilization* is an issue as the small numbers allowed by funding don't come close to covering the numbers of potential abusers. Other criteria are not relevant, but readers should not expect every evaluative criteria to apply in every policy or program analysis.

Form of Benefit and/or Service

The type of benefit this program offers is not a hard benefit (like cash or commodities) but a service. In this case, it is an *expert service*, sometimes called "psycho-education"—that is, education and skill training in understanding and avoiding family violence. It is not a personal social service because the program design doesn't call for one-on-one tutoring in this educational venture. There is no attempt to individualize program participants and focus particular kinds of service and benefit packages on their unique problems. No money (or equivalents) change hands, so this benefit form is not material goods, not credits or vouchers nor subsidies or loan guarantees, and so on. Although it concerns citizens who have been protective services clients, this program does not involve *protective regulation*, something very different from protective services for children. "Protective regulation" refers to government regulations protecting some businesses from competition from other businesses (often imports, or dairy subsidies), not protection from child abuse or neglect.

Now, how shall we evaluate this benefit form: Is it a "good" one with respect to this social problem? At the most obvious level, the benefit is a *good fit with what the social problem requires*. But we must also take a large-scale perspective here: How far could this program go in dealing with the child battering problem among the population in general; could this type of program be implemented in *every* high school in the nation? Would a public high school in a wealthy urban neighborhood tolerate a program whose very existence implies that child battering and family violence might occur among them? It does, of course; it's just unlikely to be officially reported. Notice that this suggests the possibility of *political risk* for the supporters of this program should it be more widely implemented. And, of course, that raises the relevance of another evaluative criteria: *How adaptable is this program across users?* Those are serious issues.

Analysts need to realize that this program cannot reach child batterers who have not so far come to the attention of official child protective units—that is, those who are never reported. That illustrates a problem in *target efficiency* for this benefit form: It does an excellent job of focusing services only on those who have the problem, but it must overlook a significant number of them. Although this is not a reason to avoid implementing the program, the analyst should never lose sight of what is left over after program intervention has occurred.

Finally, the good practical policy analyst must always be conscious of the immense temptation to substitute services for hard benefits as a solution to social problems. The advantage is that social services often can be implemented on a relatively small scale and thus are less expensive than broad-scale hard benefits like income supplements or medical care. Although most of the poor do not batter children, there is no debate that the stresses and constant crises for those living in poverty may set the stage for child battering. The point is that we don't know how much battering would be reduced if income adequacy were the hard benefit delivered rather than services like counseling, psycho-education, and so on. Practical policy analysts need to keep in mind that the legislative motive for services may not be altogether altruistic: Social services are never cheap, but they are usually cheaper than universal income protections and health care for all citizens.

The costs of this service are less than the costs of some personal social services because its personnel serve groups of program participants rather than single subjects. Assuming this program design ultimately proves itself to be effective in reducing child battering, this form of benefit is *cost-effective* (at least for those who receive it)—even as it may ignore most of the social problem.

Does this program have a potential for serious *coerciveness* toward clients? The answer to the question turns on the extent to which teenagers from families known to protective services are free to refuse participation without retaliation. There is nothing in the program design itself that would prohibit teenagers from opting out when their participation is solicited or thereafter. But in action it could be just the opposite; the point is that we don't know until we ask program staff the questions. If so, it might produce high dropout rates or otherwise compromise the "voluntariness" of participants. This program design doesn't appear to entail serious *intrusiveness* into program participants' lives, although participants are asked to apply the concepts learned to their own life experience. The issue is whether those in charge of the group meetings do or do not use group pressure or the pressure of their own professional status to force participants to divulge personal information against their ordinary caution. That information must come from participants themselves.

Administration and Service Delivery

Program Theory. Administration and service delivery must be in service of implementing the program design. Administration is means to an end, a vehicle for a purpose, not an end in itself. That is why we will begin with a discussion of program design for the Adolescent Relationships Program (ARP). It is derived from three general social science theories and here applied to the goal of reducing violence toward family intimates and children. They are (1) social learning theory, (2) feminist theory, and (3) attachment theory.[71] *Social learning theory* explains how violence among intimates arises as intimate relationships develop in adolescence. As children, violent males are taught hostile beliefs about women, power-assertive behavior, and how power and control over women are legitimate inside their families, culture, and subculture. *Feminist theory* explains the socialization process through which the power imbalance between genders occurs: Males are reared to be in charge, competitive, and "silent," whereas females are reared to be compliant, oriented to others' needs, and anger-denying. Thus, women are socialized to believe that the outcomes for and well-being of intimates are their task, where the point is "the other," not themselves. And, for males, rigid gender roles produce a perspective on females that is both demeaning to women and radically separates the functions females play in subroles—mother, cook, whore, and so on. Empowerment is an important concept in feminist perspectives and used in ARP design with respect to working with adolescents and health promotion aspects of the program. *Attachment theory* explains how the choice of "partners in dating relationship may be directly related to attachment experiences in childhood and early adolescence."[72] Readers should remember here the empirical fact that 70 to 80 percent of children who grow up in violent families don't abuse their children or intimates.[73] Many believe that it is being reared in a violent environment *and* in a culture that gives sanction to male violence toward women that makes the difference. For example, there is a research finding that the presence of a supportive intimate partner substantially reduces the probability of spousal and mother–child abuse.[74]

Program Design. The program design for ARP is drawn from three general (social science) theories described before. This design (illustrated in Figure 9.1) assumes that child battering and violence to intimates by males are based on learned gender roles and reinforced by cultural and media-idealized models. There is nothing much ARP can do about the latter, but it might be able to help males "unlearn" gender roles and replace them with relationship skills that promote clear communication, avoid coercion, and reduce the drive toward power and control. And it may be able to help females "unlearn" gender roles that reward the problematic male gender roles described before: compliance, other orientations, and anger repression. The program objectives are clearly reflected in the outcomes found in the element *program theory* and outlined in Figure 9.1. They are unabashedly cognitive in that they assume that "knowing" a new gender role will translate into "doing" it, that is, playing it out in real-life relationships.

Notice in Figure 9.1 that associated with each objective is a set of *program specifications* intended to achieve that objective. Here is the way this chart is to be read. The

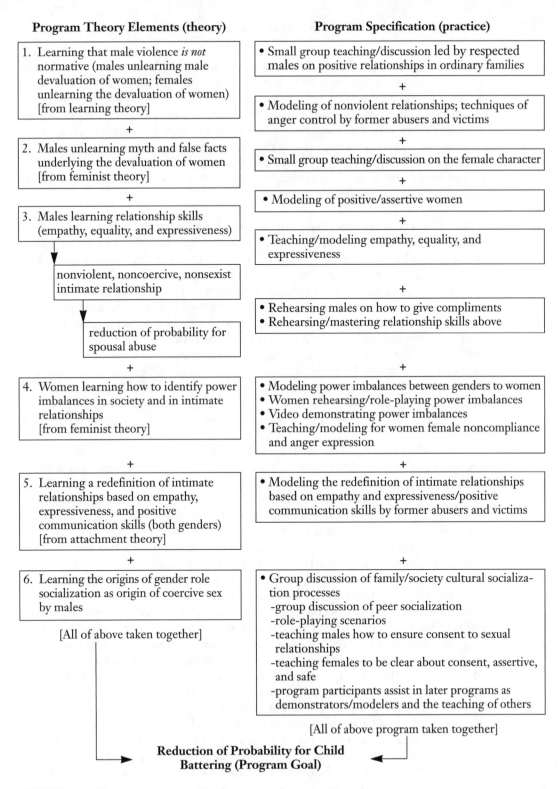

Program Theory Elements (theory)

1. Learning that male violence *is not* normative (males unlearning male devaluation of women; females unlearning the devaluation of women) [from learning theory]

+

2. Males unlearning myth and false facts underlying the devaluation of women [from feminist theory]

+

3. Males learning relationship skills (empathy, equality, and expressiveness)

nonviolent, noncoercive, nonsexist intimate relationship

reduction of probability for spousal abuse

+

4. Women learning how to identify power imbalances in society and in intimate relationships [from feminist theory]

+

5. Learning a redefinition of intimate relationships based on empathy, expressiveness, and positive communication skills (both genders) [from attachment theory]

+

6. Learning the origins of gender role socialization as origin of coercive sex by males

[All of above taken together]

Program Specification (practice)

- Small group teaching/discussion led by respected males on positive relationships in ordinary families

+

- Modeling of nonviolent relationships; techniques of anger control by former abusers and victims

+

- Small group teaching/discussion on the female character

+

- Modeling of positive/assertive women

+

- Teaching/modeling empathy, equality, and expressiveness

+

- Rehearsing males on how to give compliments
- Rehearsing/mastering relationship skills above

+

- Modeling power imbalances between genders to women
- Women rehearsing/role-playing power imbalances
- Video demonstrating power imbalances
- Teaching/modeling for women female noncompliance and anger expression

+

- Modeling the redefinition of intimate relationships based on empathy and expressiveness/positive communication skills by former abusers and victims

+

- Group discussion of family/society cultural socialization processes
  - group discussion of peer socialization
  - role-playing scenarios
  - teaching males how to ensure consent to sexual relationships
  - teaching females to be clear about consent, assertive, and safe
  - program participants assist in later programs as demonstrators/modelers and the teaching of others

[All of above program taken together]

Reduction of Probability for Child Battering (Program Goal)

FIGURE 9.1   How a program specification puts a theory into practice.

objective of "unlearning" male devaluation of women (left column) is intended to be accomplished by a program activity that has respected male models speaking in the discussion (right column) positively of women. And women model the obverse of female compliance: expression of anger and self-orientedness. *Program specifications are exactly the activities that the program staff will put into operation.* That list could be more detailed, but what is there serves as an illustration. The practical policy analyst should work to obtain program activity descriptions at, at least, this level of detail. If the staff cannot provide those specifics, it should raise questions about whether they are clear about what they are implementing.

Type of Service-Delivery Organization.   ARP is intended for high school students, and although it could be administered in various organizations, let us assume that a public high school in the United States is the host organization providing financing, community sanction, and administrative accountability. It seems reasonable to assume that public high schools are a *centralized* type of organization in which classrooms and subprograms such as ARP are embedded in a hierarchical organization with authority concentrated at the top levels of an organizational pyramid. Even so, the practical policy analyst should be alert to whether ARP has more than one "boss," ordinarily a bad idea since it requires the administrator to constantly negotiate between each authority when decisions are made or when issues of funding, evaluation, staff, facilities, equipment, and supplies are considered. That can happen if funding is from one source and direct administration is from another. ARP should have a single authority to whom it is responsible and the administrator should be clear on who that is.

Now let's consider whether the administrative arrangement is a good one for ARP. First, let's look at the evaluative criteria requiring an administration and service-delivery organization to have qualities of *integration and continuity* with other relevant social services. The practical policy analyst should consider that ARP's participants are from families who are most vulnerable to being reported for child abuse or have been reported or known to child protective services (CPS): from families who are likely to live on the edge of poverty or worse, likely to have serious health problems because medical care is not easily come by, likely to be in crisis much of the time from illness and injury, unemployment, arrest, conflict in the schools, and so on. ARP should show evidence of having done advance organizational preparation so that referrals to community helping resources can be made easily and without delay when needed—medical care for health problems, personal counseling, remedial education, and so on. That means seeking out advance understandings with various service providers about how, to whom, and under what conditions ARP participants can be referred. Without advance preparation, it can be time-consuming, clumsy, and may not achieve its purposes. Humanitarian considerations aside, unless the program is prepared to do that, program participants can drop out and good program outcomes can be completely overwhelmed when participants become preoccupied with coping with the pressing and serious negative outcomes that happen to people in constant crisis. For ARP to be integrated with other community services means the participants know people in those organizations who can help ARP participants get services when they need them.

Another service-delivery criterion is *accessibility*. Geographic location and transportation are commonly issues, although that is not the case here—the program is conducted at the high school attended by all program participants. But there are other things that can make a social program inaccessible to people who need it for example, language. For those for whom English is not a first language, a program without staff who speaks the language of, say, a recent emigrant is inaccessible to that emigrant. ARP might fail that test if its potential participants were not competent English speakers. The *helper-therapy principle*—teaching others what you yourself have just learned—is one device by which to make learning certain things accessible to people. It has been been demonstrated to be a powerful educational strategy. This program includes it in its program specification: Program participants are enlisted to help teach other adolescents the same material.

If ARP is a good service-delivery organization, it should meet the criterion of having *accountability* features. Recall that accountability is concerned with an organization's that ability to establish who made decisions and a forum for appealing them when program consumers (or staff) feel that they have not been consistent with the organization's own policies. In Chapter 6 on the analysis of service delivery, we described what a rudimentary accountability system should contain. Because we have imagined ARP as existing in the context of a host agency, we should assume that program participants (and staff) have accountability features available to them. Many, but not all, school systems have fair-hearing procedures and other accountability systems in place. ARP participants, for example, need recourse for appeal if they are dismissed from the program, and the same applies to ARP staff.

Another evaluative criterion for service-delivery systems is their ability to relate to *ethnic, gender, and racial diversity*. ARP is clearly relating to gender diversity, *but the program opposes cultural and ethnic tradition* whenever it is the origin of adolescent socialization to the acceptability of putting women at a power disadvantage with respect to men. Indeed, the program theory expects cultural differences to be an important source from which the conditions for male violence toward women and child battering originate. The objective of the program is to challenge such cultural perspectives and attempt to socialize program participants to quite the opposite perspective. It is a very large order because the program is entirely cognitive. That is, it takes no action with respect to changing cultural influences or peer group socialization factors—both powerful reinforcers of these attitudes. So, does the program "fail" on this criterion? Readers must examine their own ideological perspectives to decide where the limits are for accepting and being sensitive to cultural diversity. It is important for the practical policy analyst to pursue policy issues beyond the obvious. One way to do that here might be to put the following question to ARP staff: How would they react to, say, a traditional Muslim adolescent who was clearly adopting the ARP perspective about gender power differentials they saw in their peer group and family, but who, in all other ways, responded from her religious perspective in the group discussion?[75] The answer that might save ARP from being a form of sectarian evangelism is whether ARP group leaders would act to protect her right to change her own religious belief at her own pace and *only so far as she herself desires*. It is an interesting, difficult issue here, but it is a good illustration of the difference between various types of policy analyses. Remember, this is a value-critical analysis.

Financing

Let us assume that ARP is funded from a Children's Trust Fund (CTF). These trust funds, enacted by state legislatures, first began in the early 1980s, and early on were funded from a tax on marriage licenses.[76] Usually, an appointed board administers the trust, including the responsibility for making decisions about disbursements to projects. Much of the initial motivation to establish these trust funds was to fund prevention programs. Then or now, only a small proportion of all funds expended on the social problem of child abuse goes for prevention.[77] CTF financing would seem to be a good fit with the social problem analysis because it focuses on a type of prevention. Also, the causal analysis found here suggests that developing knowledge of prevention is a serious need because after-the-fact treatment of child battering is not reliably successful in reducing subsequent incidents or healing the trauma. But, of course, the most important issue is whether the revenue generated by the trust fund strategy is sufficient to cover the "need." Clearly not.

This type of funding is unusual for social welfare programs and so let us use the term *special revenue*. That identifies it as coming from tax revenues but sets it off as coming from a special source—*not* from general revenue funding whose sources are from taxes on, say, income and property and from the public at large. That isn't unusual—think of the special taxes on hunting licenses used to fund wildlife projects.

One of the recommended criterion for funding is its *dependability over time*. Compared to other financing methods, taxes on marriage licenses would appear to produce very dependable funds. The state legislature isn't likely to take the trouble to lower the amount of this small and seemingly uncontroversial tax. And its constancy is ensured as long as marriage rates are reasonably constant over the short to medium term (*demographic change*). But notice that this type of funding fails another of the evaluative criterion: It cannot *respond quickly to economic change* (say, inflation). Program costs increase under inflation, but the tax is set in law as some absolute dollar amount per marriage license. Thus, any change requires a special action of the state legislature, which is never quick. Notice that indexing the CTF tax rate to the rate of inflation, as for Social Security retirement benefits, would settle this problem.

Finally, let's consider the criterion that calls attention to whether financing provides *incentives or disincentives for obtaining specific client outcomes*. The answer for the Children's Trust Fund financing is "yes," because most trust funds require project proposals to specify preventive outcomes as a condition for consideration for funding.

Interactions between Basic Policy Elements and between This and Other Programs

This program necessarily interacts with the local child protective services (CPS), which identifies and refers program participants, and the local public high school, which is its host organization. But this program does not make participants either coeligible for other services or ineligible either. It is unlikely to duplicate services, given its unusual psycho-educational design. It is conceivable that there is potential for what we've called *contrary policy/program effects* given that the types of changes the program seeks to make are in the participant's perspective on imbalanced power relationships among genders. For example, an ARP participant might be simultaneously involved (at the initiative of CPS) in a family counseling program attempting to reduce internal family conflict. In contrast, ARP might well be creating family conflict around cultural and family traditions with respect to gender role issues. That isn't necessarily a bad thing but might be a contrary effect from some perspectives.

NOTES

1. Definitions of child abuse have varied over the years. See, for example, the definition of "child battering" in a major 1987 study of the incidence of child abuse and neglect by the National Center on Child Abuse and Neglect and the 1998 definition in the Child Abuse Prevention and Treatment Act (CAPTA).

2. *Definitions of Child Abuse and Neglect*, Child Welfare Information Gateway, U.S. Children's Bureau, State Statutes Series, 2007, p. 1, http://childwelfare.gov.

3. Administration on Children, Youth and Families, U.S. Department of Health and Human Services, *Child Maltreatment 2003* (Washington, DC: U.S. Government Printing Office, 2005), www.acf.dhhs.gov/programs/cb/pubs/cm05/index.htm.

4. Ibid.

5. Ibid.

6. Ibid; *Virginia Performs, Measuring Virginia, Health and Family Summary*, www.vaperforms.virginia.gov/i-childAbuseAndNeglect.php; V. Polusci, E. Smith, and N. Paneth, "Predicting and Responding to Physical Abuse in Young Children Using NCANDS," *Children and Youth Services Review*, 27(6) (2005): 667–682; B. Gessman, M. Moore, B. Hamilton, and P. T. Muth, "The Incidence of Infant Physical Abuse in Alaska," *Child Abuse and Neglect*, 28(1) (2004): 9–23; N. Trocmé et al., *Canadian Incidence Study of Reported Child Abuse and Neglect in 2003*, McGill University Center for Research on Children and Families, Ministry of Public Works and Government Service, Canada, 2005.

7. P. J. Pecora et al., *The Child Welfare Challenge* (New York: Aldine de Gruyter, 1992), p. 99.

8. Administration on Children, Youth and Families, *Child Maltreatment 2003*.

9. M. K. Rodwell, *Policy Implications of the Multiple Meanings of Neglect: A Naturalistic Study of Child Neglect* (Ph.D. diss., University of Kansas School of Social Welfare, Lawrence, 1988).

10. R. Wollons, *Children at Risk in America: History, Concepts and Public Policy* (Albany: State University of New York, 1993), p. 269.

11. Pecora et al., *The Child Welfare Challenge*, p. 23.

12. Ibid., pp. 22–24, 433.

13. E. Segal, "Adoption Assistance and the Law," in E. C. Segal (ed.), *Adoption of Children with Special Needs: Issues in Law and Policy* (Washington, DC: American Bar Association, 1995), pp. 127–134.

14. *Summary of the Adoption and Safe Families Act of 1997 (P.L. 105-89)* (Washington, DC: Child Welfare League of America, 1997).

15. L. Matheson, "The Politics of the Indian Child Welfare Act," *Social Work*, 41 (1996): 232.

16. M. Plantz, R. Hubbell, B. Barrett, and A. Dobrec, "The Indian Child Welfare Act: A Status Report," *Children Today*, 18(2) (1989): 27.

17. R. Barth, "Adoption," in P. J. Pecora et al., *The Child Welfare Challenge*, pp. 367–369.

18. Christopher G. Petr, *Social Work with Children and Their Families* (New York: Oxford University Press, 1998).

19. Ibid., p. 44.

20. Ibid., pp. 85–87.

21. Ibid., p. 167, quoting 42 USC 675 (5) (A).

22. Ibid., pp. 111–113.

23. D. Lindsey, *The Welfare of Children* (New York: Oxford University, 1994), p. 161.

24. Ibid., quoting S. Kammerman and A. J. Kahn, "Social Services for Children, Youth and Families in the U.S.," *Children and Youth Services*, 12(1) (1995).

25. Lindsey, *The Welfare of Children*, pp. 173, 177.

26. O. Tzeng, J. Jackson, and H. Karlson, *Theories of Child Abuse and Neglect* (New York: Praeger, 1991), p. vi.

27. R. Ammerman and M. Hersen, *Children at Risk: An Evaluation of Factors Contributing to Child Abuse and Neglect* (New York: Plenum Press, 1995), pp. 201–203; O. Tzeng et al., *Theories of Child Abuse and Neglect*, pp. 31–108; Pecora et al., *The Child Welfare Challenge*, pp. 133–136.

28. R. Chalk and P. King, *Violence in Families* (Washington, DC: National Academy Press, Commission on Behavioral Science, on Social Sciences, Committee on Education of the National Research Council and the National Institute on Medicine, 1998), p. 3.

29. C. H. Kempe, F. Silverman, B. Steele, and H. Silver, "The Battered Child Syndrome," *Journal of Marriage and Family*, 18(2) (1962): 17–24.

30. Ammerman and Hersen, *Children at Risk*, p. 90.

31. Chalk and King, *Violence in Families*. See also J. Garbarino, "Preventing Child Maltreatment," in R. Price et al., *Prevention in Mental Health: Research, Policy and Practice* (Beverly Hills, CA: Sage, 1980), pp. 63–80.

32. Chalk and King, *Violence in Families*, p. 44; L. Berger, "Income, Family Characteristics and Physical Violence Towards Children," *Child Abuse and Neglect*, 29(2) (2005): 107–133.

33. Tzeng et al., *Theories of Child Abuse and Neglect*, p. 35.

34. B. Egeland and K. Papatola, "Intergenerational Continuity of Abuse," in R. Gelles and J. Lancaster (eds.), *Child Abuse and Neglect: Biosocial Dimensions* (Hawthorne, NJ: Aldine de Gruyter, 1987); L. Knickerbocker et al., "Co-Occurrence of Child and Partner Maltreatment," *European Psychologist*, 12(1) (2007): 36–44.

35. L. Pelton, "The Role of Material Factors in Child Abuse and Neglect," in G. Melton and F. Barry (eds.), *Protecting Children from Abuse and Neglect* (New York: Guilford Press, 1994). See also Chalk and King, *Violence in Families*, p. 43.

36. J. Vondra, "Sociological and Ecological Risk Factors in Child Abuse," in R. Ammerman and M. Hersen (eds.), *Children at Risk: An Evaluation of Factors Contributing to Child Abuse and Neglect* (New York: Plenum Press, 1995), p. 162; Berger, "Income, Family Characteristics and Physical Violence."

37. Tzeng et al., *Theories of Child Abuse and Neglect*, p. 111. See also Vondra, "Sociological and Ecological Risk Factors in Child Abuse," p. 162; J. Crandi and L. Behl, "Relationship Among Parental Beliefs and Corporal Punishment, Reported Stress and Physical Child Abuse Potential," *Child Abuse and Neglect*, 25(3) (2001): 413–419.

38. D. Baumrind, *Child Maltreatment and Optimal Caregiving in Social Contexts* (New York: Garland, 1995), p. 80.

39. Baumrind, *Child Maltreatment*, pp. 65, 71.

40. Vondra, "Sociological and Ecological Risk Factors," p. 157; K. Henning et al., "Long-Term Psychological Adjustment to Witnessing Parental Conflict During Childhood," *Child Abuse and Neglect*, 21(6) (1997): 501–515; K. Malley-Morrison, *International Perspectives on Family Violence and Neglect: A Cognitive and Ecological Approach* (New York: Routledge, 2004), pp. 39–84.

41. A. Rosenbaum and D. O'Leary, "Marital Violence: Characteristics of Abusive Couples," *Journal of Consulting and Clinical Psychology*, 49 (3) (1981): 63–71.

42. Tzeng et al., *Theories of Child Abuse and Neglect*, pp. 57–58; J. S. Milner, "Social Information Processing and Physical Child Abuse: Theory and Research," in D. J. Hansen (ed.), *The Nebraska Symposium on Motivation*, vol. 45 (Lincoln: University of Nebraska Press, 2000).

43. Ibid., pp. 90–91.

44. Ibid., p. 92; G. Harris et al., "Children Killed by Genetic Parents vs. Stepparents," *Evolution and Human Behavior*, 28(2) (2007): 85–95.

45. Ibid., p. 94; M. Gara et al., "The Abused Child as Parent: The Structure and Content of Physically Abused Mothers' Perceptions of Their Babies," *Child Abuse and Neglect*, 24(5) (2000): 627–639.

46. Ibid., pp. 96, 97; D. J. Kolko, "Individual Child and Parent Physical-Abuse Focused Cognitive-Behavioral Treatment," in B. E. Saunders, L. Berliner, and R. F. Hanson (eds.), *Child Physical and Sexual Abuse: Guidelines for Treatment* (National Crime Victims Research and Treatment Center, 2004), www.childwelfare.gov/pubs/cognitive/cognitive.pdf.

47. T. Field, "Child Abuse in Monkeys and Humans: A Comparative Perspective," Martin Reite and Nancy G. Caine (eds.), in *Child Abuse: The Nonhuman Primate Data* (New York: Alan R. Liss, 1983), p. 171.

48. D. Besharov, *Criminal and Civil Liability in Child Welfare Work: The Growing Trend*, 3rd ed. (Washington, DC: National Legal Resource Center for Child Advocacy and Protection, American Bar Association, 1986).

49. T. Stein, *Child Welfare and the Law* (New York: Longman, 1991), p. 62; A. O'Connor, "Child Protection Investigations: Miranda Warnings," *Juvenile and Child Welfare Law Reporter*, 8(2) (April 1989): 29–30.

50. Stein, *Child Welfare and the Law*, p. 70.

51. *Stanley v. Illinois*, 405 U.S. 645 (1972); Stein, *Child Welfare and the Law*, p. 73; *Caban v. Mohammed*, 441 U.S. 380 (1979).

52. B. MacMurray and B. Carson, *Legal Issues in Violence Towards Children* (Berlin: Springer, 2000).

53. R. Wollons, *Children at Risk in America*, p. 65.

54. Lela B. Costin, "Cruelty to Children: A Dormant Issue and Its Rediscovery, 1920–1960," *Social Service Review*, 66(2) (1992): 177–181.

55. Ibid., p. 179.

56. Ibid.

57. Ibid.

58. Ibid., p. 181.

59. Ibid.

60. Ibid., p. 182.

61. Ibid., p. 183.

62. Ibid., p. 193.

63. Ibid., p. 194.

64. Wolfe's program is described in full in D. Wolfe et al., "Empowering Youth to Promote Healthy Relationships," in D. Wolfe, R. McMahon, and R. Peters (eds.), *Child Abuse: New Directions in Prevention and Treatment Across the Lifespan* (Thousand Oaks, CA: Sage, 1997), p. 114. The program design in the book you are now reading is our own work, not Wolfe's, and an invention for illustrative purposes, inspired by Wolfe's Youth Relationships Program as described in his article referenced at the beginning of this note. It is not intended to be an exact replica in any way.

65. Wolfe et al., "Empowering Youth," p. 111.

66. Ibid., p. 112.

67. J. Vondra, "Risk Factors Associated with Child Abuse and Neglect—Sociological and Ecological Factors," in R. Ammerman and M. Hersen (eds.), *Children at Risk* (New York: Plenum Press, 1990), p. 156.

68. Wolfe et al., "Empowering Youth," pp. 106–107.

69. Chalk and King, *Violence in Families*, pp. 118–119.

70. Wolfe et al., "Empowering Youth," pp. 121–123.

71. Ibid., pp. 106–107.

72. Ibid.

73. E. Zigler and N. Hall, "Physical Child Abuse in America: Past, Present and Future," in D. Cicchetti and V. Carlson (eds.), *Child Maltreatment: Theory and Research on the Causes and Consequences of Child Abuse and Neglect* (Cambridge: Cambridge University Press, 1989), pp. 52–53, 63–64.

74. Chalk and King, *Violence in Families*, p. 46.

75. It won't do to challenge this question on the basis that if people actually did that they would be inconsistent in their beliefs—few people are entirely consistent with respect to their ideology.

76. J. Poertner, "The Kansas Family and Child Trust Fund: Five Year Report," *Child Welfare*, 66 (1987): 3–12; Kansas Children's Cabinet and Trust Fund, Minutes, October 17 2007. www.kschildrenscabinet.org.

77. Pecora et al., *The Child Welfare Challenge*, Table 1.4, p. 18.

INDEX